Wakefield Press

WILD ASPARAGUS, WILD STRAWBERRIES

Barbara Santich is a highly respected food writer, culinary historian and academic, with an abiding interest in French food, cooking and eating, currently focused on eighteenth-century Provence. Her book on Australian food history, *Bold Palates: Australia's Gastronomic Heritage*, was shortlisted in the non-fiction category of the 2013 Prime Minister's Literary Awards.

By the same author

The Original Mediterranean Cuisine
What the Doctors Ordered
Apples to Zampone
Looking for Flavour
McLaren Vale: Sea and Vines
In the Land of the Magic Pudding (ed.)
Bold Palates
Dining Alone (ed.)
Enjoyed for Generations

WILD ASPARAGUS, WILD STRAWBERRIES

 *Two years in France*

Barbara Santich

At the time represented in this book, $1 Australia was equivalent to approximately 5 French francs.

Wakefield Press
16 Rose Street
Mile End
South Australia 5031
wakefieldpress.com.au

First published 2018

Copyright © Barbara Santich, 2018

All rights reserved. This book is copyright. Apart from any fair dealing for the purposes of private study, research, criticism or review, as permitted under the Copyright Act, no part may be reproduced without written permission. Enquiries should be addressed to the publisher.

Edited by Margot Lloyd, Wakefield Press
Cover designed by Liz Nicholson, designBITE
Text designed and typeset by Clinton Ellicott, Wakefield Press

ISBN 978 1 74305 533 5

A catalogue record for this book is available from the National Library of Australia

Wakefield Press thanks Coriole Vineyards for their continued support

*For John, Stephanie, Dylan
who shared, and contributed to,
this adventure*

Contents

1	Nizas	1
2	Prelude	4
3	Arrival	8
4	L'Escoute	13
5	Milk and bread	18
6	Life in Nizas	25
7	The shepherd and the gypsies	29
8	Markets	35
9	The butcher	41
10	Libraries	44
11	Gastronomic explorations	47
12	Vin du pays	52
13	Jean-Pierre and Vivette	59
14	A la française	65
15	Wild leeks and wild asparagus	73
16	Au revoir Nizas	77
17	Bonjour Caromb	81
18	Madame and Raymond	88
19	Mistral	94
20	Julian	98
21	Visa	103
22	Pot-au-feu	107

23	Feast to famine	113
24	Cooking like the locals	118
25	Snails	127
26	Cherry harvest	130
27	Progress	135
28	June at Caromb	140
29	Claret	146
30	Le Parti Socialiste	152
31	Le quatorze juillet	157
32	Courses de taureaux	162
33	Where next?	167
34	Villanueva y Geltrú	171
35	Cambrils	178
36	Home again!	185
37	La vendange	190
38	Partridge	195
39	'The cold, dark north'	199
40	A house in the forest	203
41	Work – and flying	208
42	Potatoes	213
43	Christmas	218
44	Parisian weekends	222
45	Geese	227
46	Television and politics	231
47	'Yes, we live in Europe'	236
48	Spring and salons	240
49	'Our correspondent in France'	245
50	La Belle Epoque	251
51	Wild strawberries	261
52	Summer	267
53	Au revoir	274
	Epilogue	280

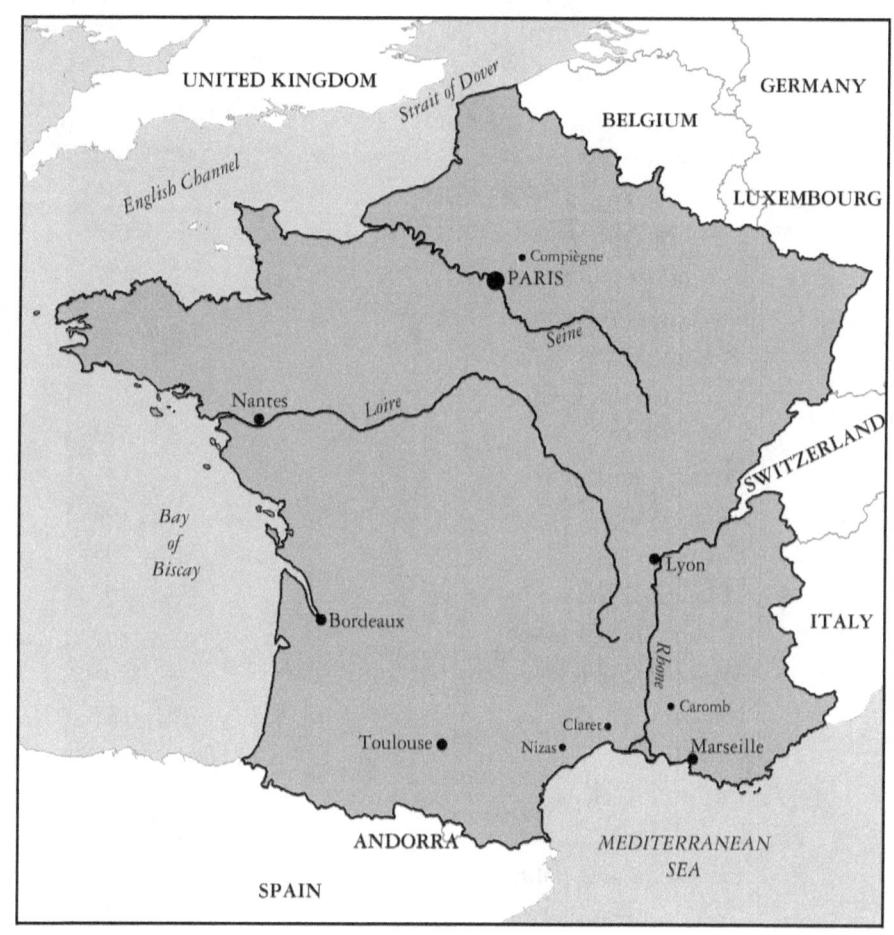

France, with my significant cities and villages

izas

It's the most exciting thing that has happened in Nizas since the massive thunderstorm during vintage the year before last, which ruined 10 truckloads of grapes on their way to the winery.

News travels quickly in French villages, and gossip even faster. It takes less than a day for the women of Nizas to spread the word: Australians, with one-year-old twins, renting Madame Molla's l'Escoute. Headscarves tied under their chins, they parade past the house and pounce on us the first day we enter the village. Once the obligatory greetings are over and done with – *Bonjour Madame, Bonjour Mesdames* – they bend down and peer into the strollers for a closer look, poking the children as if they were rabbits for the pot. *Comme il est costaud! Comme elle est mignonne!* (What a sturdy boy! Isn't she cute!) Then comes the inevitable question. They already know the answer but need to hear it again, first hand, as if they can't yet trust us to have been truthful with Madame Molla.

Ce sont des jumeaux?

Yes, they're twins, I reply. Boy and girl.

Garçon et fille? Alors, ce sont de faux jumeaux.

They say this with a triumphant certainty. I am puzzled. *Faux jumeaux* is, literally, false twins, but how can twins be false? A problem of translation? Appealing to rationality, I try to explain.

They have the same mother, same father, same birthday, they're twins. *Ce sont des jumeaux.*

Ah, oui, de faux jumeaux.

Impossible to reason. By their logic only identical twins are genuine. Different sexes cannot possibly be twins. In the end I give up. *Oui, de faux jumeaux*, I agree. It's only later, when I've come to accept the *faux jumeaux* tag, that I realise that it's simply the French term for fraternal twins.

It dawns on me, gradually, that it's not just the novelty of twins that fascinates them. Young children are as rare as diamonds in Nizas. The local school closed its doors years ago. The last generation of children have grown up and mostly moved away; grandchildren and great-grandchildren only visit in the summer holidays or for funerals. This is a village in stagnation, its population at a historic low – 391, the sign at the entrance proudly proclaims – and diminishing with every decease. It is an old village of old people, many of whom have lived all their lives in Nizas and confidently expect to end their days there, dying in their familiar bed then buried in the Nizas cemetery.

Like its inhabitants the village itself seems almost to have outlived its usefulness, its houses crumbling away stone by stone. Overlooked by the main highway from Montpellier to Béziers, it is not really on the way to anywhere. No road signs point to *centre ville*. There's only one road wide enough for a car, leading into the village square and out again, and any car that finds its way in has nowhere to go but out. But who needs a car when bicycles and Shanks's pony do just as well?

In many respects Nizas is of a piece with its neighbours, all connected by meandering country lanes that began as paths stamped by medieval feet. Perhaps all that distinguishes it are the remnants of its medieval castle – and its bells. All the local churches operate according to their own idiosyncratic clocks and

on Sundays their chimes reverberate and echo and respond in a joyful carillon.

You wouldn't live here if you hadn't been born here, explains one old crone. She's right; nothing remarkable lured me, nothing made me choose Nizas above all the other villages in this region, the Hérault. It just happened to have a suitable house to rent, and I seized the opportunity. And while I might not be Nizas-born-and-bred, it is now my village, and its very typicality is what fascinates me. Its timelessness seduces me. In its narrow cobbled lanes that twist and turn as if in defiance of town planning standards I glimpse the life of the medieval village. Its houses, built in the traditional Languedoc style with a large barn on the ground floor, bear witness to the accretions of subsequent centuries as they cluster close together for solidarity and security. Unlike anywhere I have ever lived before, it's small enough to be knowable, its characters old enough to remember past glories and relaxed enough to stop and talk and pass on accumulated wisdom, especially in relation to bringing up children. As an outsider, a foreigner, I feel obliged to allow them the right to interrogate – while I retain my right to observe.

As a child, I lived in small rural towns in Australia but never appreciated the unwritten codes that underwrote social interactions and rituals. Now, in 1977, I have to understand and respect them if I want to make a life in France.

Prelude

What wayward bus brought us here, to this deepest corner of *la France profonde*, abandoning friends, family and a perfectly comfortable life? In hindsight, it was rash, selfish, scatter-brained, impulsive, improvident, impractical, foolish and ill-advised. At the time it seemed perfectly reasonable to leave Australia on a one-way ticket to Paris – the four of us: me, my husband John, and one-year-old twins, Dylan and Stephanie.

Three years earlier I'd stepped off the train at Nice into warm spring air and the beguiling scents of jasmine and orange blossom. Suddenly, after weeks of travelling in Greece and Italy, sounds made sense. Nouns and verbs I thought forgotten tumbled back, delighted to be of use. People understood me when I asked for directions, when I changed travellers' cheques, when I requested a *tarte aux amandes* from the *pâtisserie*. The feeling of being in a foreign country gradually faded. Six glorious, carefree weeks in Paris, studying French language and culture at the Sorbonne, visiting museums on free Wednesday afternoons, walking barefoot in the gutters after summer storms, asking the friendly barman in the café downstairs for ice cubes for the refrigerator-free apartment, choosing a different cheese each day – all these only confirmed a conviction that in France I'd found a new home, a place to belong.

Perhaps I was seduced by its reputation of glamour and sophistication, but more important, I think, was its otherness, and what France allowed me to be. Speaking French, I had the opportunity and the excuse to be a different person. I could flirt audaciously. I could spend a rainy afternoon in a café in Antibes debating religion with the man repairing the cathedral organ. Hitchhiking my way around the country, I could innocently ask about the gastronomic specialities of the region's food, a topic on which all drivers were experts. Generous experts: thanks to them, I drank Normandy farmhouse cider, ate strawberries dipped in red wine then sugar, and tasted truffles and soft goat cheeses for the first time. I returned to Australia inspired to become a food writer – and, working at *Woman's Day* under Margaret Fulton, achieved my goal.

Back in Sydney, reading my letters and labouring under the weight of PhD studies, John could only dream of such experiences. He, too, yearned to travel. When I returned, I introduced him to French food: French-inspired *charcuterie* from a tiny shop in North Sydney, French cheeses from a deli in Woollahra. We married, and made an impulsive decision: when the PhD was finished we would live in France for a year, two years, indefinitely. Nonchalant, we saw no reason for the arrival of twins to divert our project.

Our plans were vague in the extreme. Leaving Australia for France seemed hardly different from moving house, changing suburbs. In my mind it was all so clear: we would board a plane, the plane would land, we would leave the airport, and in the next frame we were installed in a cute little cottage eating croissants for breakfast. I couldn't see the cottage, nor the countryside, but I could smell the coffee and the enticing sweetness of the croissants.

In preparation we attended to the necessary practicalities.

We opened an account with the Sydney branch of the French bank, BNP. We laboriously completed the lengthy applications for long-stay visas, pressing heavily with the pen so that even the last of the six carbon copies was legible, and sent them to the French consulate. We bought tickets to Paris – one-way, because at the very back of our minds was the cargo-cult vision of jobs and residence. Reducing belongings to the barest of necessities, we packed the rest into four tea chests and sent them off to Marseille, care of my friend Emil. Optimistically anticipating an extended stay, I included clothes to last the children for the next two years, along with their patchwork quilts, soft toys, and a Dick Bruna frieze of animals and numbers to decorate their room. For sentimental reasons, my handmade rug for the floor and familiar kitchenware: a couple of sturdy Le Creuset pots, the Moulinex mixer, a wooden-handled cast-iron frying pan and the Sabatier kitchen knife in its hand-sewn leather pouch. For listening to English voices via the BBC, a large radio/cassette player capable of receiving shortwave.

Most important was our library – all the books that, in our grandiose vision, we imagined absolutely necessary to life in France, indeed anywhere. First of all, dictionaries: the *Concise Oxford Dictionary*, the English-French dictionary that had belonged to my father, plus pocket dictionaries for French, Italian, German, Greek and, for no real reason, Latin. Second, guide books: *The Gastronomic Routes of France* listing the cheeses, *pâtisseries* and other gastronomic specialities of each region; my old green Michelin guides for Paris and Provence; and other, more general books – John Ardagh's *The New French Revolution*, Waverley Root's *The Food of France*, Lawrence Durrell's *Spirit of Place*, and Archibald Lyall's *Companion Guide to the South of France*. Complementing these: Carlisle's *History of the French Revolution*, Bertrand Russell's *A History of Western Philosophy* and Simone de

Beauvoir's volumes of memoir. Finally, the indispensable cookbooks: all of Elizabeth David, Julia Childs' *Mastering the Art of French Cooking*, Claudia Roden's *A Book of Middle Eastern Food*, Alan Davidson's *Mediterranean Seafood*, the word-heavy *Larousse Gastronomique*, the Penguin translation of Brillat-Savarin's *Physiologie du Goût*, and recipe cards from the French magazine *Elle*, inherited from my time at *Woman's Day*. And, on top of these, the second-hand portable typewriter I'd bought for $30 for my future food writing. I'd had a taste at *Woman's Day*; France would inspire me to follow in the footsteps of Elizabeth David.

On the first day of 1977 we boarded the UTA plane for Paris, blithely leaving parents to dispose of cars, clean the house and organise tenants, all while depriving them of the opportunity to play grandma and grandpa.

Arrival

Travelling with young children, I soon realise, is not the carefree, happy-go-lucky life I enjoyed as a student. Nor is Paris the lively summer capital of my memory. Beneath a low, grey sky the streets seem bleak and forlorn, and the solemn stone of the Sorbonne wears an icy shroud.

Our destination is the Midi, where winters are warmer and rents cheaper. Paris is only an interlude, a necessary pause in the journey to allow us to take the first formal steps toward becoming adopted citizens: registering our visas and opening a French bank account. At the *préfecture de police* the surly clerk looks suspiciously at our papers and insists on new photos, with separate ones for the children. We wait impatiently in the long, echoing corridor until he eventually returns on the dot of midday and hands over the stamped visas. He immediately slams down the shutters of his window and disappears for lunch. I wouldn't have said *merci* even if I'd had the chance.

It's a more congenial experience the next day. Monsieur BNP is only too delighted to welcome new clients, keeping up an endless patter about the benefits of living in the country while multiple documents pass to and fro across his desk. We want to link the French bank account to the Australian one and arrange for regular monthly transfers of funds; so long as we are relatively frugal,

rent from the Australian house should cover our living expenses. I don't notice until we leave, but while we have been signing interminable forms the children have amused themselves by removing the leaves from Monsieur's pot plant in the corner of his office.

I need Paris to reaccustom myself to French ways and to refamiliarise myself with the words and phrases of everyday communication. There's an additional imperative, to introduce John to the cafés and bars I used to frequent, the ones with stools at the counter where I could sit with my coffee or glass of wine and still only pay the *comptoir* price. The air is icy but the thrill of being here, of recognising *boulangeries* and bookshops, more than compensates for the winter chill and the inadequacy of our clothing. We do not yet know to wear hats, and jackets that can cope with a Sydney winter are no match for this penetrating cold. For the first time in their lives, the children need shoes, and we buy them sturdy little lace-up ankle boots in a soft caramel leather. Walking back along Boulevard Saint-Michel, we are stopped by a woman who points to Dylan, miserable and crying in his stroller. *Il lui faut un bonnet*, she commands (He needs a hat). Full of guilt and remorse, I turn into the next shop and choose him a bright red knitted balaclava. As if to reinforce my shame, his crying stops the minute I pull it over his head.

Dominique, a friend of my sister, has promised to help us find and buy a second-hand vehicle. With no idea how to buy a second-hand car in France and no technical terms in my vocabulary, I'm happy to entrust him with the task despite the long detour to Strasbourg. He meets us at the station with an invitation to his parents' apartment for tea, *un goûter*. Rich, buttery aromas ooze from the door, and as we are led to the dining room I see an overwhelmingly generous table of Alsatian tarts, apple and plum, as well as a savoury quiche. It is a far cry from scones and Anzacs and a cream-filled sponge.

His parents are kind, attentive hosts but have only a few words of English, so it falls to me to sustain the conversation, explaining that we intend to live in France for a few years. No, we don't know when we will return to Australia. No, we don't have return air tickets. No, we don't have jobs, and no, we don't have definite plans except to head south. They listen politely and refrain from offering opinions, though privately they are probably thinking 'rash, reckless and irresponsible'. The fact that Dylan is sniffling and whimpering and obviously unwell would only confirm their views. Our negligence in Paris has had its inevitable consequence, and he has a temperature and is most unhappy. They insist that he see a paediatrician and make an appointment for the next day.

Dr Levy-Silagy is very methodical and thorough and demands a complete medical history from the time of his birth, week by week and month by month. Her final diagnosis of a heavy cold and throat infection is far outweighed by her concern that, at 16 months, Dylan is not yet walking.

Do you give your children vitamins?, she asks, and there's an implicit reprimand in her voice.

I realise she suspects a vitamin D deficiency and try to explain that Australia has fresh air and sunshine, that vitamin D beams naturally through the open windows, that the children have enjoyed sun kicks since they were two weeks old. Her frown signals disbelief as she writes out five prescriptions, three for the throat and two vitamin preparations, including capsules of vitamin D. I give Dylan the most important of the throat medicines and, because of her insistence, a week of vitamins as well. Miraculously, within a couple of days he is better. And a couple of weeks later he is walking. I hesitate to thank the vitamins.

But the whole point of this detour is to buy a car, and Dominique's parents have another useful piece of information to

pass on: their local garage man has a 1968 Citröen DS for sale. They have always owned Citröens, always bought them from this garage, and know Monsieur le Garagiste to be thoroughly reliable and honest. At approximately $900, it sounds perfect – and within our price range.

Roland Barthes described the DS – *la déesse*, the goddess – as an object from another universe, a gift from the heavens, 'a new Nautilus'. As soon as I see it, even before a test drive, its breathtaking beauty wins me. Sleek, streamlined and elegant, it is all lean muscle, built for speed. It has the precision of a gymnast, able to turn a full circle on the smallest of country roads. Hydraulic suspension ensures the smoothest of rides. Its colour, the subtle pale green of sea foam or the most delicate celadon, is classic Citröen. It has real leather seats and, because its previous owner was a music teacher, a high-quality radio. *C'est une voiture de luxe*, says the garage man, fondly patting the bonnet, but we are already convinced. It seems an absolute bargain, though of course we have no idea the price will double when costs for registration, compulsory insurance and the *carte grise* – the registration certificate – are added.

On Sunday, one week after arriving in Paris, I feel that at last we are not simply marking time. The car represents respectability and permanence as well as the means to our end, a place of our own in the Midi. Optimism returns. Anywhere south will be warmer and more cheerful than Strasbourg. But in our infatuation with the DS and our eagerness to take possession, we neglect to ask the garage man if he could possibly help us by installing the children's car seats that we've lugged all the way from Australia. Without an electric drill there's no way of attaching them, so we jam soft bags around the children in the hope of keeping them comfortable while confined. Everything else can be accommodated in the spacious boot.

My spirits rise again when we reach Lyon, gateway to the Midi. After Lyon everything seems different, as if the city is home to kindly spirits who transform the grey industrial north, subdued and reserved, into a sunnier south, free-spirited and open-hearted. The road follows the valley of the Rhône, deep and narrow and what I have always imagined a valley to be. Clearly delineated by hills that rear steeply on either side, it embraces the wide, silvery river, a river so wide and so full of water that it serves as a double-lane highway for barges, an alternative road to parallel the autoroute and the Route Nationale. In all my trips up and down the N6, this valley, the opening to the Midi, never loses its power to thrill and exalt.

'The first fact of life in Provence is the sun,' wrote Waverley Root in his book *The Food of France*. The sky is clearer and bluer, the clouds untouchably high. Friendly plane trees line the highway and whisper welcome to an edible landscape of vineyards and orchards of espaliered pears and apricots. It's as though the worst part of the journey is over and we're now on the homeward stretch. The landscape and roads are familiar, and the distant profile of the Pont du Gard brings back the same sense of awe and wonder I experienced the first time I saw it, three years ago, on a warm spring afternoon. As I watch cars drive nonchalantly across its elegant arches it seems an affront to its venerable age that this ancient Roman aqueduct should become simply part of the road network, a means of crossing the river. It is heartening to see that beauty and elegance can be allied to utilitarian ends, but a monument that has lasted so long and still stands gracious and serene deserves perhaps to be spared the need to be useful.

At last, two days after leaving Strasbourg, we reach our destination, Montpellier, and claim our reward: the *Gîtes de France* guide for this region, the Hérault. Within its pages is the address of a place I'll soon call home.

4 L'*Escoute*

L'Escoute would never win a beauty contest but to me it is a palace. It is only the second place we look at in our quest for a house to rent after the first one, further inland at Péret, turns out to have only one bedroom instead of the promised two. Scratching it off the list we continue to Nizas, which has two possibilities.

I have spent hours poring over the newly acquired *gîte* guide, Michelin map at hand, identifying potential rentals that satisfy my criteria: two bedrooms, small village, not in the mountains and not too isolated. All the while I have been silently thanking the unknown French politician who, concerned by the population drift from country towns and villages to the cities in the 1950s, saw an answer in tourism and inspired the creation of a national association to assure certain minimum standards: hot water on tap, cooking and washing-up facilities, and a properly ventilated bathroom. These yellow booklets are more valuable to me than a red Michelin.

In Nizas neither *gîte* has a telephone contact or even an address, but in small French villages everybody knows everyone. I approach a group of men chatting outside the post office and have only to mention that I am looking to rent a *gîte* for them to spring to action. Within minutes the first owner arrives. I ask about her house, just a few doors away in the middle of the

village. It's only a summer rental, she explains – looking me up and down and probably wondering why anyone would want to rent a house in Nizas in the middle of winter – and there's no heating. This might be the south of France but in January it's hardly warm, and the thought of spending a couple of months in an unheated house fills me with horror. *Merci*, but no, I reply.

Then a sturdy, twinkle-eyed woman in grey stockings, a kerchief round her head, arrives on her bicycle. *Voici Madame Molla*, the men explain. She beckons and we eagerly follow her, still on her bicycle, to a stand-alone house just outside the village proper. This is l'Escoute.

Even though it must have been built quite recently the house still conforms to the standard style of the region, plain and practical. External stairs lead to the first-floor living quarters above a garage: two bedrooms, a kitchen, a living room, a toilet and shower, and a large walled terrace, perfect for the children to play outside. Windows on all sides look on to vineyards, at this time of year bare, unpromising stumps. Oblivious to appearance, I am entranced. Except for linen, which Madame promises to supply, it has everything we need. Astonishingly, this find is only 120 francs per week – the equivalent of about $23 – plus electricity and gas. It's a bargain. Without hesitation we accept.

Madame Molla must have raided her glory box for us. The sheets she supplies are of heavy, coarse linen, the surface irregular and knobbled, the kind of sheet I imagine a Penelope weaving. They are beautifully hand-embroidered and monogrammed but irregular in size, sometimes barely stretching to the end of the bed, and stiff and cold as though they had never been slept in. The house is cold and damp, too, the last occupants having left after the grape harvest in September, so we turn the oil-filled heater to its highest setting. Checking the electricity meter a couple of

weeks later, Madame Molla is aghast to see we have spent nearly one hundred francs on warming ourselves. I am shocked, too, at a time when frugality should be foremost, but rationalise that it is a necessary expense.

If I had any doubts about the wisdom of our adventure they have now vanished. Less than two weeks after landing in Paris we have a car and a place to live. But it is not yet home – not until we retrieve the tea chests despatched from Sydney care of Emil at Carry-le-Rouet, just west of Marseille. I had met Emil in Spain, and we shared laughs and dog stories during a day on the road from Valencia as far as Andalusia. Emil was on his way to Niger in Africa, accompanied by Suzy, his precious toy poodle who went everywhere with him, even – to my astonishment – into restaurants.

The day after arriving at Nizas we head off for Carry-le-Rouet. Once again on his way to Niger, Emil has written to us to say his neighbour will take care of his mail. Madame answers the door in her housewife pinafore – but instead of the expected tea chests she hands over the shipping documents we need to collect them, temporarily stored in a warehouse in the chaotic metropolis of Marseille.

No one answers when I ring the shipping company; it's midday, and everyone will be at lunch for the next two hours. When eventually I speak to someone about our tea chests, I learn that first I need to collect the *bon à livrer*, the delivery docket, from the terminal at Fos-sur-Mer, some 50 kilometres away in the opposite direction. We lose valuable minutes taking a few wrong turns but finally find the office and pay the port charges. At last, the precious document is in my hands. The sympathetic manager looks at his watch.

You'll never make it, he says. Already half-past three, and the warehouse in Marseille shuts at five.

With success so close, we are not about to give up. Despite his detailed directions, we again lose our way and need the help of a policeman and several locals to reach the *vieux port* in Marseille. With 15 minutes to spare I show the delivery docket. Our tea chests are indeed ready for collection, they tell me, but to claim them we need to get customs clearance from La Joliette, another kilometre away. We make a quick dash down to the docks, where the customs officer shows no interest in the listed contents, spare clothes and household goods, and happily stamps the forms. Another dash back to the shipping depot – which, we discover, is open until 5.30 – and, at last, after all the forms have been cross-examined and re-stamped, we take possession of the precious tea chests.

But there is another problem. One car, four of us, and four tea chests. One almost fits in the boot if we tie it down with a rope. Removing the entire back seat and advancing the front seats allows the other three to be juggled and jammed into the empty space. Now all four of us have to squash in the front seats – with only two seat belts.

Then there is the maze of Marseille to confront. Finding the way out of the city is maddeningly confusing at any time, but at six on a Friday evening, in the near dark, it's easy to miss direction signs. Twice we find ourselves on the road to Aix rather than Arles, and then on the road back to Fos, already traversed twice that day. But at last we are on the homeward stretch, and despite the unintended detours we make it back to Nizas four hours later.

Of course it is impossible to resist immediately prising open the lids and unpacking the treasures we had selected as essential to an extended stay in France. We turn on the radio and become reacquainted with our books. In retrospect, I realise it would have been prudent to include a few practical books, such as *Basic*

First Aid and *Common Ailments of Children and How to Treat Them*, but at the time common sense was the least consideration.

And among the towels and blankets, safely protected, is the large rich fruitcake my mother made for us, a memento of family and Australia.

5
Milk and bread

Madame Molla becomes our guide to life in Nizas. A kind of village elder, her approval eases our acceptance. Rosy-cheeked and motherly, she is the archetypal peasant woman, strong and resilient, capable and confident, astute and practical, thrifty yet generous, embodying French country virtue. Next to her, Monsieur Molla is Jack Sprat, lean and spare. Neither was born here – the Catalan name should have been a giveaway. Both came to southern France as itinerant grape-pickers in the 1930s, later choosing to stay during the Spanish Civil War and adopting Nizas as home.

Madame Molla is one of the few villagers we know by name. The men and women we meet in Nizas rarely introduce themselves or volunteer a name, even when we exchange greetings almost every day. *Monsieur* and *Madame* are perfectly adequate to cover the whole village, with the exception of the fat old *curé* who inevitably bales us up in the square as he returns to his church and asks about life beyond Nizas. Overhearing the salutations of the locals I realise that he is to be addressed as *mon père*, though I find it hard to accept the custom and, more often than not, revert to the automatic *Monsieur*.

In the privacy of our own conversation, we invent sobriquets to differentiate one individual from another, adopting the model

of Happy Families card games with their Ma Bones and Pa Bun and christening them according to their role in the village. For the old men, it's on the basis of personal characteristics: Basque Beret, for his distinctive headgear; Quatre-vingts, because he tells us he is over 80; Joker, who likes practical jokes; and Poireau Sauvage, who introduces us to wild leeks. Collectively, they are *les Messieurs*.

La place, where the men congregate, is the only part of Nizas to be given an address, even though it's simply a colloquial abbreviation. The whole village knows where everyone lives, which, for the most part, is where their parents and grandparents also lived. When we go to the *mairie* to have our new address registered on our visas the secretary tells us that we don't have to complete the address part. *Nizas, ça suffit.* But *la place* is important as the gathering point for the whole community. It is the only open space in the village, the obligatory fountain at its centre. Facing one another across the square are the twin poles of authority, secular and religious, as represented by *mairie* and church.

The *mairie* is like a one-stop shop, the first port of call for information about anyone or anything in the village. It's where you buy a permit to transport wine outside the *département*. Once a week it serves as bank, twice a month it welcomes the travelling library. In the absence of a pharmacy in the village, medical prescriptions are delivered to the *mairie* for collection. Its notice board carries election posters and exhortations to join the French communist party, together with advertisements for a bingo night, notices from the local *cave coopérative* and a simple, handwritten note advising locals that a shoe repairer has set up business in a neighbouring village.

The church, meanwhile, keeps watch over time, its bell announcing *midi* and tolling at random hours throughout the day, twice as often and as long on Sundays. You can't set your

clock by it; *midi* might be a couple of minutes early or late, depending on the whim of the *curé* and the rumblings of his stomach. Notices pinned to the church door announce a vineyard for sale (*Cause – Décès*) or the forthcoming marriage of a granddaughter returning to the family village for the traditional ritual.

These two institutions are central to life in Nizas, where the inhabitants still live by the rhythm of the seasons and follow customs inherited from earlier generations. They buy *ventresca*, the southern French equivalent of pancetta, from the *charcutier* de Lacaune, calling it by the same name as their medieval ancestors. At the beginning of summer they enjoy the sweet, mild onions from the nearby village of Lésignan-la-Cèbe, giant bulbs whose reputation dates from at least the 16th century.

Observing their daily routines, we quickly develop our own, though always an hour or two later with our morning activities. The first interaction of the day is always with Monsieur Maire. He's not the official *maire*, the representative of both local and national government, but rather the factotum who works at the *mairie*. Regardless, that's the name we bestow. His job every morning is to collect the village garbage, and we hear the rumble of his tractor as it lumbers up the lane to retrieve a plastic supermarket bag hung on a flimsy wire hook near the garage door. Soon after, it's Monsieur Poste on his bicycle, and we delay our stroll into the village until after he arrives. If I see him coming I run downstairs and take the letters directly; he uses the opportunity to ask questions about Australia.

While he's on his rounds, banking services at *la poste* have to wait. Temporarily in charge, Madame Poste can only take care of basics, such as the large colourful stamps that form a bright banner across the top of the square French envelopes containing our letters home. Her brief extends only as far as telegrams and phone calls, *la poste* boasting one of the few telephones in the

village. Feeling nervous about the fate of his thesis – he had dropped it in a suburban letter box during the holiday period between Christmas and New Year – John decides to telephone Australia to check that at least it was received. It's a complicated process, especially as Madame Poste never dialled Australia before. After several false starts she succeeds and waves John into the cabin in the corner of the room, handing me a spare earpiece. I'm sure it's all gobbledegook to her, but she greedily listens to every word. All's well, says John's sister; she has the formal notification of receipt of the thesis.

Surly and scowling, Madame Poste never invites a conversation and I'm always glad to shut the big heavy doors behind me and make my way to the Co-op, one of two *épiceries* (general stores) in Nizas. It's always cheerful and noisy, unlike the second *épicerie*, dark and forbidding, presided over by a bent old crone who could be a double for the wicked witch in Hansel and Gretel, casting black looks on all who brave the plastic strips protecting the doorway. Despite surviving the initial scrutiny, we return only once, and then safely in the company of Madame Molla when she wants to buy a packet of biscuits to give the children as a farewell present.

Younger than most of her customers, our Madame Co-op knows everyone intimately, what they bought yesterday and what they'll need tomorrow. She understands their tastes and habits. Her stocks are basic – tinned peas and beans, dried pasta, packets of biscuits and *biscottes*, the feather-light squares of dried bread the French dip in their breakfast coffee. Other breakfast essentials grace the back shelves – ground coffee and tins of instant chicory and gaudy yellow packets of Banania for chocolate milk. The small refrigerated cabinet holds fresh milk, a few yogurts and *petit-suisses*, thin pink sausages and minuscule packets of butter. On the counter behind Madame, next to the shiny wheel

of the slicing machine, is a roll of ham and a couple of cheeses. Apart from the obligatory foil-wrapped Tiger-brand triangles, the only cheeses are local varieties, *cantal* and *roquefort*, the town of Roquefort being only about 100 km to the north. It's not that the Co-op subscribes to an 'eat local' philosophy, but these are the cheeses the Nizas women buy, the cheeses they know and trust.

Like the local women, we visit the Co-op almost daily. it's where we get fresh milk for the children, a litre carton of *lait frais*. We don't buy much else at the Co-op, preferring the larger choice at the supermarket in Pézenas. There's not a lot of demand for *lait frais*, pasteurised and homogenised, the village women preferring the UHT milk that doesn't need refrigerating, and the Co-op stocks only a few cartons. Almost every day there's someone reproving our choice and advising us to buy *lait sterilisé* instead.

Il vaut mieux acheter le lait sterilisé; il ne faut pas le faire bouillir. (It's better to buy UHT milk; you don't have to boil it.)

But the *lait frais* has been pasteurised, I explain. You don't have to boil it. It's already been boiled. That's what *pasteurisé* means.

She doesn't believe me and shakes her head. *Il faut toujours faire bouillir le lait*, she mutters as she walks out of the shop (milk must always be boiled). It's reassuring to know that a public health campaign from the time of Pasteur has been so effective, but science has progressed. I point out the word *pasteurisé* on the carton to Madame Co-op, but I can't be certain that even she accepts my logic.

A little further on from the Co-op is the *boulangerie*, the domain of Madame Boulangère. Strictly speaking, she is not *la boulangère*, since there is no baker in Nizas and therefore no baker's wife. Ever since the wife of the previous baker ran off with the local doctor, it's been the *boulanger* in the neighbouring

village of Fontès who has baked the bread for Nizas: the everyday basics of long baguettes and sturdy *pains* plus the salt-free bread prescribed by Madame Molla's doctor for her blood pressure. In any case, a population of less than 400 hardly justifies a baker, especially when the frugal habits of the old women ensure *un demi-pain* lasts a couple of days and croissants and *éclairs* are unnecessary extravagances.

Voici une baguette. Clearly pronouncing both syllables of 'une' and all three of 'baguette' in a melodious Midi accent, *la boulangère* twists a flimsy square of tissue paper around the baguette's middle, as though tying a serviette, and hands it across the counter. She considers it her duty to gently improve my grammar and pronunciation, even when our exchanges, though still formalised, become more chatty. Immediately I break off the end – *le quignon*, it's called – and divide it between the children before leaving the shop. Outside, the temptation to 'even it up' takes over and, unable to resist the crusty freshness, we tear off chunks for ourselves.

Il vaut mieux acheter un demi-pain, advises Madame Molla, looking down at what's left of the baguette as we near home. So we switch to a *demi-pain*, arbitrarily but accurately split by *la boulangère*. It's the same quantity of bread but not only is it slightly cheaper, it keeps better for breakfast the next morning.

It's rare that are we the only customers in the *boulangerie*, and we quickly adopt the custom of greeting everyone as we enter: *Bonjour, Mesdames* – or *Bonjour, Mesdames, 'sieurs*, if an occasional male has been sent to buy bread. Conventional formalities almost inevitably lead to conversation. Unsure of the bounds of propriety, I stick to generalities – the sun today, the wind yesterday, and the prospects for tomorrow. Whatever the weather, it is always unseasonal. The wind lasted too long; the rain was too little; a warm day in January can only lead to worse vagaries. The

women are less reticent. They ask about the children, their likes and dislikes, what we think of Nizas and le Midi in general. *Il me plaît*, I reply, with genuine affection; I like it here, I am comfortable in Nizas. I want to ask them about their lives and stories, their relationships and beliefs, but I am not yet confident that they would respond. I have to remind myself that in their eyes, we are still outsiders – *étrangers*.

6
Life in Nizas

Life is simple for the inhabitants of Nizas. What they don't produce at home or buy from the general store is brought to the village by a sequence of itinerant merchants: the vegetable man on Mondays and Fridays, the *poissonier* from Agde on Fridays, the butcher mid-week. The *charcutier* (always announced as '*le charcutier de Lacaune*', a region reputed for its hams, *saucissons* and other *charcuterie*) visits on Tuesday afternoons, on his way home after a morning at the Montpellier market. Every two weeks or so the sweet seller arrives and sets up a long trestle table with bowls of raspberry drops, fruit jellies and aniseed sweets, boxes of plain and fancy biscuits and trays of dates, figs and prunes. Less frequent is the shoe van, the clothes seller with his racks of pinafores that the women all wear for the morning housework, or the mobile *droguerie*, its van opening up to display a motley assortment of household necessities, from brooms and buckets, mouse traps and potato peelers, to enormous cups for the breakfast coffee and soap for the weekly wash.

These visits are ritually announced by the *mairie*, which has a set of loudspeakers on its roof. The village silence is suddenly broken by the strident blast of a current pop song at full volume, interrupted after a few bars by *Allo, Allo*, followed by the announcement that *Le poissonier d'Agde* or *Le charcutier de Lacaune*

has *arrivé sur la place avec une belle choix de* . . . It is always *une belle choix*, a fine choice, as though nothing but the best for the people of Nizas. I stop and listen as soon as I hear the music – who will it be this time? I can't resist making my way to the square, joining all the other women who leave their kitchens, still in their pinafores. They look, touch, discuss and compare, but rarely buy. The men stand aloof, quietly watching and unconsciously detached.

The *mairie*'s system also broadcasts news of local events – that a sum of money has been found in the square and can be reclaimed at the *mairie*, that election day is approaching. It relays messages from the *cave coopérative* at Montagnac, today's equivalent of a benevolent medieval seigneur who accepts fealty from the peasant farmers and, in return for the grapes from their small patches of vines, delivers an allocation of wine. Not only does it supply their daily beverage but also the grapeseed oil and vinegar for their salads.

More importantly, since the *cave* is also a distillery, it provides the farmers with a measure of grape spirit, their legal entitlement. It's a right that their children will be denied. In an attempt to curb alcoholism, the French government recently decided to discontinue this privilege, abolishing its hereditary status. The old men shake their heads when the subject is mentioned, as if to say that no good will come of this change. Highly valued, this spirit is rarely drunk neat, like grappa, but rather is used as the base for a variety of homemade liqueurs and *apéritifs*, from *pastis* and quinine-flavoured *quinquina* to *vin de noix* and *vin d'orange*. The process is hardly complicated, and everyone makes them. Walnut and orange liqueurs are simple: sugar, wine and walnuts or oranges plus alcohol. For *pastis* and *quinquina* you buy a bottle of concentrate from the chemist to add to the sugar and alcohol. The results are variable, and I can never tell if it's the recipe or the quality of the spirit to blame. After some harsh encounters I

learn to steer clear of the *pastis*, and anyway this is considered a men's drink and rarely offered to women.

For the locals, days at Nizas follow a regular rhythm: clean clothes on Sunday and an afternoon of rest following Mass. For the women, Monday is for washing, and the old *lavoir municipal*, its tubs and scrubbing boards overlooking the shallow stream beneath, is still popular. Their weekday routine is unvarying. Mornings are taken up with household chores, buying the day's foods and preparing the main meal to be set on the table at midday. The afternoon is more leisurely, and they gather in threes or fours in a sunny corner, mending and knitting and patching and gossiping. On a fine day they might discard the household pinafores to go for a stroll. In keeping with their 'waste not, want not' maxim, the women keep one eye alert for young dandelions or chicory to add to the evening's salad bowl, or cut fresh grass to take home for the rabbits. Sometimes they bring their chooks to give them fresh air and a peck of green.

The men, shooed out of the house in the morning, have a different routine. They meet outside the church, where a low wooden bench catches the winter sun, and watch over all the activities happening in *la place*. Later they might idle across to the café or to the *tabac* that operates from someone's front room, selling cigarettes and matches and the thin lengths of liquorice root that some of the men chew as a substitute for smoking. Or they choose the morning for their walks, ambling in groups and sometimes inspecting their patches of vines or garden plots on the way. Their strolls are more aimless than the women's and at the slightest provocation they stop for a chat, whether to discuss the weather with the local shepherd or debate a contentious or particularly engrossing topic.

Their morning walk often takes them past l'Escoute and they dawdle as they approach, hoping to catch us and pose the queries

they've saved since yesterday. They are curious, these men, and ponder ideas and mysteries for which they cannot find explanations. Will man ever be able to fly to Mars? Are there fish in the deepest parts of the ocean? Is it possible to tunnel beneath the equator and come out the other side? Even without answers, at least we provide diversion and entertainment. Other questions are easier. Is it true that the Queen of England is also Queen of Australia? *Impossible!* What language do Australians speak? What's the time in Australia right now? Is it winter in Australia as it is here? It's hard to tell whether they accept our responses. After a while they move on, but we watch them stopping every few metres to review and dispute the new facts they have learnt, which inevitably generate another series of questions.

One day the men pass by l'Escoute in the company of a couple of dogs. They are scruffy, gangly animals, biting and teasing one another in obvious enjoyment of their outing. John meets the men in the lane and greets them, shaking hands one by one. Although his French is still rudimentary, he has enough confidence to test it in a simple exchange. How do you say, what breed of dog? he calls to me, as I lean out the kitchen window upstairs.

Quelle race de chien, I reply.

Quelle race de chien? he repeats to the men, pointing to one in particular.

C'est un bâtard.

Un bâtard? echoes John, as he racks his brain to find a possible equivalent in English. Then, haltingly, as if reading from a beginner's grammar, he manages to put together a whole sentence. *C'est la première fois que je vois un bâtard.*

The Messieurs burst out laughing. Puzzled, John looks to me for an explanation. It's a bitser, a mongrel, I tell him. It's not a breed.

The men notch up one for Nizas and continue on their way.

7
The shepherd and the gypsies

I used to think shepherds inhabited only fairytales or romantic pastoral scenes in the style of Boucher, but Nizas has a real-life shepherd. We never learn his name; he is universally referred to as *le berger*, the shepherd. He lives *sur les causses*, on the bare, windswept plateau above the village where the Aéroclub de Pézenas-Nizas maintains a primitive landing strip. *Les causses* seems to refer to a particular geographic formation, and in this part of France there are many areas of *causses*, all similar in appearance and vegetation, with some, far more extensive, classified as natural parks.

On this unwanted patch of ground the shepherd has staked a claim and built a basic hut attached to ramshackle sheep pens. With no land of his own, he takes his sheep to pasture every day, sometimes letting them browse along the roadside or the old railway line, sometimes in the pruned vineyards near l'Escoute or on the airstrip. We hear his approach from a distance, the bells around the necks of the leaders tinkling as they move. In winter there's no risk of the sheep nibbling the vine leaves and they do a service to the vigneron in keeping the weeds down, but some owners, says the shepherd, are now preferring to spray with herbicides. He shakes his head, bemoaning the inroads of technology that will deprive his flock of feed.

A solitary individual, the shepherd does not invite immediate contact. It's thanks to Madame Molla's son Vincent that we first exchange formal *bonjours*. Vincent is on his tractor when we stop to talk to him on the side of the road, while behind us the shepherd approaches, leading his musical flock. The shepherd also stops to talk – but in a language that is totally incomprehensible to me. Puzzled, I strain to interpret one word, unsure whether it's because he is speaking too quickly or his accent too strong.

I had trouble understanding the shepherd the other day, I say to Vincent next time he comes to the garage beneath us. *J'avais beaucoup de mal à comprendre.*

Ah, says Vincent, *il parle en patois.*

This local patois is my first encounter with the original language of the Midi. It's a version of the Occitan spoken, in one variant or another, throughout the south of France and into Catalonia in the medieval centuries. Though French was decreed the official language of the whole of France in the 16th century, people continued to use Occitan in daily life. Eighteenth- and nineteenth-century travellers who wrote about the differences between North and South in France commented on the incomprehensibility of people they met on their travels. Never in my wildest dreams did I imagine that this chance encounter with the shepherd would eventually inspire me to study this ancient language, and certainly never could I conceive that a course in Ancien Provençal would eventually lead me to culinary history.

Once we've been introduced, in a fashion, the shepherd is happy to talk, using his heavily accented French. He tells me he has about a hundred sheep, plus a few goats – just enough to earn a living. Long-legged, sparsely fleeced, the sheep produce lambs that are born throughout the year, except in summer when it's too dry. One day, looking out the window, I see him in the vineyard opposite, bending over one of his ewes that had just given

birth, so I quickly dress the children in outdoor clothes and take them downstairs to inspect the new lamb. Perhaps exhausted by her effort, the mother is not at all concerned by this small crowd of spectators.

You have sheep in Australia? the shepherd asks.

Yes, sheep for wool as well as for lamb and mutton.

How many sheep would a man have in Australia?

Well, I explain, we don't have shepherds. The sheep are in paddocks, enclosed by fences, and so a farmer might have a couple of thousand sheep.

He rolls his eyes and shakes his hand in that typically southern gesture that shows disbelief and amazement.

Impossible! Un homme, et trois mille moutons?

But he has sheepdogs to help, I explain, and he manages the sheep differently. He doesn't have to bring them home every evening.

He scratches his head and leans on his crook, puzzled, trying to envisage a flock of two or three thousand sheep. It is clearly a concept beyond his imagining.

But how, he asks tremulously and incredulously, how can the farmer remember all their names?

It's a mystery that stays with him. He has no reason to doubt my answer but it is so far outside his understanding of the world that, however often he returns to ponder the concept, it defeats him.

We often come across the shepherd on our afternoon walks, after Stephanie and Dylan have woken from their afternoon nap. Exploring beyond Nizas is my way of getting to understand this region, though I tell myself that I'm educating the children at the same time. Unlike the narrator of Proust's *In Search of Lost Time*, who had only two routes for his walks – the path on the Guermantes side or the one past Swann's house – I have multiple

options. Almost any direction will lead me to something of interest – a weed I recognise, the pattern of lichen on a stone wall, a view of l'Escoute from a different angle, an ancient iron cross by the roadside.

The easy route skirts the edge of the village to arrive at the *terrain de boules* at its eastern end. The *terrain* is quiet now, in the middle of winter, and the tall plane trees on either side are bare, but I can imagine it loud and boisterous in summer as holidaying visitors compete with locals, a cool and shady retreat at the end of the afternoon. The homewards circuit takes us past our neighbour's house. She's not a near neighbour, living about half a kilometre from l'Escoute, but it's the only other house outside the village on our side. Madame la Voisine, as I name her, is also something of an outsider. Unlike the other women of the village, she is not from Nizas, nor is she old. She is educated, drives a car and reads books, which she offers to lend us. In addition, her husband has an important white-collar job at the *cave coopérative*. All these qualities distance her from the other women of the village. Yet like them she is curious about *les Australiens* and stops us as we pass. Sensing less of a social distance between us, I'm less diffident about asking questions, though her knowledge of Nizas and its affairs is more limited.

If we take the opposite direction, toward Caux, we come to the stream and its *lavoir municipal*. There's nothing remarkable about the Nizas *lavoir* – most villages in the Midi have a set of tubs like these, either next to a stream or an underground spring – but the idea of a dedicated public place for women to do their washing strikes me as both enlightened and controlling. I thought my mother's washday work enough when the only aids were a copper and a wringer. The prospect of soaking and scrubbing and rinsing in icy water to the elbows sends shivers down my spine.

The dirt track on the western side of l'Escoute takes us up a slight rise and around a bend to the remains of the old railway line. At the turn of the century, when trains promised escape and new horizons, Nizas had a regular service, but now thorny weeds poke up between the tracks. The stationmaster's house is just visible beneath rampant vines and the two platforms, barely the length of a single carriage, are slowly dissolving into the natural vegetation. Here, on this windswept plateau, I discover wild herbs – thyme, rosemary and sage. It's a miracle that they survive in such hard, stony ground. Like the village women, I collect small bunches and take them home, tying them with string and hanging them above the kitchen bench. Thyme, say the women, is obligatory with rabbit.

There's another path that we take far less often. It starts on the opposite side of the village, beyond *la place*, and runs alongside the high stone wall enclosing what I like to think of as the *château*. The wall is thickly covered in ivy and far too high to scale, and what lies behind it is a mystery; perhaps a spidery old miser and his faithful retainer, living among cobwebs and tatters.

If we were to continue beyond the end of the wall, we would end up at the caravan of *les gitans*, the family of gypsies. We have seen their encampments, sprawling and unkempt, on the outskirts of towns such as Montpellier, where a near-permanent settlement has been established in the wedge of land where two highways meet. Fringe dwellers and outside society, by their own choice as much as by community will, gypsies are not beholden to its norms. *Attention aux gitans!* Madame Molla tells us, and I am reminded of the poems of A.A. Milne, where gypsies are 'other' and vaguely unsettling. So we avoid their sinister territory and keep following the wall around the other two sides of the estate to return to the village. Occasionally, in the square, we see the gypsies, the man as swarthy as any encountered by

Christopher Robin, the woman aloof and proud. *Comme elle est belle!* exclaims Madame Molla. *Elle est superbe.* Broad-hipped and firm-breasted, *la gitane* epitomises Bizet's indomitable Carmen, strong and resilient, and I realise that Madame Molla's standards of beauty are based less on aesthetics and supermodels, and more on utility and functionality.

Markets

Our nearest 'big' town is Pézenas, a somnolent centre that seems to have scarcely changed since Molière and his troupe performed there in the 1650s. The closest thing to celebrity that the town has ever known, Molière is duly honoured with a formal statue overlooking the river, his fame now appropriated by hotels and restaurants.

Pézenas has a variety of shops and even a supermarket, on the very edge of town on the road to Béziers. It's new and it's never busy when we choose to shop. The inhabitants of Pézenas are reluctant to change their ways, preferring small individual businesses and, most of all, the weekly market.

Every town in the region has a designated market day and for Pézenas it is Saturday. Saturday has been market day in Pézenas since 1434, and its status is inviolable. In Béziers the big day is Friday; in Agde, Thursday; in Clermont-l'Hérault, Wednesday; and in Marseillan, Tuesday. Equally resistant to change is the standard pattern of markets, with mornings devoted to the main business of the day, the essential food shopping, and the afternoon to leisurely browsing. After 1 pm, when the empty crates and crushed cardboard boxes have been cleared away and appetites have been fed, a second wave of merchants open their stalls, tempting customers to part with their discretionary

francs. Out come the desirable but less immediately necessary goods, from socks and slippers to tablecloths and thread, saucepans and shampoo, handkerchiefs and hairbrushes. Wandering among these stalls is like taking a surreptitious peek into someone's house – even into the intimate recesses of a wardrobe. Clothing for every member of the family is on display, for work and for Sunday best, from hard-working pinafores to undies and pyjamas. No false modesty, no embarrassment – though it takes me a while to get accustomed to the sight of a stall festooned with brassieres, D-cups billowing exuberantly in the breeze.

We make a weekly pilgrimage to Pézenas on Saturdays. The whole town is transformed, its broad boulevard a bustle of activity. It must have been like this in Molière's day, when shops were few and the townspeople relied on travelling merchants to bring luxuries such as silks and spices and other goods they didn't produce for themselves. Stalls take their habitual places in front of the town's permanent shops, and no one seems to resent an interruption of normal business since market day means more customers.

Professional merchants, the mobile *charcuteries* and *crèmeries* and the sellers of spices and olives, who do the rounds of local markets each week, open their vans to reveal their treasures. Weather-beaten farmers stand behind small trailers of apples from their orchard, or mounds of onions and potatoes, though potatoes are scarce and expensive this winter when all over France crops have failed. Women armed with sharp elbows and capacious bags are intent on completing their shopping as efficiently as possible; there's still the midday meal to prepare. Men idle and chat before repairing to the corner café to observe.

For me, used to a supermarket culture, the market is another world. Shopping is less a tedious chore, more a social occasion. Regular customers chat with the *charcutier* or the onion man as

if old friends, and perhaps they are. Conversation is an essential part of the transaction, indeed of the whole market experience. You can't avoid talking to the man who offers you a slice of *saucisson*, telling you that it's pure pork and a traditional product of Lodève, nor the honey man who asks about the children (Are they twins?). Since any trip to the market involves at least six different stalls, even for a brief list that includes only carrots, apples, biscuits, ham, nutmeg and cheese, the business takes well over an hour as each purchase involves a patient wait and, at a minimum, the exchange of pleasantries. Before I know it, it's time to dash back to the butcher and the Washmatic before they close at midday.

It takes only a few visits to be recognised by market sellers, to become a regular. As good customers of the cheese van we are warmly welcomed; Monsieur and his wife take time to tell us about the *comté* on special this week and a particularly fine *bleu des causses*. While many customers have very localised tastes, rarely venturing beyond Auvergne, we have no such inhibitions and range freely and widely. And because our custom is worth encouraging, the cheese man gives us free samples, such as a wedge of an Auvergne cheese I've never heard of, Savaron. It turns out to be a new marketing invention, a would-be Saint-Nectaire, if only it came from the prescribed area for that cheese.

There's always one last treat to buy from the Pézenas market: a bag of biscuits from the sweets and biscuits van. Miniature shapes, round and oval and square with scalloped edges, lightly dusted with superfine sugar. I pretend they're for the children, a sort of substitute for Milk Arrowroots but less expensive than Petit Beurre. I rationalise that their size makes them more suitable for the children, that two or three small biscuits will seem more generous than a single larger one, but if pressed I would have to admit that they are my particular indulgence. Like

conversation lollies, each biscuit bears a phrase or a couple of words, and in reality I buy them for the fun of constructing a series of mini scenarios. It's like playing Scrabble with phrases instead of single letters. Spreading a handful on the table, I select two or three to create suggestive messages: *'Tiens polisson/embrasse-moi'*, *'Venez danser/dans le bois'* and *'Voulez-vous/dans les vignes/avec le patron'* (Kiss me, you naughty boy; Come and dance in the woods; Would you like to, in the vineyard with the boss).

I'm thankful that Pézenas and its market are so near, but for all its advantages the town has a significant deficiency: there is no branch of the BNP bank. This is also propitious, giving us an excuse to visit other towns and other markets. I'm well aware that markets change with the seasons but less prepared for the variations from town to town, even over distances as small as 20 kilometres. Each one has its personality. To the north, the farming centre of Clermont-l'Hérault shows us a rustic, agricultural market complete with tractors and specialised tools, trays of seedlings and potted vines for immediate planting. Stalls here display goods I never see at Pézenas – local olives and walnuts, hand-knitted woollen caps and sturdy wooden clogs.

To the south, the Mediterranean port of Sète offers the spectacle of yet another different market. With its large population and important fishing industry, Sète merits a permanent, six-days-a-week market. There are more *poissoniers* than *bouchers* at this market, and they are all busy – sending scales flying from a whole *daurade*, selecting the shiniest sardines, loudly spruiking their wares. Spread before us, in row after row, are shimmering, silvery, luminous displays of bright-eyed bream and blushing red mullet and, under the catch-all name of *poissons de roche* or *soupe de poissons*, tubs of miscellaneous fish only a few inches long whose legality I silently question. I recognise some as similar species to Australian fish, but many others are totally unfamiliar.

Later, with the help of Alan Davidson's *Mediterranean Seafood*, I manage to identify many of the unknown species, though he fails to reassure me as to the edibility of knobbly *violets de mer* and *escargots de mer*.

Watching the local women make their choices, I am in awe of their confidence and expertise, and realise the limits of my own understanding and experience. These women know exactly what to do with each species, which fish they need for the dish they are cooking for dinner, and how it is to be prepared. Eavesdropping, I learn more ways than I ever imagined for cooking fish; frying is not the only option. I also learn an important lesson: just as different cuts of beef or lamb demand cooking techniques and certain accompaniments, so do different varieties of fish. Mackerel is best grilled over coals, tuna steaks should be pan-fried with garlic, and large cuttlefish are always stewed with tomatoes.

Sète also has a seafood auction, *la criée*, that takes place in the afternoons when the boats return. Only professional buyers are allowed but I can watch from the wharves as strong, solid, no-nonsense vessels laden with men and nets pull in to their allotted berths and start to unload. The catch, already sorted by species and size into grey plastic trays, is stacked on trolleys and wheeled away to the auction room, though a large and mischievous octopus keeps trying to escape. Enormous tuna, stiff and blue, are carried individually, resting on a broad shoulder. Some of this seafood will be on restaurant tables in Paris tomorrow.

I soon realise that most of the crowd assembled on the wharves are not simply onlookers. Men and women carrying discreet plastic bags try to make themselves useful and are rewarded with damaged or unwanted fish. As a boat's hold is hosed out, the rejects and leftovers rain into the water of the canal and a fat elderly gentleman with a long-handled net fishes for those that take his fancy.

Béziers is further away and we never quite manage the morning market there. Browsing the afternoon market, however, I find an implement I never before knew I needed: a *mouli-légumes*, a food mill with three discs for purées of varying texture. It's exactly like the ones I see outside houses in Nizas, hanging on a nail to dry. Now I can make soups like the locals.

The butcher

At the Washmatic in Pézenas I can do a large load of washing for only seven francs. Since I'm not ready to join the women at the *lavoir municipal*, it's always first stop on market day.

Next to the Washmatic is a butcher, and he becomes My Butcher. His shop is old-fashioned and authentic, not a bandsaw in sight: instead, a sturdy, slightly uneven chopping block and, above it, a row of choppers of different sizes and weights. In his one-shouldered apron, the butcher is as solid as his chopping block and lord of his domain, gravely dispensing culinary wisdom. Like *la boulangère* at Nizas who gently rebukes my French, the butcher corrects my gastronomic grammar, making sure I choose the right cut for the dish I want to cook and checking that I know how to prepare it.

My first lesson is about lamb. Entering the shop one Saturday, early in our relationship, my eyes light on a loin of lamb on the chopping block. Instantly I know what I want on my dinner plate and my mouth salivates at the prospect. Having patiently waited my turn, I point to the rack, still on the chopping block, and confidently place my order: *Quatre côtelettes d'agneau, s'il vous plaît.* At least I assume it's lamb. It looks exactly like the lamb I'm familiar with, but the butcher is clearly offended. He draws himself to his full height and puffs out his chest. *Ce ne*

sont pas des côtelettes d'agneau, madame, he replies, *elles sont des côtelettes de mouton.* Not lamb chops, mutton chops. Reprimanded and roundly humiliated, I can only reply, *Oui, quatre côtelettes de mouton, s'il vous plaît.*

French lamb, I'm made to understand, is not the same as lamb in Australia, which can be as young as three months in spring or as old as 13 months at the end of the following winter. So long as it still has its baby teeth it can be branded as lamb. No matter what the season, in Australia it's always lamb chops we buy. No one goes to the butcher and asks for mutton chops. Only when it's in meat pies or disguised in some other form do we unwittingly eat mutton.

Here in the south of France things are clearly different. Lamb in January is inconceivable, it's simply not the season. Lamb invariably implies a young animal, and it is indissolubly associated with spring. It's a seasonal delicacy, a luxury meat. The baby lamb we inspected in the Nizas vineyard will be ready to eat at Easter, around March. If allowed to enjoy life for a little longer it would become *mouton*, a completely different beast. Never disparaged as old lamb, mutton has its own respectable place in the seasonal repertoire.

Yet if I'd served these chops in Australia I'd be praised for the quality of the lamb. My four *côtelettes de mouton* are superb: tender, meaty and flavoursome. I grill them on an improvised barbecue in front of the house. Having smelled the distinctive aroma in the streets of Nizas on the day the butcher makes his weekly visit, I've learned from the old women that there is only one way to cook *côtelettes de mouton*, and that is to make a little fire outside your house and grill them in the open air over hot coals. It's not because their stoves don't have a grilling element, although they don't. Rather, it's because this is the way it's always been done

and, most of all, gives better results. I heed the lesson, and never again do I do I try to 'grill' chops on a gas or electric stove.

The Pézenas butcher doesn't hesitate to reprimand me if he thinks I'm making the wrong choice. One Saturday I ask for *tendrons de veau*, veal brisket or flank, as I want to cook a recipe from my collection of *Elle* cards: *Tendrons de veau bordelaise*, a slow-cooked dish that includes mushrooms and red wine. Approving my choice of cut, the butcher tells me that *tendron de veau* is good when slow-roasted on a bed of potatoes and onions. And how will I cook my veal?, he asks. I explain that my French recipe uses red wine and mushrooms. He is appalled, shaking his head in disbelief. *Non, Madame, jamais du vin rouge. Avec le veau il faut le vin blanc.* And he appeals to other customers for support. You never use red wine when cooking veal, do you? And they all nod silently, condemning me as a heathen.

At least I'm not banned from his shop; he considers it his duty to enlighten the ignorant. Now that we have a relationship of sorts, an implicit trust in one another, I decide to save precious market time and leave a verbal order: *une queue de bœuf, s'il vous plaît*. Returning at two minutes to midday, I am shown the heart, *le cœur*, that he's wrapping. Horrified, I try to explain that it was the tail I wanted, *la queue*. Clearly, it's my pronunciation that's at fault, and *une queue* is very different from *un cœur*. The butcher laughs it off and finds me an oxtail before completing my order, whizzing a blend of beef, veal and pork in his electric *hachoir* to make the children's special *viande hachée*.

 Libraries

Eager to immerse myself in the Midi I am determined to find a library. There's only so much I can learn from the locals; my horizons stretch further. I know how libraries function in Australia, not only providing books to consult and borrow but also serving as a kind of community centre, an information exchange with details of community activities and groups and clubs to join. French libraries, I confidently expect, will provide the same services. Perhaps I'll find a mothers' club in a nearby village. But even if I draw a blank on this – the example of Nizas is not propitious – I'm sure there will be plenty of books that will enlighten me about the Midi and life in general in France. That there will be shelves of cookbooks to borrow goes without saying.

The first town we try is Béziers, suspecting Pézenas is not quite advanced enough to have a library. Certainly, says the helpful man at the *syndicat d'initiative*, as he marks the library's position on the map and outlines the route we should take. It's not far and we find it easily – but it's definitely not the kind of library I envisaged, open and welcoming and filled with people. With the exception of a stern-looking man sitting at a high desk, the place is empty. Glass-fronted bookcases filled with ancient, leather-bound volumes reach all the way to the tall ceiling. There are no new books to be seen, no bright dust jackets on display.

I get the feeling that libraries in France are for serious edification rather than entertainment.

In the vestibule I meet a man who looks like a librarian. Are French libraries so starved of funds that they can't afford to update their collections? I ask. He's puzzled, not understanding the sarcasm in my question, and shows me a couple of recent publications. New they may be, but these are heavy, scholarly works with tiny print and no illustrations. They are not for the general reader.

I explain the kind of library I'm looking for, and the kinds of books I'd like to borrow. He seems to understand and is sympathetic to my project, directing us to the *bibliothèque pour tous* a little further on. Although not optimistic, I thank him and persevere.

The *bibliothèque pour tous*, as the name above the door reads, is even less like a library. It is tiny, no bigger than a child's bedroom. Open shelves line three sides of the room, and at a table in the centre two old ladies dutifully keep watch. I find the catalogue and peruse it. So far as I can see, the *bibliothèque pour tous* stocks mostly novels, but under the heading '*Classée*' I can see histories, biographies and other non-fiction.

Do you have any books on food, any cookbooks? I ask.

The librarians look at one another in amazement, then slowly turn toward us. What planet do we come from? A library having cookbooks is as inconceivable as a *boulangerie* selling sausages.

No, they reply. Everyone has their own cookbooks. Why on earth would they want to borrow a different one? And they mutter to themselves as their eyes shoo us out of the room, obviously thinking, 'Good riddance'.

Pézenas, it turns out, does have a library. In fact, it has two libraries, the municipal library and the *bibliothèque pour tous* lending library, though each is open only a couple of mornings or afternoons per week. The municipal library is free to join but

there's a charge of about 10 cents to borrow a book. It's still nowhere near my idea of a library. None of its publications are even remotely recent, and it has no cookbooks, but browsing the open shelves I discover some musty histories of the town. John is delighted to find a book on mathematics written in 1788. Any volume this age would be under lock and key in Australia but here it's treated like any other book. Not even its venerable age gives it the right to rest in comfort in the library stacks. Of course you can borrow it, says the librarian, but take good care; it is irreplaceable.

Eventually we come across the second-hand book merchant who does the rounds of the local markets – Pézenas, Marseillan, Béziers. This goes some way toward solving the library problem. The selection is idiosyncratic, cheap paperbacks and obsolete reference works, among which John finds a well-worn two-volume set of the Code Napoléon, the basis of the French legal system, and buys it for himself as a belated Christmas present. Most of the French novelists are unfamiliar to me but I choose a classic romance, George Sand's *Elle et Lui*, a thinly disguised fictional account of the author's affair with the poet Alfred de Musset – whom she abandoned, ill in Venice, to run off with poor Alfred's doctor.

And then, at the market in Sète, I find my cookbook, a damaged paperback copy of *La Cuisine pour Tous*, first published in 1955. Its author is Ginette Mathiot, '*Inspectrice Générale de l'Enseignement Ménager*', Chief Inspector of Domestic Science Education. A French equivalent to the *Commonsense Cookery Book*, it promises '*1200 recettes simples, originales, faciles à réaliser*' (1200 original recipes, simple and easy). As soon as I read her recipe for fresh fruit tarts, where Madame Mathiot recommends filling the pastry case with dried cherry stones before baking, I know she will be a trustworthy, practical guide.

11 Gastronomic explorations

In the Pézenas supermarket the butter counter presents a dilemma: *beurre d'Isigny* or *beurre des Charentes*? I have the luxury of choice. I also have the luxury of not being obliged to choose. I can have both.

Beurre d'Isigny comes from Normandy where, so the locals say, the grass grows overnight, the meadows magically renewed as fast as the cows eat them. The pastures are lush and verdant, soft and tender, and give a particular savour to the milk, cream, butter and cheese. You can taste the characteristic flavour in the buttery apple tarts and crumbly *sablé* biscuits from Normandy *pâtisseries*. *Beurre des Charentes* is produced in the Poitou-Charentes region further south, and is less pronounced in flavour. Both are unsalted; only Brittany butter is salted, more often *demi-sel*, lightly salted. Some French prefer Normandy butter, others the Charentais brands.

In the households of Nizas, butter is still not commonplace. At the Co-op it comes in tiny 100-gram packets. In the Midi people use oil for cooking. Two hundred years ago, when the new post-Revolution government sent public servants all over France with a standardised form to record food prices, the official sent to Avignon wrote, next to the space for butter, '*on n'en nye mengue pas*', people here don't ever eat any. Even now at the Pézenas

supermarket, the selection is restricted but varied enough for me to do a side-by-side of Elle & Vire from Normandy and l'Escure from Charentes.

Butter-tasting is a serious test demanding much concentration and quantities of baguette. I focus my senses, searching for differential nuances of flavour and texture. In the end, I cast my vote in favour of Elle & Vire but every so often, to avoid cellar palate, I buy l'Escure.

Exploring through food offers another way of getting to understand this new environment. A whole vocabulary of new tastes awaits, with so much unfamiliar to our palates that we almost need a spreadsheet to plan a series of scientific experiments and methodically record the results. After butter comes *fromage frais*, a light, delicately flavoured fresh cheese the consistency of softly whipped cream. It can vary in fat content from 40% and 60%, as in Petit Suisse, to 0% in brands such as Jockey and Taillefine. This no-fat version is the *fromage frais* championed by chef Michel Guérard in the low-calorie dishes of his *cuisine minceur*. I sample them all, from 0% and 5% mg (*matière grasse*, fats) through to 15%, 20% and 30%, and settle on 20% as the perfect partner to dollops of apricot jam on slices of baguette. The Co-op, I am delighted to discover, has a fantastic apricot jam, big chunks of apricot in a thick, syrupy gel. It might not be very French to eat bread and jam and *fromage frais* but I haven't yet lived here long enough to have become blasé about baguettes.

The Pézenas supermarket also has a range of *pâtés* and I start by buying the cheapest. To a novice it is amazingly good. With baguette and *pâté* for lunch every day I could be in the Land of Cockaigne. Gradually I progress up the price scale, sampling ever more expensive versions of the same soft, smooth-textured delicacy, and start to appreciate the subtle variations from one to the other. As much as I consider my tests objective, the inevitable

conclusion is that the most expensive *pâté* is distinctly superior. It is impossible to go back to the cheap one. This teaches me an important lesson: in France and in food, quality and price have a direct relationship.

This generalisation applies to fish, too, where price depends on the species and its desirability. *Loup de mer*, or sea bass, has lovely white flesh, few bones and is easily filleted. It's upper class, 'an admirable fish,' writes Alan Davidson. Mackerel is working class, a popular species. At Sète *loup de mer* costs 30 francs per kilo, mackerel only 6 francs. I buy one of each. The comparison is unfair since they are so very different, the fine, clean flavour of the sea bass contrasting with the slight oiliness and coarseness of the mackerel. I understand why sea bass costs five times as much as mackerel but for me, each has its appeal.

Increasingly I begin to appreciate the subtleties of quality in food in France. In Australia there are different brands of butter and cheddar cheese but discerning a difference from one brand to another is almost impossible. Similarly, chicken is always the same standardised product regardless of brand, regardless of origin. Here in France the variations are multiple. I can choose a *poulet fermier*, a free-range chicken, at the market, or I can buy a branded chicken from the supermarket or butcher. And among brands I can choose my chicken according to breed, diet and region of production, the label giving me all the details I need. The butcher recommends yellow-skinned corn-fed chickens as having a superior flavour, as well as chickens from the odd-looking 'Cou nu' breed with knobbly red necks.

It's with cheese that flavour variations are most evident, and especially camembert. Is it made with raw milk, or pasteurised? In Normandy or in Lorraine, on the other side of the country? Industrially, or by hand? *Moulé à la louche*, says the label on my Normandy camembert, meaning the curd has been scooped out

and turned into the mould by hand. Does this make a difference? I'm not sure, but there's no doubting the superiority of Normandy raw milk camemberts.

Although price gives vital clues to quality and place in the French food hierarchy, I'm not content to rely on price alone or on other people's judgments (unless, of course, it's the butcher). I need to taste and assess for myself in order to understand, to develop my own discerning palate. As a wine judge cultivates his skill by tasting and reflecting and remembering, so must I. And cheese is as good a place as any to start.

Here in the Hérault it's obligatory to eat the almost-local *cantal*, which comes in three stages of maturity. I sample them all. The youngest is *cantal jeune*, mild and milky and springy-soft, the sort of cheese that might have been called soapy by my parents when they expected a sharper, more mature cheddar. After eight months or so it hardens and the colour becomes more intense, especially close to the rind; this is the tangy, peppery *cantal vieux*. In between, having a bet both ways, is *cantal entre-deux*, firmer than *cantal jeune* but not so strong as the aged version. Like Goldilocks, I prefer the in-between option. *Cantal jeune* is an acquired taste, but I later learn to like it in the traditional pairing with fresh *chasselas* grapes.

I buy *cantal* because it is possibly the closest cheese to cheddar, which Stephanie insists on for her melted cheese on toast. If not *cantal*, then *mimolette*, a spherical orange-red cheese from the region of Lille, in the very north of the country. She is very definite in her tastes and, although I have to make do with only two gas rings and no toaster, I manage to supply her favourite food for breakfast every morning. At this stage she rejects *comté* and won't even look at brie or camembert or any of the other cheeses that I avidly consume.

Each week there's a different selection. Over a couple of

months our cheese board is a moveable feast: garlic-studded *gaperon*; camembert and *coulommiers*; ash-sandwiched *morbier* and a vine-wrapped *bandol*; *saint-ambray* and *saint-nectaire*; *saint-marcellin*, *crottin*, *picodon* and other goat cheeses undistinguished by name; and a palette of blues: *bleu d'Auvergne*, *bleu des causses*, *bleu de Bresse* plus three different ages of *roquefort*. We taste and compare and discuss, and then taste again. Which means another sip of wine.

12 *Vin du pays*

Living in France naturally means wine with meals. Especially with vineyards all around us. What they produce is an ordinary, unpretentious wine, *vin de pays*, a simple, natural beverage that is perfectly acceptable for everyday drinking. Everyone here drinks wine. It's the lifeblood of the Languedoc, a source of both sustenance and income. Drinking wine is actively and enthusiastically encouraged. *Buvez du vin, le boisson de santé* (Drink wine, the health drink) exhort advertisements, and bumper bars carry slogans such as 'Water is polluted – drink wine', and 'Drink the wine of the region, it's full of vitamins and good for you'. Wine is also a powerful political presence, and there is even an Association de Propagande pour le Vin whose bold slogan is 'Fight pollution – drink wine'.

It is almost always red wine, though the *bourse des vins* in Béziers – like a stock exchange exclusively for wine – deals in red, white and rosé varieties. We follow the market prices, *les mercuriales*, in the pages of the *Midi Libre*, where wines are ranked according to colour and to percentage of alcohol, from about nine degrees to thirteen. Red wine is more valuable than rosé, which in turn is more valuable than white, and the higher the alcohol the higher the market price. I cannot believe how little it costs, around two francs per litre. Nine degrees is almost as low as wine

can go; any less alcohol and the wine would barely last the year. I begin to understand why, from ancient times, the noble wines, the most valued, were also the wines with higher alcohol – which also explains the old custom of adding water to wine.

Wine has been flowing through the veins of the Midi for many centuries, ever since the Romans introduced grape vines around the fifth century BCE. One of these was the esteemed *muscat à petit grains* variety that today yields the perfumed and complex *muscat de Frontignan*, from the region just behind the port of Sète. The muscat wines of Frontignan have been produced and traded since at least the 12th century, and their reputation has endured. Even earlier, Béziers, known as Baetarrae in the first century AD when it was a Roman city, exported its local white wine to the imperial capital, Rome.

I read in one of the dodgy local histories that the -as, -ac and -an suffixes of many local place names indicate that it was once the site of a Roman camp or farming estate, and may possibly derive from the Latin word for water, *aqua*, since a source of water would have been crucial to any settlement. If I close one eye and look out the corner of the other, I can almost see Nizas as an ancient Roman farming estate, and in the vineyards surrounding l'Escoute I can almost hear the wine-fuelled stories from almost two thousand years ago.

Despite being in the heart of wine territory, it is not easy to buy wine in Nizas. Everybody has a connection to the *cave coopérative* and sources bulk wine direct from the *cave*. The local Co-op has half a dozen bottles, but with customers for it few and far between they could be well past their prime. The supermarket in Pézenas has wines from Bordeaux, the Loire valley and the Rhône but, disappointingly, very little local wine. The reason, I realise, is that wine in the Languedoc is rarely bottled. It doesn't benefit from an appellation. It's a bulk commodity for buying

and selling, in accordance with the quotations of the *mercuriales*. In Béziers we discover a *cave*, a wine merchant with wine in bulk – take your own bottles – but fail to locate a similar one in Pézenas. I mention the dilemma to Vincent, Madame Molla's son who works for vineyard owners in the district and also manages the family's small holding. He immediately goes into the garage beneath and retrieves a bottle of his wine, made from grapes he delivered to the Montagnac *cave coopérative*. In return I give him a slice of Christmas cake.

A few days later, on the way to Caux, we come across a crude sign by the side of the road: *Vin du pays rouge*. (The 'du' signifies that it's from this particular patch of country, rather than a generic *vin de pays*.) It's so close, on the other side of the plateau where the shepherd lives, that I puzzle why I missed it earlier. Following the sign takes us to Mas Laval, a sizable complex of stone buildings on the crest of a small hill, completely surrounded by rows of vines. The high and handsome wrought iron gates suggest an important estate but its days of glory look to be past. There's no bell but to one side is a small door. We enter the courtyard, scattering the hens scratching in the dirt, and are greeted by a dark-haired young woman from the house beyond. When she hears we've come to buy some wine, she calls her husband from the vineyard at the back. They're about our age, Jean-Pierre lean and sinewy, Vivette olive-skinned and as vivacious as her name suggests.

We shake hands and introduce ourselves, and Jean-Pierre immediately disappears into the *cave* with an enamelled pitcher and fills it direct from the tank. Tumblers serve for the tasting – nothing fancy for *vin du pays*. He explains that he makes it himself and that it's a natural wine, fermented with the yeasts on the skin of the grapes. In this way he hopes to offer wine of a better quality and at the same time make more profit than if his grapes

had contributed to the universal blend from the *cave coopérative*. The wine is good: clean, fresh, uncomplicated, authentic, and only 1.80 francs per litre – in bulk. We have to supply bottles, or else buy a plastic container, known locally as a *cubitainer*.

When we return in the afternoon with our five-litre *cubitainer* from *la droguerie*, the hardware store, at Pézenas, Jean-Pierre and Vivette are expecting us. They invite us into their house and suggest a glass of *clairette du Languedoc*, a white wine from the *cave coopérative* at Adissan where Jean-Pierre takes his small harvest of *clairette* grapes. While the children amuse themselves with a few toys – Jean-Pierre and Vivette have a daughter and son, France and Vincent, aged six and three, who are currently staying with her parents at Fontès – we sit around the large oval table talking, yet again, about France and Australia and the differences between them, and learning about Mas Laval, which has been in Jean-Pierre's family for many generations.

The property is called a *mas*, which the dictionary translates as 'farmhouse' or 'country house'. A legacy of Roman occupation, the term is particular to the south of France and Catalonia. But it means more than just 'farmhouse'; perhaps 'homestead' is a closer approximation. At Mas Laval the term seems to encompass the whole complex, the barns and outbuildings that, with the house, form the four sides of a rectangle around a central courtyard complete with windmill and well, today obsolete and boarded over. The scale of the construction confirms that this was once a substantial holding that would have grazed sheep and produced cereals and fruits as well as wine. Over the years, sections have been sold off or gone to other branches of the family. On the death of Jean-Pierre's grandfather the property was divided between two brothers, and now part of it belongs to Jean-Pierre's uncle. Jean-Pierre has only seven hectares of vineyard.

Vivette shows me through the house, which occupies part of

one wing and has three storeys. The top floor is a large, airy attic, completely empty. Vivette anticipates my question. *Autrefois, c'était la magnanerie* (formerly, this was intended for raising silkworms). If the row of trees in front of the house had been in leaf, I might have recognised them as mulberry. Silk weaving was a thriving industry in the Midi from the 19th century, and it made sense for family farms to take advantage of it, especially when the daughters of the family had idle hands and the summer shade trees might as well be mulberry as anything else.

Dating to the 18th century, the house is practical rather than pretentious. At one end of the large living area is the fireplace, nearly as tall as me, and about two metres wide. It was built for cooking, and in winter Jean-Pierre and Vivette use it to grill chops and coils of *saucisse de Toulouse* from the local butcher. The heavy iron tripods and long-handled grills, whose designs go back to Roman times, have lost none of their functionality. In summer the sausages cook over a fire of *sarments* (dried vine prunings) in the courtyard, especially when there's a crowd for dinner. The modern kitchen is a narrow gallery on one side of this living space, running almost the whole length. Once it might have served as scullery and pantry but it now has a gas stove and a washing machine. But what catches my eye in the main room is a kind of side table, tiled, with three deep square cavities inset into its top. Noticing my interest, Vivette explains its function. 'It's a *potager*. In the old days you took hot coals from the fire and placed them at the bottom, then put your pot on top to simmer or keep warm.' So simple, so sensible. Later, when I start to research the food and cooking of Mediterranean Europe in the medieval era, I discover that the design goes back to the Arabs and came to France via Spain, where Arab civilisation thrived for over five centuries.

Vivette comes from Fontès, where her father was the village

doctor – not the one who ran away with *la boulangère* from Nizas. She completed her education locally then spent time at a kind of finishing school in Switzerland before getting married. Jean-Pierre also went to local schools but experienced life in other parts of France when he did national service. Their world view stretches further than most of the population of Nizas, but they are still patriotically attached to the Midi, with its accent and practices and way of life, which means red wine with meals and oil rather than butter in cooking. I couldn't stomach fried eggs when we were stationed in Normandy, Jean-Pierre says. They cooked them in butter.

Just as we think we might be overstaying our welcome, a grey-haired lady wearing the standard French housewife's uniform of cover-all pinafore appears at the door. I can see she's cradling a large, furry, black bundle. It's a rabbit, I realise as she offers it to me. *Non, non merci*, I politely refuse, but she's only showing it to me before she holds it out before Dylan and Stephanie, who immediately want to touch it. She leads us across the courtyard to one of the outbuildings, which houses a hundred or so rabbits of all sizes and colours, even small kittens. Row upon row of boxes, with pink ears and timid pairs of eyes just discernible in the dim light of late afternoon.

Mamie – Jean-Pierre's mother – takes some of the small rabbits out of their cages and the children stroke their soft, trembling fur. Here rabbit is a much more prestigious meat than chicken and costs about twice as much. From each female they get four litters a year, and at about four months the young are ready to sell for a 1.5 kg family roast. Looking after the rabbits is Mamie's responsibility; her contribution to the family enterprise. Scorning commercial feeds she feeds them her own thrifty concoctions plus green discards from the kitchen, both morning and night, and she knows the age and breed of every single one.

Once upon a time a property this size would have provided a comfortable living for a large family and its dependants, but when your wine sells for only 1.80 francs, about 35 Australian cents, you look for other ways to earn a living. Jean-Pierre supplements their meagre income from wine by raising chickens and ducks as well as rabbits. It's all sold by word of mouth; he doesn't advertise, nor does he have a stall at the local market. Customers come to the gate asking for a rabbit or a chicken, which can be despatched on the spot. Ducks, more complicated to pluck and dress, are done to order. On another visit we find Vivette bent over the ironing board, holding the steam iron over a lifeless duck carcass, the spread wings covered with a damp cloth, and as the steam rises so does the nose-wrinkling smell of damp, dirty feathers.

With Stephanie and Dylan getting hungry and restless, it's time to leave with our full *cubitainer* and the six fresh eggs Vivette presses upon us. And then, as if today has not already bestowed its rewards, Jean-Pierre mentions that Vivette's brother Henri is a geologist and works at the University of Montpellier, in the School of Mining. Since John's thesis relates to mining, this is a coincidence almost too miraculous to believe. Even if I secretly hope for more, the experience of living in France for as long as the money holds out would be enough. Now, on the distant horizon, I can almost see a pot of gold holding the offer of a job and the prospect of an extended stay. With Vivette's offer to make introductions the vision starts to take shape.

13 Jean-Pierre and Vivette

Jean-Pierre and Vivette become our new best friends. We see them a couple of times a week, sometimes dropping in to buy wine but more often just for a chat, usually toward the end of the afternoon when they are finishing their chores. Sitting around the table, the fire softly crackling behind us, we discuss grapes and children and sausages and local politics. Municipal elections are coming up, and there's talk of change, left-wing parties favoured to poll highly. The Midi, if Jean-Pierre is any guide, is strongly socialist, if not communist.

As the days lengthen so do their working hours, and the lateness conflicts with the children's routines. *Our Babies*, the booklet I was given when I first took the children to the baby health clinic, the standard reference issued to all new mothers in New South Wales, advises that toddlers should be in bed by seven each evening. It's my only guide, and I follow its routine: a small snack after the afternoon nap, evening meal before six, then bed.

You should give them a *goûter*, says Vivette.

In France the *goûter* is seen as the fourth meal of the day for children. Unlike a small afternoon snack, it is substantial enough to keep them going until eight o'clock, the usual time for the evening meal. Traditionally, it's a length of baguette stuffed with a slender bar of chocolate, sometimes simplified to bread spread

with Nutella. I have my doubts but start offering the children an Australianised *goûter* – a cheese sandwich, or bread and *pâté*, or yogurt and a handful of the conversation biscuits. The effect is miraculous. The next time we visit Mas Laval, Dylan and Stephanie happily play with Vivette's two children, or with their toys, while we enjoy a glass of wine and talk until dark.

Until now, our explorations of this micro-region have been superficial – towns and villages, markets and *mairies*. With Jean-Pierre and Vivette as guides, we get to see behind the scenes, to begin to understand the places and stories and rituals that coalesce in local culture. One Sunday they take us to the Cirque de Mourèze, an ancient limestone formation of bare, weathered rocks that resembles a moonscape, bleak and windswept. The soil is fine and powdery, easily blown away, and the only vegetation is low shrubs and stunted herbs. Thanks to centuries of wind and rain, the site has been eroded into sheer pillars and grotesque forms that start to resemble weird and imaginary animals. There's a viewing platform on one of the peaks, and although the wind is fierce I want to climb to the top. Beneath me stretches a magnificent panorama from Montpellier to Sète. The landscape is a mosaic of browns and greens, and here and there a brighter patch of pinkish red indicates the new roofs of the *lotissements*. I recognise Nizas by the line of the stream and pattern of roads leading in and out, by the patches of scrub on *les causses*. From this height I start to appreciate the individuality of each of the tiny villages, islands in a sea of vineyards. At ground level, they are almost identical, but each has a particular profile, a particular complexion.

Without Jean-Pierre and Vivette's precious local knowledge we would never have been aware of the Chartreuse de Mougères monastery just outside Caux. Vivette and Mamie take us one sunny afternoon. Dating from the 14th century, it was abandoned

in the 15th, rebuilt in the 17th and shut down during the revolution of 1789. It could have suffered the fate of other religious establishments, pillaged and ransacked by a peasant rabble intent on destruction, had not a devout and a wealthy woman from Pézenas decided to buy it. She instructed in her will that on her death the monastery was to be returned to the first white-robed monks to return to France after the turmoil, and thus it passed to the Carthusian order who promptly re-established its vineyards.

It's not so much the monastery that interests us; more the wine that it produces. The winemaker is Brother Paul, the only monk who has not taken a vow of silence and is permitted to interact with visitors. A newcomer to the order, he was an electrical engineer in his former life and spent two years working in America; his English is very good. He takes us first to the simple chapel, which I dutifully admire, though it's the monastery's vegetable garden beyond that takes my attention. Row after row of cabbages, some deep green and crinkly, some narrow and pointed, some like a tight ball in a neat nest, give a clue to the monks' austere diet. They are allowed wine with meals, but the main purpose of the monastery's winemaking activities is to yield income. As in most of the vineyards here, the main grape variety is *cinsaut*, and from this they make both red and rosé wines. At around 13 degrees, these are superior wines; most local wines struggle to reach 11.5 degrees. Even more unusually, the monastery's wine is bottled rather than sold in bulk. I want to buy a bottle of the rosé – at eight francs, it must be a top drop – but Brother Paul makes a present of it. I tell him I will return to lend him my copy of Waverley Root's *The Food of France*.

As promised, Vivette introduces us to her brother Henri, inviting us all to Sunday lunch. I'm nervous; it's the first time we've been asked to join another French family for a meal, and I feel obliged to make an effort. Despite the limitations of my

wardrobe I try to choose something a little more stylish than the practical, comfortable clothes I usually wear, and dress the children in their best pants.

Lunch is a rather more formal affair than our impromptu end-of-day visits. The table is set with the best plates on a tablecloth that reaches the floor. We are offered *apéritifs* – *pastis* for the men, sweet wine for the women, then a platter of hors d'œuvres, all prepared by Mamie – *salade russe, œufs mayonnaise*, olives, slices of *saucisson*; the homely classics of countless hotel dining rooms. Vivette has pot-roasted one of Mamie's rabbits, and accompanies it with an intensely green salad from her garden. Then cheese, and apple cake, and coffee.

Sitting next to Henri, John has a good chance to ask questions about the University of Montpellier and its activities. Henri's speciality of geochemistry is vaguely associated with mining but far removed from John's engineering research. Nonetheless he offers to arrange a meeting with the professor of rock mechanics who works in the same building. It's beginning to sound promising, especially when he adds that Professor Jouanna has worked in an American university and speaks very good English. John is making excellent progress but his French is still at a fairly elementary level.

As it happens, Jean-Pierre has a dentist appointment in Montpellier the next week and offers to take John with him and drop him at the university while Stephanie, Dylan and I spend the afternoon at Mas Laval. The professor is away so the visit is brief, but long enough for John to get some understanding of the kind of research the faculty does and how and where he might find a niche.

A week later Henri lets Vivette know that he's arranged a meeting with Professor Jouanna and all four of us go to Montpellier. We don't have a map of the city but we find the

university, on the northern outskirts, with only a little difficulty. It's a new university, or at least a new campus – the medical school of the University of Montpellier was one of the earliest in Europe, renowned from the 12th century – and its isolated multi-storey cubes seem rather soulless, with little sign of student life. John meets some of the researchers in the morning before we return to Henri's for lunch, then John accompanies Henri back to university. Meanwhile I take the children to the open-range zoo, just beyond the university. Like the campus, it's new and not yet fully populated. Best of all, it's free, and the animals are at semi-liberty in natural surroundings, separated from visitors by deep moats. It's the children's first visit to a zoo and they revel in the freedom and space of the park and its sights, even though the distant and partly camouflaged animals have to be pointed out to them – zebras, llamas, kangaroos and a lakeful of pale pink flamingos.

I arrive back at the campus just in time. The meeting is finished and, bringing Professor Jouanna over to the car, John introduces me. His English is indeed excellent, and he enthusiastically praises John's qualifications and expertise before abruptly disappearing back into the building. I assume this is goodbye but a few minutes later he's back with something wrapped in tissue paper. In a totally unexpected gesture, he presents me with a bottle of Mumm champagne. I've never before been offered a bottle of Mumm. Champagne is so far beyond my humble horizons I consider it the summit of extravagance. As I mumble effusive thanks, he turns to John and casually remarks, 'Of course, if you wanted a place I could probably help you'.

At first I think he's suggesting a house to live in, which might be useful, but gradually it dawns on me that he's talking about a job. It might only be temporary, he adds, a research assistant, six months or so, and it might depend on the success of a

grant application, but it would be a start. I can hardly believe this serendipitous stroke of fortune – especially since it would mean that we could stay in the part of France we like. Driving back to Nizas we start to dream elaborate scenarios that see us living here for the next five years.

14 À la française

Despite my eagerness to embrace Frenchness, to integrate myself into a new culture, I perversely persist in eating the main meal in the evening. I defy French custom by having soup for lunch. It's incomprehensible to Vivette that I reverse the natural order of things. In retrospect, I realise it is totally inconsistent with my desire to live *à la française*, but soup is a practical response to our basic cooking facilities. A pot of soup can be left to look after itself while we do our daily business in the village, and even the children will sometimes eat soup.

Now that I have my *mouli-légumes* I can cook the vegetable purées that the French know as *potages*. The vivid, deep orange *potiron* from the Pézenas market inspires a pumpkin soup and Madame Molla's leeks become *potage bonne femme*, leek and potato soup. I vary the menu with turnip soup; *potage Crécy* made with carrots; pea soup, with raw ham from the *charcutier* de Lacaune; and potato, leek and tomato soup. John decides to rate the soups, one to three stars, and we pin the list to the inside of the kitchen cupboard door. Pumpkin soup, turnip soup and *potage bonne femme* all get three stars, as do the rich broths from the slowly simmered beef and the *poule au pot*, made with a large and inexpensive hen from the market. Garlic soup also earns top rating.

These are all authentic, typical French soups – or so they

seem. But in reality this is French cuisine in translation, as mediated through the words of Elizabeth David and Julia Child. Lack of success at local libraries means these two writers are my only guides, at least in the early days before I acquire my copy of *La Cuisine pour Tous*, and before I make the acquaintance of Tante Marthe. Garlic soup comes from *French Country Cooking*, turnip soup and *potage Crécy* from *French Provincial Cooking*, *poule au pot* from *Mastering the Art of French Cooking*.

Helpful interpreters as they are, Elizabeth and Julia fail to prepare me for *poulet fermier*, free-range chicken, from the market. It's properly plucked and the intestines have been removed, but often it still has head and feet, and always the desirable internal bits, heart and liver and gizzard. A *poule*, a hen, might still have its egg duct with unlaid yolks. If I buy my *poulet fermier* from a butcher, he will dress and truss it but market sellers don't bother with such refinements. I learn to plunge my hand into the cavity, feel around for the soft organs and gently dislodge them. Since the children like chicken, we buy it reasonably often, initially from the market and then from Jean-Pierre. Stephanie is very attracted to the hens and chickens at Jean-Pierre's, chasing them and trying to catch one, and the first intelligible word she says, a week or so after our first visit to Mas Laval, is *poule*.

It's chicken I choose to serve when Jean-Pierre and Vivette come to dinner at l'Escoute, Julia Child's *poulet en cocotte bonne femme*, a simple dish I've done many times previously. It's a one-pot dish, perfect for the large oval casserole, and although the recipe specifies oven cooking our primitive facilities mean cooking on one of the gas burners. Julia calls for a chunk of bacon, her substitute in America for the piece of pork that the original French recipe would require. But what do I request from my butcher? Should I ask for fresh pork, *lard de poitrine frais*? Or the salted version, *petit salé*, or even smoked *poitrine fumée*? Would

cooks in the Midi naturally use *ventresca*, the southern French equivalent to pancetta, in such a recipe? Not even my know-all butcher can give me an authoritative answer this time.

Jean-Pierre and Vivette are surprised by this way of cooking, which is quite different to the way they might pot-roast a rabbit. Perhaps I am too cautious in regulating the gas – another one of the lessons I eventually learn in France is not to be afraid of high heat – but cooking in a sealed pot with vegetables creates steam and is no way to produce a crisp-skinned bird. The flavour is good, but perhaps too buttery and delicate for our guests. And Julia's *bouquet garni* – four sprigs of parsley, half a bay leaf and a quarter teaspoon of thyme – is far too subtle for the robust tastes of this part of France.

The gap between French cuisine as practised in France, in particular in the Midi, and French cuisine via Elizabeth David and Julia Child might be as thin as a truffle shaving, but it's clear there is a discrepancy. In England and America, compromises are necessary with respect to ingredients and the way they are prepared; substitutes have to be found. French butter has a slightly higher fat content and less moisture than butter in America and Australia; the cuts of beef are not the same, with no real equivalent to the *entrecôte*; and *crème fraîche*, naturally thick and about 30 per cent milk fat, behaves in sauces in a completely different way to pouring cream of similar fat content. Further, like all cookbook writers, Elizabeth and Julia have to consider the preferences and practices of likely readers as well as envisage how a recipe can be made to succeed in a modern English or American (or Australian) kitchen.

Translating a recipe from one culture to another is not as simple as it might appear. Cuisine is like a language, with a vocabulary and rules of grammar; in the same way as words are arranged in a particular order to make a meaningful sentence,

so ingredients are put together to make a dish that accords with cultural norms. And as with novels and film subtitles, the translation might not exactly coincide. Were I not living in France, observing and listening and tasting the foods around me, I would accept Julia Child and Elizabeth David as perfect translators in the culinary sphere. Now I recognise the limitations of their recipes and look around me for French ones.

Even before I buy my copy of *La Cuisine pour Tous*, I find French recipes in the most unlikely places. At the market in Sète I pick up a brochure of fish recipes, *Le Poisson Facile*, and the *poissonier*'s wrapping paper gives me more: *soupe des poissons, seiche à la rouille*. When she learns of my interest in food and cooking, Vivette lends me some old copies of women's magazines – *Femme Pratique, Modes et Travaux, Modes de Paris* – and tells me I can keep the recipe pages. The 1970s *nouvelle cuisine* revolution is in full swing but the magazine recipes are almost defiantly traditional, faithful to the well-mannered *cuisine bourgeoise*. While the colour images are unappetising, far too fussy and formalised in comparison with the ones Margaret Fulton presented in *Woman's Day*, I accept that they represent the food that ordinary French housewives in the provinces might aspire to. I am all too happy to absorb the knowledge that these magazines can impart.

Then, in the pages of the *Midi-Libre*, the local paper of this region of France, I discover Tante Marthe, Aunt Martha. There's no clue to her identity – Tante Marthe might be the Betty Crocker of the Midi – but her name alone inspires confidence. I envisage her as practical, sensible, with an old-fashioned, no-nonsense understanding of what is right and proper. Who would dare disobey when she commands: 'Leave the cake for several hours before serving'. Each week she proposes a menu and provides the recipe for one of the dishes, usually the main course but occasionally a cake or dessert, and also recommends a wine to accompany

it. Nothing fancy, no appellations or vintages, just a good, unpretentious, local wine. With *coq au vin, vin rouge V.D.Q.S.*, a better quality red wine; with veal liver brochettes, she prescribes *vin rouge de consommation courante*, ordinary, everyday red.

It's through Tante Marthe that I discover a classic of French cuisine, *bœuf aux carottes*, that calls for one kilogram of beef and one kilogram of carrots. I'm sceptical of the proportions – one carrot would be considered enough in Australia – but decide to try it, and ask my butcher for an appropriate cut of meat. This time he thoroughly approves my intentions. The result is a revelation, the carrots contributing their sweetness to the soft and succulent meat, a harmony of flavours and textures. *Bœuf aux carottes* becomes a staple of my winter repertoire.

Bœuf aux carottes
Beef with carrots

I am dubious when I read Tante Marthe's recipe, with its equal quantities of beef and carrots, but my first taste evokes an apology.

Serves 4–6

500 g stewing beef, cut into reasonably big cubes
olive oil
½ to 1 tablespoon flour
1 cup white wine
salt and freshly ground pepper
bouquet garni (if desired, include a couple of cloves of garlic)
500 g carrots
2 onions, chopped

Bœuf aux carottes (continued)

In a large heavy casserole, brown beef all over in oil, sprinkle with flour and toss meat to seal. Add wine and ¾ cup water, season, add *bouquet garni*. Cover and simmer over low heat for about 1 hour.

Peel and slice carrots, add with onions to the casserole and cook for a further hour or more, until the beef is very tender.

Serve with mashed potatoes, *purée de pommes de terre* in French, or more simply, *purée*.

Little by little our meals are Frenchified. One of Vivette's magazines provides a recipe for *ragoût de mouton*, lamb cooked with haricot beans in the style of a *cassoulet*, another success. From a *charcuterie* at Pézenas we buy a *boudin aux oignons*, a blood sausage made with a hefty proportion of onions, and eat it with yet more softly cooked sweet onions and slices of apple. A cabbage from Vivette's garden inspires a dish of *chou farci*, cabbage rolls, following the recipe on one of the *Elle* cards.

On one of our afternoon visits to Mas Laval I find Vivette in the kitchen with Fifine, who was a kind of nanny to her and her brother when they were young. Until recently Fifine cooked at a hotel in the mountains nearby and seems to be recognised as something of a local authority: a competent, instinctive cook. Tiny, stooped, with darting black eyes and crooked teeth, Fifine is teaching Vivette to make *pacquets*, a tripe dish, and *civet de lapin*, rabbit cooked in red wine in a similar way to *coq au vin*. The *civet* is almost finished when Fifine takes the rabbit liver, tosses it in oil in a blackened pan then mashes it to a kind of purée, adding this to the simmering sauce. I ask Fifine about the recipe but her way of talking out of the side of her mouth, together with

her thick accent, is an obstacle to my understanding. It's for the sauce, Vivette explains.

Adding liver to a sauce – and barely cooked liver at that – is completely foreign to me and to my cookbooks. Julia's American readers are likely to recoil at the idea of rabbit, let alone *civet de lapin*, and she gives it a wide berth. It's well outside the common-sense repertoire of Madame Mathiot. Elizabeth David reproduces a 19th-century recipe for hare *civet* that relies on the blood and liver for thickening, but it's not one she has made herself. Cookbooks, I realise, are useful guides, but they are neither infallible nor totally comprehensive. There's merit in old-fashioned ways of learning by observing, listening and experimenting.

About five years later, when I start delving into medieval recipe manuscripts, I discover that thickening sauces with pounded liver was a characteristic feature of Catalan cuisine. I remember Fifine's *civet* and things fall into place. At that time Catalonia extended into what is now southern France, and the courts of Barcelona and Toulouse shared family connections. I start to see food and cuisine as lasting threads in the fabric of history.

Ragoût de mouton aux haricots blancs
Lamb with haricot beans

This recipe, from one of Vivette's magazines, illustrates for me the essential simplicity and economy of French home cooking. The butcher unhesitatingly approves my choice.

Serves 6–8

Ragoût de mouton aux haricots blancs (continued)

> 300g white haricot beans
> 100 g salt pork or flat pancetta, thickly sliced
> 750 g lamb forequarter or shoulder, diced
> salt and freshly ground pepper
> 2 to 3 large tomatoes (about 350 g to 400 g), peeled and roughly chopped
> 1 clove garlic (or more, if desired), crushed
> generous *bouquet garni*
> 1 carrot, sliced
> 1 onion, roughly chopped

Soak beans overnight in plenty of water.

Remove rind from salt pork or pancetta, cut into small pieces, cook slowly in a heavy pan over low heat for 2–3 minutes to render the fat. Increase heat, add lamb and brown all over (add a little olive oil if necessary). Season with salt and pepper. Add tomatoes, garlic, *bouquet garni*, carrot and onion and about 2 cups water (or stock, if preferred). Cover and simmer gently over low heat for about 1 hour.

Meanwhile, drain beans, turn into a large saucepan and cook in plenty of water, lightly salted, until they are half done, almost tender to the bite but still retaining a raw taste (about 40 minutes). Drain and add to the lamb and continue cooking for a further 1 to 1½ hours, until the meat is very tender. The beans should absorb most of the liquid, but if necessary add more, or increase heat to evaporate excess. Check seasoning, remove *bouquet garni* and serve very hot.

If desired, add a little tomato paste in addition to tomatoes, or substitute canned tomatoes for fresh.

15
Wild leeks and wild asparagus

In just a month at Nizas the landscape has become increasingly familiar, and I start to appreciate the almost imperceptible changes that accompany the cycle of seasons. With February come the first hints of spring. The harshness of winter softens. The sun is stronger and the days distinctly warmer. White and pale pink blossoms cluster on the wild almond trees lining the road to Pézenas, and the local women collect huge armfuls to decorate the church. Along the roadside and in the vineyards wild flowers appear, purple anemones, deep violet-blue hyacinths, wild marigolds and small white flowers growing close to the earth.

Also growing in the vineyards – unless they've been sprayed with herbicide – are wild leeks, *poireaux sauvages*. Since they're not part of my repertoire of known and edible foods I would never think of looking for them, certainly not among the straggly weeds of the sheep-grazed vineyards. To the people of Nizas, however, they are a delicacy.

One day, as I'm sitting in the sun with a book after lunch, one of the old men of the village approaches me, one of the regulars who walk up our laneway. Earlier in the day he had passed by and seen Madame Molla giving me some leeks from her garden. He stops and announces, conspiratorially, that wild leeks are in season.

Aimez-vous les poireaux sauvages? he continues.

I have to admit I have never seen, let alone eaten, wild leeks.

I'll bring you some, he replies. I harvested plenty this week.

And almost immediately he returns with a bunch of wild leeks, pencil thin, pale green stalks ending in small bulbous swellings. Some are almost straight but most of them are crooked and twisted. From the look of astonishment on my face it must be clear that I have no idea what to do next.

Il faut les laver, he says, you have to wash them.

So, as he gets out his trusty pocket knife – every male here carries a pocket knife – I get some plastic tubs of water and bring them downstairs. He trims the top and the outside layer of leaves then demonstrates the cleaning process, which is to dunk them in clean water three times.

On such a sunny Sunday almost half the village is out for a walk, and with each passer-by our friend gains a little glory from his role as benefactor, explaining that he has supplied these wild leeks to us who have never before eaten them.

You know how to cook them?

He's itching to tell me so I let him go on.

You boil them till they're soft and tender, about half an hour. Then you drain them well, and when they've cooled a little, pour over your vinaigrette. You make your vinaigrette with oil and vinegar and pour it over while they're warm.

I follow the instructions to the letter, and we eat the leeks for lunch the next day. They're more stringy and tougher than garden leeks, less delicate in flavour, but unmistakably leeks. I'm not sure I'd bother with them again, but when you've lived in Nizas all your life you don't turn up your nose at free food.

Late February is the season for *asperges sauvages*, wild asparagus. Vivette casually mentions *asperges sauvages* at Mas Laval, and in Nizas I see the villagers returning with big bundles wrapped

in tea towels. This time I'm determined to gather my own, but where it grows is still a mystery. There are probably many secret places but we find just one, and only after a tip-off: up near the old railway culvert, where the wild thyme grows. You have to pick them very early in the morning, says our informant. This seems an unnecessary detail. I don't see why harvest time should be so crucial.

Of course it turns out to have nothing to do with the intrinsic quality of the asparagus spears; they're no better at ten o'clock than they were at seven o'clock. Harvesting early, however, means getting to the site before anyone else has visited, the benefit being that you can choose the best, the palest and most tender shoots, as well as the most accessible. Having ignored the advice I am faced with the seconds.

Gathering wild asparagus is not much fun. The ferns are prickly and like cohabiting with blackberry bushes, and the cost of the harvest is scratches all over my hands and arms. Collecting enough for more than a tiny taste takes time, as each stalk is only half a centimetre in diameter, and you have to hunt for the youngest ones, the smallest shoots that poked their heads through the soil and pebbles overnight. Yesterday's shoots are already 30 cm high and almost too fibrous to bother with.

I select and trim the most tender stalks, boil them and serve them with butter, as I would fresh asparagus in Australia. The flavour is almost identical to that of the cultivated variety but, like the wild leeks, they are less tender, less delicate. My lack of experience with wild asparagus doesn't earn the same headlines in the village as wild leeks, but I am gently reprimanded when Monsieur asks me how I have eaten them. As with wild leeks, there is only one way to cook the wild asparagus, and that is to stew them gently in oil then add them to an omelette.

The reward of these foraged vegetables is less in their intrinsic

quality than in what they represent: nature's gift on a plate gathered by one's very own hands. For the people of Nizas there's the added bonus of them costing nothing, but more important is their role as a marker in the seasonal calendar. February is just a label arbitrarily attached to a particular four weeks, but the time of wild leeks and wild asparagus is deeply embedded in the memory and therefore more real. Next year, when the old men remember an exceptionally warm spring day the year before, they'll say, *C'était au temps des poireaux sauvages*, it was when the wild leeks were ready.

One of these exceptional days occurs near the end of the month, a mild, windless afternoon when the thermometer rises above 20 degrees for the first time since last autumn. This early burst of proper sunshine inspires John to remove his shirt and soak up the warmth, and the children are let loose to play in the vineyard downstairs, *sans culottes*, bare-bottomed. Passing by, Madame Molla is shocked, or at least feigns shock, smiling at the foreign ways of the Australians. In Nizas, as in the rest of France, one changes clothing not with the actual weather but with the official change of season. There will be no men *sans chemise* in Nizas until June.

16 *Au revoir* Nizas

You must be blessing the day you saw the sign, *vin du pays*, remarks Vivette, as we sit beneath the mulberry trees, now beginning to show pale leaves.

I give her a hug. Thanks to Vivette's introduction to her brother Henri and the subsequent introduction to the University of Montpellier, I am blithely confident in the prospect of a job for John. But even without this, and without the gifts of eggs, of clothes for the children, I am immensely grateful to Jean-Pierre and Vivette for their generous hand of friendship.

We are sharing Professor Jouanna's bottle of Mumm with them, having just stored the last of the repacked tea chests in their garage in preparation for a brief visit to England. Following a small operation three months ago, my doctor in Australia has ordered a check-up – and not knowing any French doctors has referred me to one in London. When we return it will not be to Nizas. Tearing ourselves away is difficult, but the plan was to experience life in different regions of France, and our next home will be in Provence.

I didn't tell Vivette and Jean-Pierre that there was a reason for our little excursion to Provence a few weeks earlier: to find a new gîte for spring. Having left Nizas on a Monday morning and spent a couple of hours wandering through the flea market at

Nîmes, we reach Aix-en-Provence for the evening. Always with an eye on the budget, I have a hunch that the eastern half, around Saint Maximin and Brignoles, will be cheaper, so that becomes our destination. Supremely optimistic, I feel certain that we will fall upon another *gîte* as easily as we found L'Escoute. The first *gîte* we inspect is a second-floor apartment, hardly suitable for children and strollers; another is isolated in a pine forest. I've identified a dozen or more possibilities in the *gîte* guide but each is inappropriate in some way, or is being repaired, or the owner is absent, or the house is not available for rent outside summer. It's dispiriting. I begin to feel ambivalent about the prospect of living in this region. The houses are too new, the inhabitants too recently arrived, the towns too towny. In short, it's not Nizas.

Disillusioned, we retreat to the Provence I know and love, the fertile Rhône valley around Avignon and Carpentras, with its landscapes of vineyards and orchards, stoic olive trees that survive in shallow, stony soil and constant reminders of a proud Roman heritage. Plenty of places to rent round here, says the owner of the hotel in Beaumes-de-Venise where we spend the night. It's a very popular holiday destination in summer, he adds. Belgians come here in droves to hunt butterflies and insects on the hills above the village.

I have a good feeling about Beaumes-de-Venise and its surrounding region, and this positive response brings its reward. The next day we find the perfect place at Caromb, about five kilometres away. It's half of the first floor of a spacious old house at the edge of the village, light and airy with two large bedrooms and a proper stove with an oven. In the yard outside Madame keeps the almost obligatory rabbits plus a cat, and there's plenty of space for the children to play near the garden and the orchard of cherry trees. Most importantly, it's within our budget, only 600 francs per month; most of the other properties are around 1000 francs.

I think Madame takes pity on us, though this doesn't stop her insisting on a hefty deposit.

Back in Nizas we announce the news to our friends, sugar-coated with little gifts bought in Arles: nougat wrapped as a *saucisson d'Arles* for Madame Molla, and for Jean-Pierre and Vivette a bag of sugar-coated marzipan olives, black and green. Small gestures, compared with the help and support they have given us, but I hope they understand, despite their disappointment, that we have to move. I reassure them that they will see us in September, for the grape harvest, *la vendange*.

The business of packing and repacking all our goods and chattels reminds me that I have no tangible souvenir of our stay here – nothing I could send back to family in Australia. Having observed some of the old village women working at a kind of crochet as they gossip in the afternoon sun, I ask Vivette and her mother about the traditional local handicrafts of this part of France. They pause then shake their heads.

L'artisanat, ça se trouve plutôt en Provence, Vivette replies sadly, and her mother agrees. That kind of thing you'll find in Provence rather than here.

She sighs, a fatalistic sigh that betrays her thoughts, that once we leave for greener pastures and taste the culture and prosperity and joyfulness of Provence, we will abandon the Languedoc and never come back. It's as if she believes the Languedoc doomed always to play second fiddle to Provence, that this region west of the Rhône is somehow less privileged, less blessed than the eastern side.

It's a common sentiment in these parts, as if the Languedoc is forever condemned to be on the losing side. The people know what it's like to be the underdog. In the early 20th century Languedoc winemakers objected to the practice in other regions of adding sugar to the fermenting juice. It was unfair, they argued, when

nature blessed their vineyards with plenty of sun and the grapes ripened on the vine to full sweetness. It put them at a disadvantage, they continued, especially at a time when there was a glut of wine and no checks on the quantities of sugar used. They got short shrift in response, the authorities deciding that from 1929 vignerons in Bordeaux and other wine regions could continue to add sugar. Rubbing salt into the wound, they decreed the practice strictly forbidden in the Languedoc.

I feel Vivette's censure – that I could be so disloyal, after all the help they have given us! – but more compelling is the need to understand France through tasting life in its different regions. It's only a temporary departure, I assure everyone. We'll be back for *la vendange*. I hesitate to promise more, despite my confidence in the success of Professor Jouanna's research grant.

Farewells are prolonged and tearful. Madame Molla insists on a cup of coffee with her – the first time we've been inside her house – and on chocolates and biscuits for the children, *pour le voyage*. There's one last goodbye and *au revoir* to Jean-Pierre and Vivette. And as we drive away from Nizas, we see the old men, Monsieur Molla and his mates, sitting in the sun on the wooden bench next to the road, and wave as we pass. Their eyes signal their disappointment. What will they talk about now, I wonder?

17 Bonjour Caromb

In comparison with Nizas, Caromb is a modern metropolis. With a population of over 2000, it can support two *boulangeries* – which means fresh bread every day, since the two make sure their days of closure don't coincide. It also has three very small hotels, three café-bars, two *boucherie-charcuteries*, one *tabac*, a *maison de la presse* for newspapers and magazines, a Casino mini-supermarket and an even smaller *épicerie*, two hairdressers, one camera shop, one *droguerie* for household hardware, one bank (not BNP), one pharmacy, and two garages – one Citroën and one Renault. It even hosts a small market every Thursday.

Most of the shops are on the main street, in effect a continuation of the main road from Carpentras to Malaucène. Our new address is on the edge of the village, and to reach the centre with its shops we have to climb the hill then turn left. Once we discover it, I prefer the less direct route, turning right and continuing on a meandering path through the old town, past the fountain with its water pump, beneath the stone archway, then along one of the narrow passages that affords peeks into tiny courtyards and the back of the *boulangerie*, where I sometimes see the flour-dusted baker at work. A low tunnel – I think of it as a secret passage – leads to the main street, *boulangerie* to the left and *boucherie* to the right. It's a daily pleasure, this behind-the-scenes

glimpse of old Caromb. In this part of Provence, where there are high and low hills and even smaller rises, towns and villages are all of a pattern, all clustered around a hilltop *château*. In Caromb the *château* has long since disintegrated, its building blocks invisibly incorporated into other structures, but the maze of narrow laneways in the old town preserves the imprint of medieval centuries.

Dominating Caromb, and the whole countryside for many kilometres, is Mont Ventoux. Bleak and forbidding, it is largely bare of vegetation, as though the fury of the mistral has, over the years, gradually denuded it. In fact it was the shipbuilders of Toulon to the south who systematically stripped it of trees many centuries ago. Nearly 2000 metres high, it is almost a perfect cone, crowned with a gleaming white cap. The mountain is clearly visible from Madame's, and I develop the habit of checking it every day: is it clear? Is it hazy? What is it promising for today? Its personality changes, sometimes scowling and malevolent, sometimes beaming its blessings on all below. I assume the name means 'windy mountain', since it is certainly that, until I discover later that Ventoux is a corruption of the name of an ancient pre-Roman deity believed to live on high mountains.

Beneath Mont Ventoux, as far as Avignon, is a fertile and well-watered plain crisscrossed with streams and irrigation channels. A fine network of roads leads to places with romantic names like La Roque Alric, Crillon-le-Brave, Saint-Pierre-de-Vassols. Vineyards, cherry orchards and olive groves stretch to the horizon; asparagus, melons and tomatoes thrive in the sunny climate. Caromb is known for its cherries, and the succulent strawberries of Carpentras fetch high prices in Paris. Little surprise that the region is known as 'the market garden of France'. Its wines also enjoy great repute: Côtes du Rhône, the fabled

Châteauneuf-de-Pape, the formidable Gigondas and the luscious Muscat de Beaumes-de-Venise.

The variety and abundance of its agriculture bring prosperity to the Vaucluse in general, and it's clearly evident in Caromb. Nizas, in comparison, is moribund, and the Hérault languishing. It's this imbalance of fortunes that Vivette and her mother lamented, as if the fairy godmother bestowed her gifts too generously at the cradle of Vaucluse, leaving little for the other regions.

Caromb has a different demography, too, with a far higher proportion of active workers than Nizas. Only once, around one of Caromb's lovely fountains, do we come across a group of women who want to know where we come from, whether Dylan and Stephanie are twins, and how old they are, but their confusing Australia with Austria means we are less exotic, less of a novelty, and they have no interest in us. We don't have curious locals walking past our house, as we did in Nizas, because few people bother to walk this way. Beyond us is only the *cave coopérative*. Flourishing gardens mean no one has to forage along the roadside for greens for their rabbits. In any case, foraging is discouraged by signs in the vineyards warning *vignes traitées*, the vineyard has been sprayed.

Nevertheless, we gradually make a few acquaintances. There's Monsieur and Madame Benz, whose house we pass every morning on our trek up the hill to the shops. Both from Alsace, they have retired here after spending 12 years in China, and have a couple of grandchildren about the age of Dylan and Stephanie. Monsieur Benz is eager to claim us as compatriots, having recognised the '67' registration plates of our DS that indicate the Bas-Rhin *département*, their original home.

Monsieur Benz asks us how we're settling in, how we like Caromb. Even after living here for 10 years, he grumbles, he does not feel accepted. I listen sympathetically to his protests: that

he's still considered an outsider, that the locals seem to treat him with suspicion. I don't dare suggest that he underestimates the residue of anti-German feeling in Provence – and Alsace, though now part of France, has an ambiguous past, alternatively French and German. Even the Vaucluse was invaded by German and Italian forces in 1942 and occupied by them for nearly two years. Memories last long here, and the strength of local sentiment is powerfully expressed in a simple plaque in Carpentras in memory of Rene Pasculin '*jeune patriote*' who in 1944, at the age of 19, was shot and killed 'in the most cowardly way' by *les barbares Nazis*.

If he's outside his house we stop and talk to Gilbert, retired *boulanger-pâtissier* who lives opposite les Benz. Gilbert collects stamps and we save ours to give him. Apart from stamps, his interest is food and cooking and he lends me some of his old cookbooks, including *La Cuisine Provençale* – as soon as I can, I buy a copy for myself in Carpentras. Often, when it's close to midday as we return down the hill, he invites us for an *apéritif*. Never a choice, he always pours Muscat de Beaumes-de-Venise for me and *pastis* for himself and John, but it's a recognised brand rather than homemade. Instead of asking if we have ever eaten wild leeks, he asks if we have ever eaten partridge. Opening his freezer, he invites us to look inside. It's full of game: pheasants and partridges and hares, all still in their plumage or furry coat. He beams with pride, but I find it somehow repellent, and although I politely express interest and admiration I am not disappointed when he fails to offer me one of his prizes.

In a more formal way, we also get to know some of the local business people, inside and outside of their shops. There's the man who runs the camera shop where we take film to be developed, whom we baptise Monsieur Photo 84. Business is slack and he is often glad of a chat. As a result we buy a second-hand Polaroid Instant camera, only 100 francs, so we can send more photos

home to family and friends. Not far from him is the *boulangerie* we favour, having tested baguettes from both. Recognising that we're new, and also regulars, Madame la Boulangère promotes her specialities. Have you tried our crusty olive-studded *fougasse*, she asks? It's available only on Sundays and holidays and sells out quickly, but I can keep one for you if you'd like to try it.

Our next stop is usually the *boucherie-charcuterie* whose speciality, but only in truffle season, is *andouillette aux truffes*. We like his sausages and *merguez*, the spicy North African sausages, and grill them over vine cuttings in Madame's yard. Madame la Charcutière takes a great interest in the children, since she has a six-month-old son whose christening is celebrated with a big bowl of sugared almonds for shop customers. She means well when she asks after Stephanie and Dylan, but it seems to me condescending; she beams too brightly and speaks to us rather too slowly and loudly. In the back of the shop we occasionally glimpse her mother-in-law, the deposed Madame la Charcutière, whose role now is to look after children.

We meet Madame and Monsieur Flour on one of our afternoon walks along the network of rough tracks, *chemins des prés*, between vineyards and orchards and market gardens. While not made for cars, the tracks aren't so unmade that we can't take strollers along them, and they offer glimpses into the working life of the countryside. When one day we linger by a fence watching a flock of hens in a large backyard, Madame spots us and brings out two warm eggs *pour les enfants*. Eventually we move beyond formalities, exchanging names and chat about local news and events, the weather and the progress of the cherry harvest.

On another walk we stop to watch the gardener harvesting asparagus. I'm intrigued by the special digging tool he uses that allows him to cut the stalk 20–30 cm below the soil surface. The best asparagus, he explains, is completely white, which is why he

inspects the beds morning and afternoon, looking for the telltale cracks in the surface of the mounded soil that indicate a new shoot about to burst through. If I miss one, he says, the sun will get to it and turn it green at the tip, and I won't get as much for it. This is the asparagus we buy at the Carpentras market: the seconds, bruised or slightly green, the crooked and misshapen stalks that cost so much less than the pristine white asparagus.

If Monsieur Benz feels like an outsider he should spare a thought for the North African workers employed to do much of the manual work in the gardens. They're almost invisible in Caromb, rarely leaving the farm and the rough stone huts they're given to live in, as far removed as possible from the farmhouse. They cultivate their own small patch and grow mint for mint tea. It's not a herb embraced by the French, but I'd like to have some in the little herb garden where Madame has allowed me to grow parsley and basil. Their reticence and my diffidence are constraints on conversation, but when I ask about mint they pull out a stem, with roots, and give it to me. It thrives, and becomes the ancestor of the patch of mint in all our houses in France.

Nizas was our kindergarten but we have learnt quickly and, skipping primary school, have now advanced to high school, from which we will soon graduate as fully fledged and responsible French citizens. We now understand the systems, the way life is lived in France, where to go for what service or product. Sanitary pads, for example, are found in the pharmacy; don't bother looking in the supermarket. We know what to do when the gas cylinder runs out, what an electric fuse is called (*fusible*) and where to buy a new one. It's now second nature to pull the knob up to flush the toilet, to turn the 'C' tap for hot water. We have adapted to French business hours, understanding that shopkeepers need a siesta if they're going to open from four to eight o'clock in the evening.

Not that we haven't had our share of frustrations. We argue about French grammar, which John is trying to master, though he refuses to accept its rules. I wish he would progress more rapidly; I'm tired of taking responsibility for every interaction. Our time for reading is too limited, and I might as well forget any ideas of writing. My typewriter sits forlorn, and my puny attempts to describe the idiosyncrasies of life in rural France go nowhere near capturing its complexities. French pharmacies do not stock the medicines we are familiar with, and once the last bottle of Panquil is emptied I have nothing to give the children to get them to sleep; I'm not yet ready for the suppositories French mothers use.

Our weekly spending, which I record day by day, invariably exceeds our self-imposed budget, and we've made no allowance for exceptional expenses. When the DS stops dead – fortunately, very close to a Citroën garage – there's no alternative but to replace the faulty part; Citroëns are too intricately engineered to accept a quick fix. I gasp when the mechanic tells me the cost: 760 francs! He takes pity on us, and offers to look for a second-hand part. In the end the repairs cost only 120 francs.

Yet despite these difficulties and disasters, I know we have made progress. We are getting closer to our goal and, indomitably optimistic, we are resolved to make this experiment work.

But perhaps we've become over-confident, since France has surprises in store still.

18 Madame and Raymond

Our new landlady is simply Madame. Only when we're talking to others do we refer to her as Madame Nicolaud. Thin and scrawny, with short white scarecrow hair that seems to be combed only on Fridays when she goes to town, Madame does not encourage conversation. Living in her big old house with her son Raymond, who looks to be about 50, she rarely leaves the property and rarely has friends to visit; she's too busy working, morning and afternoon, six-and-a-half days a week. If it's not the rabbits to feed twice daily it's the orchard and garden to tend, snails to collect in the right season, jams and tomato paste to make in summer. When we arrive she is checking the grape vines she grafted last year.

Madame is the complete antithesis to Madame Molla, though she must be at least the same age. And she has not reached her venerable age without sharp wits. Shrewd and practical, she is well aware of the value of things. Unlike Madame Molla, who waves away our offer to pay the second month's rent in advance, saying 'we'll sort it all out at the end', Madame insists on payment up front. When we ask her about olive oil – Caromb being in olive territory, with an old press in the town – she advises us not to bother. At 20 francs, it's too expensive. Like most of the locals, she prefers grapeseed oil. Eventually she gets us a bottle of olive

oil from the neighbours opposite, their own production. *Il faut la couper*, she insists, in admonition of our extravagance; you have to dilute it with grapeseed oil.

I suspect there's a story here – if only I could find a way to get her to talk. She's clearly no peasant; the cutlery in our apartment is Christofle, only silver plate, but Christofle all the same. When we tell her one day that we're going to Aubignan for a drive, her face brightens. *Aubignan, c'est mon pays*, she tells us with patriotic pride, as if an impassable mountain range separated her village from its neighbour, Caromb, instead of a mere five kilometre expanse of vines. Her father was the butcher there, she adds. It must have been a good business, as he left her a vineyard property at Suzette, in the hills behind Beaumes-de-Venise. I'd love to learn about her girlhood, her marriage, about life before and during the war, but she's not one for intimacies.

Even with her son, Madame is a woman of few words. Their exchanges, or at least what we hear, are peremptory and often hostile, as though Raymond thinks her requests or orders unreasonable. In this household, her word rules. One evening I overhear an argument – not the actual words, just the raised voices, followed by a door slamming and Madame's *Tant pis!* Too bad! Then Raymond's car leaving the drive. But nothing is said the next day, and I have no clue as to the source of their disagreement.

Raymond, too, is difficult to engage in conversation. Habitually clad in workmen's blue overalls, he departs on his tractor almost every morning, too early for our greetings, and rarely returns before sunset. Dylan is entranced by this new set of wheels, and *tac-ta* is his first word. He rushes to the window as soon as he hears the motor starting up, and I have to lift him up to follow its jolting progress out to the road. I never know quite where Raymond goes, but surely not to the vineyard at Suzette, which is about seven kilometres away up narrow winding roads.

Too many mysteries in this household. Even when we start to know some of the locals and raise oblique questions, we don't get far. Madame Flour tells me that Raymond married a local girl, and they were divorced over six years ago. From someone else we learn that Raymond has a daughter aged about 25 but now never sees her. Nor does Madame. The estrangement is total. No one can tell us why. Was Raymond too taciturn to live with? Did his wife run off with someone else? I wonder if Raymond and his family once lived in the apartment we are now in, and if living with mother-in-law finally proved too much.

To my surprise, Raymond does very little work about the house. The orchard and garden, and the rabbits, are clearly Madame's responsibility. When she needs someone to help she calls on *le bonhomme de Carpentras*, an odd-job man, to help pick and pack the cherries or scythe the tall grass in the orchard. He's a good worker, the *bonhomme*, but like the shepherd at Nizas, he's a simple soul. We never learn his name. For us he is only ever the *bonhomme*, and his place is definitely downstairs; Madame is not concerned with formal introductions.

The orchard is mainly cherry trees, but opposite the front door is a gnarled old fig tree, and in its broad umbrella of shade is Madame's summer table and chairs. It's a black fig particular to Caromb, *la figue longue noire de Caromb*, and over the next couple of months I watch the fruits forming and swelling and regret that I will miss the harvest in July. Beyond the orchard is a vast vegetable garden, far bigger than necessary for two people. In April it yields artichokes and lettuce, broad beans arrive in May, followed by peas, then green beans in June. Tomatoes and courgettes are still young but promise a bountiful summer harvest. But the most flourishing plants in spring are the nettles that grow alongside the irrigation channel near the garden, up to my waist. *Attention aux orties!*, Madame warns if we go down that

path – and it is such a narrow path, and the nettles so vigorous, that it is almost impossible not to be stung.

Guarding the entrance to the house are two venerable pots, their original deep green glaze now evident only in isolated patches. Each proudly bears a simple inscription: *Fait par Boisset, potier à Anduze, 1864.* They're beautiful pots, perfectly proportioned, simply ornamented with an elegant garland. Some years later, I visit Anduze, north of Nîmes, and see exactly the same pots still being made in this village totally dedicated to pottery. Madame's pots, however, have a dignity about them that is absent from the modern ones that sell for a small fortune in London's trendy suburbs.

The double doors open on to a black-and-white tiled hall and the staircase. To the left is Madame's formal sitting room, always kept locked. Only twice are we invited to enter: first when we initially agree to rent the place and pay a deposit, and later when we renew for an additional month. Madame's kitchen is on the right, and it's here that she lives when she's not sleeping or working. It's a large, sparsely furnished room with a table in the centre and a comfortable chair for Madame to watch the television in the corner. Upstairs is our quarter of the house, together with Madame's and Raymond's bedrooms on the left. We never get so much as a glimpse inside, Madame always up and about before us.

Until we move in, Madame has relied on Raymond to take her into Carpentras on Fridays to go shopping. She seems not to patronise the local shops, though Raymond must go up the hill and buy bread. In our first week, since we are going to Carpentras for the bank and the big Friday market, I tentatively invite Madame to come with us. She replies with one word: *Merci,* and turns back to her work. I am puzzled. Does this mean 'Thanks, but no', or 'Yes, thanks, I will'? Her answer is clarified when we

come downstairs on Friday and find her waiting. I have wondered if a trip to town means a change from the old working clothes she wears every day, and this morning sees her smartly dressed and wearing an expensive silk scarf, face washed and hair combed. Like a small girl, her eyes are shining in anticipation, and she is almost a different person.

The Friday trip to Carpentras becomes a weekly routine. Once parked, we go our separate ways, having agreed on a time to meet back at the car. It's such a vast and intricate market, the big square near the cathedral and every little street leading to it packed with stalls, that we lose all sight of Madame. I have no idea what she buys, what she does there; perhaps she treats herself to an elegant morning tea. But I know what she buys at the supermarket, which is the main reason for her outing. Unlike Pézenas, Carpentras is big enough for several large supermarkets – Intermarché, Leclerc, Carrefour. Madame's usual favourite is Leclerc, although she prefers Intermarché for meat.

On our first joint visit I delicately suggest that Madame might like to take Stephanie in her trolley. I'm delighted that she accepts so willingly. It becomes part of the ritual, that we hand over a child and Madame goes happily up and down the aisles with a wide smile on her face as she shows her new accessory a box of sugar cubes or a packet of soap powder.

From this day Madame adopts Stephanie as a stand-in granddaughter. She invites her to help feed the rabbits, taking her inside their little shed and holding a rabbit for her to pat. *Stephanie est très sage*, she says, very good and obedient. Stephanie can now say *lapin*. When the rabbits are in the outside enclosure she gives them grass, imitating Madame's actions. Dylan tries to do the same, but pokes his finger through the wire as well as the grass and is not pleased when a bold rabbit jumps up on hind legs and nips him.

A couple of weeks into our stay, returning home from a walk, we find Madame talking to neighbours in front of the house. We mumble the usual *Messieurs, 'dames* as we pass but as soon as the children are out of their strollers she calls to Stephanie and, as if showing off a prized new possession, presents her to her friends. Stephanie revels in the attention and the special relationship with Madame, and we benefit as well, with Madame's growing fondness expressed in the form of gifts from the garden – lettuces and broad beans at first, fresh peas and plenty of cherries later.

In my idle, musing moments, I imagine opening a letter one day in the future and discovering that Madame has willed Stephanie the Anduze pots. Or the property at Suzette. If only!

19 Mistral

No one who writes about Provence fails to mention the mistral. 'There is something of Olympian Zeus about the way it roars and rages down from Mont Ventoux, always unexpectedly and always at full force, rolling boulders and dust ahead of it and whistling down the river valleys like a herd of mad bulls,' writes Laurence Durrell. 'It is upon you at a moment's notice, cramming the words back into your throat, sending the dust-devils spinning and whirling like so many dervishes among the vineyards.'

For the first couple of weeks at Caromb, it's an idyllic existence in this most privileged part of France. The days are warm in April, and I sit on the windowsill after lunch in shorts and t-shirt, soaking up the sun as I read. When the children wake from their afternoon nap we go for a walk along lanes and between fields. One day we decide to take the direction toward the *cave co-op*. In Madame's yard there is hardly any wind, but we start to feel it hitting our backs as we walk southwards. It's a chill wind, but most winds blow cold. It's only when we turn around to head home, when it takes all our effort to battle against its brutal force, that we realise that this wind is exceptional.

Never having experienced one, we don't know it's a mistral at first. It's simply a cold wind from the north, but it builds up with a violent fury, whistling around the house and threatening

to blow the children's clothes all the way from Madame's clothes-line to the Mediterranean. I remember the stories Archibald Lyall tells in *The Companion Guide to the South of France*, about the engine-less train that was pushed backwards from Arles to Port Saint-Louis by the mistral; about the mistral that blew down the bridge between Tarascon and Beaucaire; about the three shepherds and 800 sheep that perished in a January mistral in 1786. Surely hyperbole, I persuade myself, exaggerations to persuade simple and superstitious peasants. It might be strong, but not that strong.

That evening the news on the radio confirms that this bitterly cold and powerful wind is a genuine mistral. But we are innocent of its ways, and see no reason to modify our plans to drive to Marseille the next day to collect some friends arriving at the station. I have broached with Madame the possibility of them staying with us; they can have the children's bed, I propose. For a couple of days the children can sleep with us. Madame is adamant, perhaps envisaging invasion by a tribe of gypsies, and firmly says no. Instead, we've booked them into the Auberge Saint-Roch at Beaumes-de-Venise, where we stayed earlier, and look forward to showing them around our new home.

I start to worry when road signs between Caromb and Carpentras warn to look out for falling branches because of the high winds. At the entrance to the autoroute we see a more dire notice: *Attention – vent violent*. The DS is a solid, heavy, well-balanced car and we don't feel any wind but I see the odd branch and other debris by the road, and begin to think that Archibald Lyall's stories are not so melodramatic after all.

This time we have no trouble finding our way in Marseille and manage to park close to the station. Our friends have forgotten to specify a time, so we wait for several trains to arrive from Nice before we spot them. They've also forgotten to tell us

that they have rented their own car, although a delay with their luggage means they need to stay in Marseille for a few hours until it arrives on the next train. We'll have plenty of time to talk later, as they are coming to our place for dinner that evening. We give them instructions and a mud map so they can find us in Caromb.

With boldness born of limited experience, we offer to take them sightseeing in the city before we return home. Planning to show them the *vieux port* and the rugged Mediterranean coast, we drive around the Corniche until we come to a seafront viewing area, which looks out across the sea to the sinister fortress where the Count of Monte Christo was imprisoned. Here the ruthless mistral reaches the full intensity of its rage and whips the sea into a matching turmoil. White-tipped grey waves splash over the low stone wall and on to the road. It is impossible not to be in awe and admiration of this force of nature.

From the comfort of the car we don't appreciate the power of the mistral. Wanting to take a photo, John winds down the window and opens the door a chink to lean out with the camera. This is just enough invitation for a wild gust to grab the door and smash it against the car parked next to us. No damage to either car, but the side window is completely shattered. It's a long, slow drive home on small roads instead of the autoroute, the cold air curling around us and reminding us of our folly. On our return we light, for the first time, the big oil heater that does double duty as stove, its warmth safeguarding us from the savagery outside.

The mistral has made sure we know who is boss but we get off lightly, finding a second-hand window in Carpentras for only 30 francs. For only a few francs more the man at the local garage installs it, and everything is back as it was. Except that now I know why the mistral inspires so much folklore. It might be a wild, intolerant, malevolent spirit but the mistral also has a certain

majesty, as absolute a ruler as Louis XIV in the 17th century. It is relentless, pitiless; while other winds might pause from time to time to offer a few moments of respite, the mistral scorns such finer feelings. Its authority will not be countermanded.

'Even Provençal tempers fray after 72 or 96 hours of this constant buffeting', writes Waverley Root. According to the locals, a mistral always lasts three days – or sometimes six, or nine, one can never tell, but always a multiple of three. By Thursday, exactly six days after we set off on our walk toward the *cave co-op*, the wind has vanished and the sky is clear and blue.

It might be an ill wind, but it is not totally evil. *Le mistral balaye le ciel*, says Madame; the mistral sweeps the sky. Mont Ventoux presents a sharp, clear profile, as if having undergone an annual spring clean. The paths among the vineyards sparkle with freshness; with white daisies, yellow buttercups and red poppies dotting the green verges. I have a new respect for nature and peasant wisdom.

Julian

As we are now more habituated to French ways, so are the inhabitants of Provence more used to outsiders, at least in comparison with the Languedoc. There's a long history of English writers and expatriates retiring to sunny Provence, or at least wintering there; Lawrence Durrell lives just across the Rhône, at Sommières. New inhabitants tend to keep to themselves and quietly blend in. Locals accept occasional eccentricities. Nobody raises an eyebrow at the presence of the odd Englishman, or other foreigners, with the possible exception of Germans, who are definitely unwanted.

Some of the foreigners are artists, like the Egyptian potter and his Swiss painter wife who live in the middle of a vineyard between Caromb and Le Barroux. We pass their roadside sign, *Poterie-Soie*, many times before daring to enter; there's no way we could afford any of their work. That we're not potential customers seems not to bother them and they welcome us to their workshop and showroom, demonstrating their techniques and tools: the potter's wheel and oven and dying vats. Taking pride of place in the showroom are wide, shallow bowls and large platters decorated with bold motifs, but my eye is caught by the iridescent scarves and exquisite silk shirts, softly flowing, hand-painted in shades of blue and aqua and purple that manage to be

both vibrant and muted at the same time. I might not wear them myself, but I would love to give one to my mother.

They're generous with their time and share their experiences as expatriates in France. It's the first time we've had such a conversation, and it's gratifying to know that others have made the same mistakes, have puzzled at the same customs. We don't know them well enough to be on first-name terms and, since the common language is French, they remain Monsieur and Madame. They ask about Stephanie and Dylan; they have a boy and girl, too, old enough to attend school. From time to time we drop in for a visit, and sometimes run across them shopping in Caromb. One day at the Thursday market, Madame Poterie-Soie calls to me. I have a bag of clothes our children have outgrown, she says, would you like them? I hope we don't look so destitute as to be dependent on charity, but I'm very thankful all the same.

At the *cave coopérative* at Mormoiron, I meet one of the English expatriates as we both order refills of our ten-litre *cubitainers*. Overhearing me talking to John in English, he immediately switches from French and we compare opinions on the Mormoiron wine (one of the best, we agree) and on other *caves* nearby. Life is good here, he says; the climate, the lifestyle, the wine. There are quite a few of us in the region now, he adds, though to me they are largely invisible. Nevertheless, on yet another wine-buying expedition to a local *cave* I recognise, from the slight nuance of accent, that the other customer at the counter is English. That I am not French must be equally obvious to him. Yet on this occasion we keep up pretences, offering polite pleasantries on the weather and wine – *C'est un très bon vin, n'est-ce pas?* – and wishing each other *Bon après-midi*.

The oddness of this exchange is not immediately apparent. Only when I recount it to John, waiting in the car with the sleeping children, do I realise that in our four or five months

in France I have become used to speaking French everywhere outside our little family unit. And even when we're conversing in English at home, it's actually a mixture of French and English. Do we need to get *mazout* for the heater, I ask, since that's the name of the fuel it takes and I have no idea what might be the equivalent in English. The stinging nettles are always *les orties*, broad beans always *les fèves*. This is the language the children pick up and repeat, unaware of its idiosyncrasies.

The expatriate diaspora must be well scattered and self-sufficient, as we get to know only one English speaker around Caromb. We meet Julian one Sunday at Le Barroux, a hilltop hamlet crowded around a massive 12th-century *château*, an intimidating fortress that looks as though it hewed itself out of the elemental rock. Le Barroux is known as an artists' village, and its steep cobbled lanes are home to tiny galleries and craft shops. In April customers are few, but it's easy to visualise the throngs of tourists in summer, leaning over the worn stone walls and snapping the panorama to Carpentras and beyond. Idly wandering, we follow the signs to an art exhibition at the *mairie*, where conventional watercolour scenes of Provence are juxtaposed with dark, turbulent paintings that seem to depict exploding satellites in violent colours of orange and red and yellow. At 1000 francs or more, they're not inexpensive. They're all by my husband, says the lady at the door, and these ones – pointing to the colliding colours – were in an exhibition in New York. He will be back soon, she adds, right now he's acting as a chauffeur for an Englishman who has already bought two paintings.

Out of politeness, we stay until the return of the artist/chauffeur and his wife eagerly makes introductions. I ask a few questions about the New York exhibition but it's difficult to find the right words to show the appreciation he feels his art deserves. It's the Englishman who takes over, inviting us back to his house

for tea. Since he lives outside the village proper, on the side of the hill, we have to drive him home. On the way he starts to tell us his story.

Julian has lived at Le Barroux for eight years. His reason for moving to Provence, he says, was to escape exorbitant English taxes. At first his wife and young children lived with him in the house, but after a few years she left him to live with the owner of the *château* above. It's all beginning to sound like a B-grade melodrama.

His house is a big old Provençal *mas*, partly renovated. The swimming pool, today muddy and leaf-sodden, is an ongoing project. One of his first changes was to convert the adjoining barn into a new kitchen, for which he drew up a design that included a row of windows in the solid north-facing wall. The local builder was aghast, Julian was adamant, and the end was inevitable. With the first mistral the windows were blown away. They've used stronger glass this time, he tells us, but I suspect the mistral has other tricks up its sleeve.

Inside is a scene of utter mayhem, as though the place had been ransacked by a burglar. The floor is littered with family-crested silver: trays and jugs, meat dishes and carving knives. Pieces of a dinner service balance tenuously on chairs and sideboard. My sense of foreboding is not helped by a glimpse of a huge, hairy boar's head, grimacing from the end of a dark hallway. It terrifies the children and I have to persuade them it's only a *sanglier-cochon*, like the picture in one of their books. The kitchen is a mess but Julian waves away the chaos and manages to produce a pot of tea, and leads us to his living room.

Julian's conversation is jumbled and incoherent, sometimes lucid and logical, sometimes totally incomprehensible, but I'm starting to fit bits and pieces together. One day, he says, he crashed his car into a steamroller. It was stationary, parked on

the side of the road while the workmen were having lunch. A freakish accident, I imagine, but not implausible. It's the next part that starts to raise my suspicions as to his sanity. So I commandeered the steamroller, he continues, and managed to get a couple of kilometres down the road before the police came. They immediately arrested me for DUI. He tells the story with a mixture of pride and regret. Now he has neither car nor licence, and I realise why he needed a chauffeur; why he asked us to drive him home.

The chances of his regaining a licence are slim. In his next ramble Julian tells us he's an alcoholic. Perhaps he was crazy even before the drink did him in. At one moment he seems to suggest we drop in to see him from time to time, that he'd be happy to see us at any time, that he enjoys our company; the next, it seems he would rather not know us. Right now, however, he desperately needs a lift to his 'watering hole', so we drop him at the Café du Cours in Caromb. Later that evening John checks the café and Julian is still there, in dire need of a ride home; local taxis take a night off on Sundays. His legs won't carry him down the hill to our apartment.

Over the next couple of months we run into him occasionally in the street or in the café. Le Barroux is too small to have permanent shops so Julian has to come to Caromb or another close town for supplies. He seems to live on beer and wine; rarely do I see solid food pass his lips. His extravagant bonhomie has to be balanced against the kaleidoscope of his moods but in good times he has plenty of stories of his exploits, always entertaining if sometimes straining credulity. I wonder how much longer he can continue.

Visa

The episode with the mistral, and our ineptitude, make a small and temporary dent in my self-confidence. I am still a P-plater, although I feel more at home here in France than I did on the brief sortie across the Channel. Despite the commonality of language, England remained foreign. I loved the bookshops but was out of my element when it came to eating. And Stephanie, who had desperately wanted cheddar for her melted-cheese-on-toast breakfast, decided that she preferred camembert after all. Life in France might be more challenging, but it's definitely more pleasurable.

Even more positive, John's job prospects are improving. Not only does Professor Jouanna invite him to meet his colleagues at a thesis presentation in Nîmes but another possibility surfaces at the same time. Chris, a colleague who facilitated vital computer access during John's doctoral research, has been transferred to IBM offices in France and suggests he might find a way for John to work with him in Paris. His suggestion comes with reservations: it's only a possibility, only a short-term summer job with minimal pay, a position usually offered to a student, but it's a foot in the door, a step toward a real job. Our optimism goes sky high. The snag is that John would have to obtain a work permit before he could start. For foreigners in France, being granted a work permit is normally contingent on the job being offered

first. Since our visas explicitly forbid us applying for one, we need to find a loophole.

Not a problem, I tell myself. All I see is a rosy future that becomes even rosier when John receives a letter from Professor Jouanna telling him he has submitted a tender for the research contract, believes he will secure it, and would like John on his research team at a salary of 4500 francs per month, starting at the beginning of October. This is better than winning the lottery! Not only is it the research area John enjoys, it will bring him into contact with a whole network of European specialists who, in my sunny vision of the future, will demand his expertise as soon as they get to know him. Professor Jouanna says he will set in train the process of applying for a work permit, and in my foolish dreams I imagine that the mere submission of the forms will also help open doors at IBM.

Of more immediate importance, however, is the registration of our new address at Caromb and renewal of our visas for another six months. It's hard to believe that we have lived in France for almost four months already. It should be a simple formality, but it's the first time the *mairie* at Caromb has had to deal with such a request and the secretary thinks we should return to Australia for renewals. As a mere provincial clerk, what would he know, I mutter. The French consulate in Sydney assured us visas could be renewed at any *mairie* in France, and I trust this advice.

My response is to approach a higher authority, and we present our visas to the *sous-préfecture* office at Carpentras. Again, shoulders are shrugged. *Il faut retourner en Australie, Madame.* That is certainly not what I want to hear, and at my request the man telephones the *préfecture* in Avignon to ask for advice. Hanging up the phone he repeats to us what he has been told: there is no way the visa can be renewed in France. *Impossible!* I respond, in righteous rage. We immediately set off for Avignon.

At the *préfecture* in Avignon the first person I speak to happens to be the very same one who advised the Carpentras office. I persist, explaining the promises made in Australia, not knowing how else to respond. Eventually, and perhaps to escape my haranguing, he relents and agrees to transfer us to his superior. I start to worry. Did I misunderstand the consulate's advice? Did I neglect a section of the visa application? Will I have to make an ignominious return, tail between my legs, whimpering mea culpas?

This is serious, and after this meeting there will be no higher authority I can appeal to. It doesn't help that I don't understand the reasons that make renewal impossible. What I do understand, only too well, is that non-renewal will mean going back to Australia, and we don't have a return ticket. And it would be impossible to return to France subsequently, to pick up the threads of the life we're establishing. Desperate for a solution, John and I confer furtively and agree on a plan. There's an element of truth in it, and I can name names in justification. I will say we are in France in order for John to make contact with universities and academics doing similar research.

My mouth is dry and I'm shaking as I'm summoned to the office. The chief is a kindly man with friendly eyes, but he restates the official line that it is not possible to renew temporary resident visas. I bluster, repeating again the advice given by the consulate. They're wrong, he says bluntly. I can see the rosy future evaporating. I try to envisage other options, but by this time my eyes are filling and my voice is wavering. But I haven't forgotten the agreed strategy. Taking a deep breath, I reel off John's qualifications and credentials and explain that we are here in France so that he can consult French experts: Professor Jouanna at the University of Montpellier, IBM in Paris. Ah, says the chief, smiling and perhaps taking pity on me, professional

reasons! That is completely different, an exceptional case, and I will renew the visas for six months. But, he warns sternly, wagging a metaphorical finger, a condition of the visas is that you do not look for work. I remind myself that the offer of a job in France is completely different.

My gratitude is heartfelt. I want to wrap my arms around him and give him a hug, but I can feel the tears coming and after mumbling *merci* and shaking his hand I quickly back out of the office, down the hall to where John and the children are waiting. By this time jubilation has overcome the tears. Look! as I show them the newly stamped visas, all done. I need a coffee to calm down.

22 Pot-au-feu

Like bicycles, baguettes and black Basque berets, the *pot-au-feu* symbolises Frenchness. Or so I am led to believe when I read Waverley Root, though perhaps I should take warning from his comment, 'Progress is threatening this dish'. I resolve to cook one, somehow imagining this to be another stage in the naturalisation process, a necessary test, like baking Anzac biscuits. *Pot-au-feu*, the classic that I naïvely imagine to be as much a ritual in France as the Sunday roast leg of lamb in 1970s Australia, will be the subject of my first piece for *Epicurean* magazine.

As my understanding of ingredients and my repertoire of local dishes expand, I rely less on Elizabeth David and Julia Child, except when it comes to *pot-au-feu*. I've read about *pot-au-feu*, absorbed both sides of the roast-vs.-boiled debate, but never cooked nor eaten this archetypal bourgeois meal, the epitome of ordinary French family cooking embodying all the myths of the prudent and economical French *ménagère*.

I consult all my cookbooks to identify the cuts of meat to use, the processes of preparation and cooking. With Julia Child I go no further than the first paragraph. Her *pot-au-feu* adds a piece of pork, a chicken and a kilogram of lightly smoked sausage to the beef, and ends up feeding at least a dozen. There's no way I'm going to attempt a scaled-down version of this extravaganza. In

French Provincial Cooking Elizabeth David devotes six pages to the *pot-au-feu*. Ginette Mathiot is much more economical, summarising all in less than a page.

Start with brisket, or brisket plus topside or round steak, specifies Madame Mathiot. The down-to-earth Elizabeth David acknowledges the desirability of having two different cuts of meat but also recognises the practical difficulties, especially for a 'modest family', and suggests brisket or silverside. Both authors agree on the inclusion of a piece of veal knuckle and a beef marrow bone, tied in muslin or sealed at the ends with a wedge of carrot to stop the marrow escaping.

Two adults and two very young children make for an extremely modest family, and I start to have second thoughts about an experiment that demands at least two kilograms of meat – anything less than one kilogram, says Elizabeth David, is hardly worth cooking. What will I ask for? And how much?, I wonder. I had been hoping that I could simply walk in to my friendly butcher and point to a tray of meat labelled *pot-au-feu*, but these are rare. Only once or twice, at the butchery counters of large supermarkets, have I seen meat designated *pot-au-feu*, and then it has been a large piece of silverside or a neatly tied roll, rather like a rolled rib roast. I'm beginning to mistrust the cliché. *Pot-au-feu*, I suspect, has gone out of fashion as today's customers favour more quickly cooked steaks and chops, or tidy roasts. In all the times I've waited my turn while the butcher expertly prepares a *rôti de veau* for this customer, two *entrecôtes* for that, the only person ever to ask for meat for a *pot-au-feu* has been me!

This transfer of allegiance, I write in my *Epicurean* article,

> ... has not been hindered by stove manufacturers, who have accelerated the demise of the old fuel-burning slow combustion stove and prompted its replacement by a modern apparatus,

usually gas. Often, however, the gas jet has only two flame-regulating positions, high and low, and even on 'simmer' the heat can be too much. Consequently, you can't leave the *pot-au-feu* to slowly and gently *mijoter* on the back corner of the stove for three or four hours; on today's stove it needs continual attention, regulating the heat so that it shudders just enough.

Another reason for the *pot-au-feu*'s slide down the popularity scale is the change in family customs. Not so long ago, 'midi' was the big meal of the day, when all the family assembled around the table at home. Now, people travel further to work or to school; there may not be time, even in the customary two hours break, to get home, eat, and return – and anyway, staff canteens often provide a hot meal to save this travel. So midi becomes less and less a family affair.

In the interest of proper journalism and accurate reporting, not to mention the prospect of a good dinner, I timidly ask Madame la Charcutière for meat for a *pot-au-feu*. Since she deals only in *charcuterie* and chit-chat, she passes the request to her husband, the butcher, who carefully selects the required cuts and holds them up so I can indicate how much I want. He saws through a shin bone to give me a length with marrow and finds a piece of veal with plenty of bone. My experiment is about to start.

When it's not part of your way of life, *pot-au-feu* carries with it something of the mystique of the sorcerer's cauldron but, at its simplest, it is nothing more than beef cooked with vegetables and herbs. Abundant and varied vegetables, instructs Ginette Mathiot, and obligatorily leeks, onions, carrots and turnips. None of these poses a problem, and nor does the bouquet of herbs. Fortunately I have a very large stockpot. The meats go into cold water that is slowly brought to the boil, all the scum is removed, the vegetables, herbs and salt are added, and the whole business is left to look after itself, gently bubbling, for a couple

of hours. I lift the lid every so often to check and inhale the rich, beefy aroma that promises a comforting bowl of broth.

Pot-au-feu is a midday meal, and normally the broth would be served as the first course, an exception to the French custom of soup as evening meal. I decide to deviate from French usage and save the stock for the following day, but follow tradition to the letter in serving slices of the spoon-tender beef with its vegetables plus steamed potatoes and the obligatory accompaniments of mustard and cornichons. Perhaps I set my expectations too high but, after all the planning and preparation, I have to admit to disappointment. It's the first time I've eaten *pot-au-feu* so I have no basis for comparison; as *pot-au-feu* goes, my version is probably fine. Sadly, I have to conclude that boiled beef is not my cup of tea.

Still, Elizabeth David says that a salad made with the leftover beef is 'one of the most delicious of dishes', and this is what we enjoy for lunch the following day. Cold, the beef seems to have more flavour, though I could be misled by the tangy dressing that includes mustard, capers, cornichons and lots of parsley.

The broth lives up to its promise, but even after the salad I have to find uses for the remaining leftovers. Some is reheated on a bed of slow-cooked onion as the classic *bœuf miroton*, and the last of the beef, finely chopped and mixed with onion and vegetables, goes into improvised pasties. By this time, although we've enjoyed our *pot-au-feu*, we're happy to give it a rest.

In fact, having cooked it once, I don't cook another *pot-au-feu* during the rest of my time in France. I'm satisfied that, in discarding the pot-au-feu from my list of favourite recipes, I have both proven my Frenchness and demonstrated my solidarity with modern French *ménagères*.

Pot-au-feu

Epicurean, August/September 1977
Serves 6, with leftovers for another meal or two

Meat
1.5 kg beef topside or silverside, in one piece
1 kg beef shortribs, in one piece
beef marrow bone, cut into 5 cm lengths
oxtail (optional)

Vegetables
2 onions
4 leeks
4 large carrots
2 small white turnips
1 stick celery, including leaves
bouquet garni of 3 to 4 sprigs thyme, 2 to 4 stalks parsley,
2 to 3 bay leaves
1 tablespoon salt and a few peppercorns

For serving
additional onions, leeks and carrots
potatoes
coarse salt, mustard, horseradish, pickled cornichons
and capers

Tie each piece of meat into a neat shape. Wash oxtail, if using. Peel onion, wash and trum leeks, and peel the carrots and turnips.

Place all meats except marrow bones in a very large pot and pour over cold water to just cover. Bring to the boil very slowly, removing scum as it rises. Continue to skim surface until no more

Pot-au-feu (continued)

scum is formed. Add prepared vegetables, salt and peppercorns. Place lid on pot and adjust heat so that the liquid barely simmers. Leave for 2½ to 3 hours, then add marrow bones and cook for a further 45 minutes.

Meanwhile, prepare additional vegetables for serving with the meat and either cook separately or with the meat (first discarding the ones added at the beginning). Steam potatoes.

For serving, carefully remove meats and marrow bones and keep warm. If vegetables have been cooked with meat, take them out of the stock and keep warm. Carve topside or silverside into fairly thick slices (about ½ cm), spoon over a little of the hot stock, remove marrow from marrow bones.

Serve meat and vegetables with accompaniments.

When stock has cooled, strain through muslin-lined sieve into a clean bowl and place in refrigerator. When cold, remove layer of fat from surface. This stock can be used for subsequent soups and sauces. If you want to follow French custom to the letter and serve the broth as first course, remove as much fat as possible from the surface, reheat quickly and serve very hot.

23 Feast to famine

A comfortable home, renewed visas and a job in the wings: all the cards are falling our way. In high spirits we spend recklessly on toys for the children – a small tricycle, a wheelbarrow, and a bucket, spade and rake for the new sand pit I construct with handy logs and a couple of bucketfuls of spare sand from a building site. For ourselves we stock up on wine, splurge on eight new cheeses, buy thick pearly stalks of the best quality asparagus and indulge in deeply perfumed Provençal strawberries. I find a second-hand copy of the Gault/Millau *Guide Gourmand de la France* (1970), an exhaustive guide to the specialities of thousands of towns and villages throughout France, and add it to my library. Caromb, I learn, is the vine-grafting capital of France and is reputed for its game. It also has its own dish, traditionally eaten on Saint Maurice's day, 22 September, a slow-cooked *tian* of pork, tomatoes, onions and white beans. Carpentras is known for its *berlingots* (boiled lollies to us), melons, strawberries and jams, and its truffle market is one of the most important in France.

The following week, cashing our weekly cheque at BNP, I am shocked to discover that our bank balance is only 200 francs. Having blithely assumed that there would be money coming into the account every month from the rent of the house in Sydney I have never bothered to check. Only a temporary hiccup, I

rationalise; we still have £90 in travellers' cheques and the April funds should arrive within a week. We resolve to live frugally for the next seven days.

This nonchalant optimism is misplaced. Our next visit to the bank reveals that no funds were transferred in April, and our total wealth, including travellers' cheques, is now only 300 francs, around AU$60. Never before have I been on the brink of destitution, and I suddenly realise how fragile, how flimsy is the basis to our life in France, how easily the dream could evaporate.

Requesting an urgent transfer from our Sydney bank account costs 84 francs, but we have no choice. More disturbing is the discovery that no money has been transferred from Australia since the account was established. The staff at Carpentras are equally puzzled. I try to remember the initial meeting with the bank manager in Paris, how I explained that the Sydney branch of BNP would transmit a standard amount to France every month to go into our new French account. It seemed so simple and straightforward, the rent from the house funding our quixotic adventures, that I never considered anything would go wrong. Still, with the problem now identified, I trustingly assume the bank will fix it.

It takes only five days for the cash to be received, and the following Wednesday we are able to spend again: more cheeses, 10 litres of wine – expensive wine, 3.30 francs per litre – fresh pasta and parmesan from the pasta shop in Carpentras, and French magazines to read. We pay Madame the second month's rent, for May. And we treat ourselves to lunch at the little restaurant we've been wanting to try at Saint-Pierre-de-Vassols, just a couple of kilometres away, all the while trusting that the rest of our cash will turn up soon.

A week later the bank has still not received any additional funds, has no explanation why the regular monthly transfers that

should have begun in January have not occurred, and has not bothered to investigate. Once again, carefree affluence comes to an abrupt end. I have to turn to my parents, asking them to request another transfer from the Sydney bank. Almost destitute, we ration petrol to 20 francs a week, just enough to get us to and from Carpentras and perhaps allow one excursion no further than two kilometres beyond Caromb.

Food is rationed, too, except for the children. Meat, even chicken, is out of the question. Fortunately I had stocked up on pantry staples when we first arrived – chick peas and lentils, white haricot beans and Camargue rice. I still have plenty of oil and vinegar and mustard from Nizas, together with sugar, flour and a few spices, plus the wild herbs I collected on the hilltop plateau. Gifts of broad beans and lettuce from Madame's garden are a bonus, and we have enough wine for one glass a day. 'You'll look back on this time as one of the best in your life,' writes my mother. It can hardly be worse, I think, gritting my teeth. As a diversion, I start a list of what I will buy when the money comes through – sandals for everyone, child-size chairs for D and S, hats for summer, more wine and steak!

Inventiveness rises to the challenge of making ends meet and our meals are wonderfully varied and flavoursome. I make salads of chick peas, of lentils, of beans. From Claudia Roden's *A Book of Middle Eastern Food* comes recipes for lentils with spinach, chick peas with potatoes and tomatoes. Tomatoes are now affordable, the first of the French crop arriving about the end of April. I cook courgettes with tomatoes – and since we've been given some eggs, add a couple of eggs to poach in the rich liquid.

Flicking through my cookbooks I find a recipe for *bouillabaisse d'épinards*. Elizabeth David says it is a typical Provençal dish, eggs poached in a soupy vegetable mixture of spinach and potato slices, generously flavoured with garlic. It's eaten with a

spoon, the soft-cooked eggs mixed into the liquid to be mopped up with bread. Simple but perfectly balanced, it's a revelation. The recipe calls for a few fronds of green fennel, and I remember seeing some plants by the roadside, near the *cave co-op*. Foraging lessons from Nizas return, and I mark the locations of potential food resources on my mental map of the neighbourhood.

Charcuterie is not off limits, and even a small addition can give a huge flavour boost. The *ventresca* of Nizas is less common here, and instead I buy thin slices of *poitrine salée*, salted pork belly, and *poitrine fumée*, the same but smoked. *Poitrine fumée* goes into a risotto-style dish I make with Camargue rice, a large grain that has a vague but particular flavour, not as distinctive as basmati but more pronounced than standard Australian rice. *Poitrine salée* accompanies a pot of lentils, in an adaptation of Elizabeth David's recipe.

The period of penury lasts for a nearly a month. At the bank my questions find no answers, and correspondence is slow. Not until the end of May does the branch in Carpentras offer an explanation, having traced the negligence to Paris. The Sydney office has done its job in transmitting the funds to France, and there they have languished; the Paris office has forgotten to credit them to our French account. The bank offers a superficial apology but no compensation for its oversight. After we receive the May payment we cancel the automatic transfer arrangements. From now on we will keep a closer eye on the account and request transfers as and when we need them. It's some consolation that, looking back, we've enjoyed our meals more at this meagre time than at any other.

Bouillabaisse d'épinards
Spinach and potato stew

This recipe comes from *La Cuisine Provençale*, by Irene Borelli.

Serves 2–3

500 g spinach
3 medium potatoes, waxy if possible
1 small onion, finely chopped
2 tablespoons olive oil
salt and freshly ground pepper
a good pinch of saffron
1 clove garlic, finely chopped
1 to 2 fennel fronds
1 egg per person

Wash spinach and cook in boiling water for about 5 minutes. Drain and rinse under cold running water then chop roughly. Peel potatoes and cut into slices about ½ cm thick.

Heat oil in a large pot and cook onion until golden. Add spinach and cook for about 5 minutes over low heat. Add potatoes, season with salt, pepper and saffron then add two cups of boiling water, garlic and fennel. Cover and simmer for about 15 minutes, until potatoes are soft.

When the potatoes are cooked, reduce heat and carefully slide eggs into simmering liquid to poach.

Serve over slices of bread.

24 Cooking like the locals

Imperceptibly I find myself cooking as the locals do, accepting advice and suggestions from Madame and Gilbert, the butcher and market stallholders. When I buy pork to roast Madame tells me to cook it with sage, and gives me a few fresh sprigs from the garden. I rarely cooked pork in Australia, but here it's tender, flavoursome and economical. The next time I buy a piece of pork I stud it with slivers of new garlic, big fat bulbs glistening white and pink, in a version of Ginette Mathiot's *rôti de porc à la provençale*. It is perhaps the best pork I have ever eaten.

Our table at Caromb reflects the subtleties of the season, augmented by contributions from Madame's garden. At the beginning of our stay, when she's still not quite sure whether we might run off with her silver, Madame offers me a kilogram of freshly dug potatoes but asks for two francs in return. They're worth every centime, especially when I cook them in a *gratin dauphinois*. Later, satisfied that we're trustworthy, she presents us almost daily with fresh lettuce, broad beans, peas and beans, each in their time.

The first broad beans come in mid-May, and the basket contains at least a kilogram. Stephanie likes helping to shell them. *Il faut enlever la deuxième peau*, instructs Madame, you have to remove the grey-green skin enveloping each individual bean.

Rôti de porc à la sauge
Roast pork with sage

(*Epicurean*, February/March 1978)

Serves 6

1 kg pork loin, boned and trimmed of fat
6 or more young fresh sage leaves
1 dried bay leaf
½ teaspoon dried thyme, or 2 teaspoons fresh thyme leaves
1 teaspoon salt
olive oil
garlic cloves

Prepare the pork the day before roasting. Make small slits in the meat and insert sage leaves, rolling each into a cylinder and pushing them well in. Crumble bay leaf, mix with thyme and salt, rub over all surfaces of pork. Drizzle with a little olive oil, cover and refrigerate for at least 12 hours.

Next day, preheat oven to 160°C (140°C fan-forced). Peel and bruise as many garlic cloves as desired.

Warm a little olive oil in roasting pan, place garlic in pan and pork on top. Roast for about 1½ hours, basting from time to time with pan juices. The meat is done when piercing it with a skewer yields a clear juice. Remove from pan, together with garlic, and allow to rest before carving.

If desired, deglaze roasting pan with a little white or rosé wine and serve with pork.

It's a tedious task, easier to do when the beans are cooked, but Madame insists on doing it before cooking. If I admit to not bothering I know she will tut-tut in reprimand. I suspect that even if I tell her yes, I have done them properly this time, she will still suspect I'm lying, too lazy to remove the internal coat.

In Provence, broad beans go with fresh *sarriette*, savory, another herb that grows wild in this region. I learn to identify it, and find some growing on our walks. For a change I also cook them with little cubes of *poitrine salée* from the Caromb *charcuterie*. These broad beans are so fresh they cook in a couple of minutes, and their flavour is sweet and green. For Madame and Raymond, a dish of beans is an evening meal, and so it is for us, especially at the height of the season when she gives us about two kilograms every couple of days. As the harvest diminishes, around mid-June, the beans are bigger and tougher, and Madame advises making a soup. I draw on my understanding of French soups to invent a recipe, cooking the beans with onion, potato, and outside leaves of cos lettuce in chicken stock and using my *mouli-légumes* from Béziers to make a purée. Garnished with a little *sarriette*, it's as good as I hoped for.

Fresh peas arrive in early June and Madame offers a generous basketful. I find it odd that the children refuse to eat them, since they like broad beans, but we make a meal of fresh peas. The end of the month sees the first of the beans, stringless and almost round in cross-section. I have bought local beans from the market but Madame's, spanking fresh, have a deep clarity of flavour missing from the bought ones, even though they are probably only a couple of days old.

In this part of France the usual way of cooking green beans is to add them, cooked and drained, to a fresh tomato sauce, not enough to swamp them but just enough to coat. The recipe for *haricots verts à la provençale* in *La Cuisine pour Tous* prescribes

cooking in boiling salted water for 15–20 minutes followed by another 20 minutes simmering in the sauce. This, apparently, is the way the French like them; even Paul Bocuse, one of the standard-bearers of *nouvelle cuisine*, believes in cooking them for 15 minutes.

Haricots verts à la provençale
Green beans, Provençal-style

Since Madame makes us gifts of her fresh green beans, the perfect accompaniment to roast pork, I do them in the Provençal way, adapting the recipe from *La Cuisine pour Tous* – 40 minutes of cooking is impossible!

Serves 4

500 g green beans
1 to 2 tablespoons olive oil
1 clove garlic, crushed
1 to 2 tomatoes, peeled and diced
1 cup tomato purée made with fresh tomatoes, garlic, herbs
salt and freshly ground pepper
parsley, finely chopped

Trim beans, remove strings if necessary. Boil in salted water for a couple of minutes, until just tender. Drain and keep warm. Return empty saucepan to heat, add oil and garlic and toss for 30 seconds, then add tomato and purée and cook for about 3 minutes. Return beans to pan, check seasoning and toss through chopped parsley.

I like my beans firm and slightly crunchy; five minutes is my preferred timing. Later, when picking beans with Vivette, I ask her about the way she cooks fresh beans. Five minutes in the pressure cooker, she replies. Aren't they overcooked, the flavour drained out of them?, I venture, but Vivette cannot conceive of any other way. We agree to a comparison: I cook half my way, she does half her way, and we dress both with the same vinaigrette. Mine are still *croquant*, slightly crisp and vivid green; Vivette's are grey, limp and lifeless. We take votes around the table and unanimously, overwhelmingly, all the French – which is everyone except John and me – prefer Vivette's dish. Futile to argue against majority opinion, I realise, but the experiment teaches me the extent to which 'taste' is acculturated. It also opens my eyes to the inflexibility of the French in matters of food.

Beans aside, my repertoire of local dishes expands and I rely less on Elizabeth David and Julia Child, more on *La Cuisine pour Tous* and my new copy of *La Cuisine Provençale*. In the latter I find a recipe for *soupe de poissons à la marseillaise* and make fish soup for the first time, At last I have an opportunity to buy a kilo of the marine miscellany known as *soupe de poissons*, the tiny bait-size fish I had admired at Sète. The soup is a revelation. Clean, pure, intense in flavour, it becomes the benchmark for all future *soupes de poisson*.

Another first is quail. I've eaten them only once before and found them all bones and fiddly to eat with knife and fork, as manners require in France. These I buy from the egg lady at the Carpentras market, plump and well rounded, and pot-roast them. At home I allow myself to use fingers, and I'm surprised how meaty and succulent they are.

By now we know all the little lanes and alleys of *centre ville* Carpentras and where to go for what – including *burgl*, available from the North African shop, which adds tabouli to our menu.

Soupe de poissons à la marseillaise
Fish soup, Marseilles-style

La Cuisine Provençale prefaces this recipe with the warning: 'The flavour of this soup is totally dependent on the quality of the fish selected. It can only be made with fish from the rocky depths, namely *poissons de roche*.' In other words: first, catch your fish!

Serves 6–8

1 kg assorted small fish (if large, cut into smaller pieces)
1 large onion
1 leek
2 large tomatoes
2 or 3 cloves of garlic, crushed
2 tablespoons olive oil
1 bay leaf
1 piece dried orange peel
1 frond of fennel
salt and freshly ground pepper
good pinch of saffron
1 tablespoon *pastis*
250 g vermicelli or spaghetti, broken into short lengths

If necessary, clean and scale fish.

Finely chop onion and leek. Peel tomato, squeeze out seeds and chop finely.

Heat olive oil in a large pan, add onion and leek and cook over moderate heat until golden then add tomatoes. Cook for a few minutes longer then add garlic, bay leaf, orange peel, fennel and fish. Season with salt and pepper. Cook over moderate heat, stirring from time to time, until the fish starts to break up. After 10

Soupe de poissons à la marseillaise (continued)

to 15 minutes cooking, add 3 litres of boiling water together with saffron and *pastis*. Cook over high heat, uncovered, for about 30 to 35 minutes or until liquid is reduced by about half.

Strain soup through a fine sieve into a large bowl, pressing down on the fish to extract all the liquid (alternatively, remove all bones and pass through a fine *mouli* for a thicker soup). Return soup to saucepan, check seasoning and bring to the boil. As soon as it boils, add pasta and cook until pasta is tender.

Serve sprinkled with grated cheese. According to *La Cuisine Provençale*, past tradition dictated gouda or edam cheese, an indication probably more of availability than preference. Gruyère is now more common.

And we've settled on a favourite *crèmerie* in the Rue des Halles and on 'our' brand of camembert, *Isigny Sainte Mère*, made by the Cooperative d'Isigny. I buy butter from the same cooperative, and love watching Monsieur guide the thin strip of wire through the golden cylinder, a curled wedge of butter falling softly on to the sheet of waxed paper.

Monsieur at the *crèmerie* soon recognises us as regulars and gives us tips on choosing a perfectly ripe camembert: it should have risen slightly above the edge of the box so there's a small overhang. *Il est sorti de sa boîte*, he shows us. He tests the consistency; it should be not too firm, not too soft, slightly springy. And then he loosens the wrapping and sniffs the base; it should be a rich, intense, dairy smell, with no hint of ammonia. This knowledge stays with me, but I never quite become as comfortable with the sniffing part as the French, who will sometimes upturn the box, unwrap the paper from the bottom of the camembert

and bury their nose in it – and then, if it's not as they want it, rewrap the cheese and put it back on the shelf.

The *crèmerie* owner chooses his cheeses well and guides us to the almost-local cheeses from neighbouring Savoy, *tomme de Savoie* and *reblochon*. In Provence, however, he can hardly avoid specialising in goat cheese, and alongside the nameless local *fromages de chèvre fermier* are traditional goat cheeses: *rigotte*, *picodon*, the *banon* wrapped in chestnut leaves. The panorama is almost overwhelming, but after a couple of months in France we are more mature in making selections. No longer like kids in a lolly shop, we make – we think – rational and economical choices, secure in the knowledge that whatever we miss today will still be there next week.

There's a goat cheese lady at the Caromb market, her humble stall just a small table with a couple of trays of small white discs, each with a peppery sprig of sarriette pressed into the surface. She seems lonely, isolated from the busier stalls, and I stop to chat when I buy a couple of her cheeses. Her farm is at Méthamis, high on the Plateau de Vaucluse, and she invites us to visit. It's a precariously narrow and winding road to the tiny, windswept, five-household hamlet. Even from inside the car we smell the goats as we approach, and indeed the whole farm seems permanently imbued with their characteristic odour. Calling the goats by name so we can pat them, all 13 of them, the lady points to the rocky hills above the farmhouse where she takes them to feed on the low, stocky herbage whose tang contributes to the individuality of her cheeses. In the farmhouse kitchen she explains how she makes the cheeses, warming the milk, adding rennet and leaving it to set. The curds are turned into small moulds and salted, then left to mature for a week or so in her cool, airy cellar. It's as primitive as you get, but none of us ever gets ill from eating goat cheese.

The learning curve at Caromb is perhaps not as steep as at Nizas, but I now have a deeper understanding and appreciation of practices and customs, especially in this part of France. I remember what attracted me to Waverley Root and his book, *The Food of France*, when I first read it: it was the way he showed that recipes are not created out of thin air, magicked into existence by a culinary fairy's wand. All recipes, all dishes, have a story, an ever-evolving story, and that story depends on the climate and geography of a region and the foods it produces; on its trading relations in the past as well as in the present; on the origins and histories of its people, with their beliefs and values and religions; and on a whole web of other intangibles. It's a complex business, what people eat and why, and I have so much more to learn.

Snails

'When you pull a snail out of its shell and pop it piping hot into your mouth,' writes Waverley Root, 'you are likely to consider it a simple dish, and to have no idea how much effort has gone into its preparation.'

I've eaten the snails that come in cans, with a separate bag of shells for serving them, in restaurants in Australia. And in a pension in Spain I was given a taste of the family's supper that, if I correctly interpreted the hand actions, was made with snails collected on the rooftop after the rain of the previous evening. But no, I never stopped to wonder how snails got on to my plate.

One morning at Caromb, after a couple of days of rain, I see a big saucepan of small grey-brown snails in Madame's laundry, and a couple of days later a pile of empty shells in the rubbish. Yes, she says, she collects the snails, as though surprised that the offer of a free meal would be ignored. Especially when it's a luxury meal. I've seen snails in the Carpentras market priced at 27 francs per kilo, which makes them at least twice as expensive as chicken. If you know where and when to look, she adds, they're easy to find; they love new young vine leaves. She has several secret sites on her land and promises to take me with her after the next rainy period.

I wait for the next rainy day, but no invitation comes, and the

next one, and still Madame does not summon us, so John ventures into the vineyard by himself and collects about three dozen of the biggest. He shows them to Madame; are they the right ones? Madame and the *bonhomme* sort through them, rejecting those with soft shells. About half the harvest is thrown away. Now you have to purge them, she says, fast them.

In *La Cuisine pour Tous*, Ginette Mathiot says to fast snails for a week. Another source quoted by Elizabeth David refers to 30–40 days, though I interpret this as ironic exaggeration. The *bonhomme* says he doesn't bother about the fasting, but then, nor does he bother with any of Madame's refinements when he cooks them. Madame advises a cleansing diet of thyme rather than a total fast, so that they take on some of the flavour of the herb. We keep the snails downstairs in Madame's laundry and give them five days of fresh thyme to clear themselves out.

Five days pass, and the snails don't look any different. They haven't eaten much of the thyme, either. What's next, I ask Madame. First, you have to wash them, she replies, wash them in clean water three times, make sure the shells are clean. Then you drop them into boiling water for about five minutes, drain them, and when they're cool you take them out of the shell and lift off the dark strip of intestine.

It seems a lot of work but I follow her directions to the letter. There doesn't seem to be much left by the time I've removed the inedible bits but I persevere to the next stage, simmering the snails for hour or so with onion and carrot and herbs for flavour. In the meantime I make a garlic butter, as Madame suggests. The cooked snails go back into their shells, I top them with garlic butter and slide them into the oven. The scent of garlic fills the kitchen.

Happy enough to be involved with the gathering and the thyme treatment, John has distanced himself from all subsequent

stages. If I were totally honest I'd have to say that I don't blame him; I've had moments of disgust, and I'm not looking forward to the taste test. If I could gracefully bow out I would. Yet I cannot admit to Madame that I squibbed out. I have to face the challenge.

My cooked snails don't make my mouth water when I put the dish on the table. They're grey and shrivelled and totally unappetising. John is repulsed and can't bring himself to taste one. He can't even bear to watch as I eat them, one by one, almost all of them, about a dozen in total. They're very small, no more than half a teaspoon in size, and surprisingly tender, unlike tinned ones I've eaten in Australia. I can't taste any thyme; in fact, I can't taste much of anything except the garlic butter. Perhaps they are an acquired taste, or perhaps it's in the genes of the French to appreciate snails.

The snail experiment is not one to be repeated.

26 Cherry harvest

It starts suddenly, almost taking me by surprise. Even after months of watching the cherry trees change from bare to blossoming, from pale leafy green with masses of tiny, hard fruits to the first hints of pink, it still comes as a shock to see, a week later, boughs touching the ground under the weight of their scarlet load. In *pâtisseries* I start to notice tarts filled with thick, dark, cherry purée, and little cherry tartlets, enticingly glazed.

Unseasonal rain just before the first cherries are ready ruins much of Madame's early harvest, splitting the fruit that was almost ripe. We have permission to pick the split ones and stew them, although we have already been relishing clandestine cherries straight from the tree. For every box of perfect cherries ready for market there are three boxes of spoiled ones that will be sold to the kirsch distillery for a much lower price. Madame picks the cherries mainly by herself, working until 9 pm, using a narrow triangular ladder to reach the fruit at the top. Sometimes the *bonhomme*, the odd jobs man, comes to help for a day. It's a seven-day-a-week job; Madame doesn't even take time off to come to the market with us, instead giving me a list of things to buy for her at Leclerc.

The cherry harvest involves the whole community. Cars and trucks laden with buckets and boxes head for the orchards as the

pickers set forth to gather in one month what nature has spent 11 months preparing. It's women's work, an annual ritual for the wives and mothers and daughters and sisters, as normal a role as preparing the midday dinner. Though they still have to cook, and in cherry season the Carpentras market begins business as early as 7 am so that they can get their shopping out of the way and have the rest of the day for cherries.

Stephanie accompanies Madame in the wheelbarrow when she goes picking and tells us she is helping, but for her 'helping' means 'eating' and she consumes far more than is good for her. I'm sure it's only because Madame dotes on our daughter that we are offered a token sample every few days. Unlike the vegetable garden whose sole purpose is to supply the household, the cherry orchard represents income, a cash crop to be sold at market.

More unseasonal rain arrives to damage the harvest, a heavy fall that also threatens vineyards so that vignerons have to do an additional copper sulphate spray on their vines. They're in such a hurry that they misjudge soil conditions, and the local newspaper reports 16 tractors bogged in and around Caromb on a single day, a record. Raymond is more cautious and avoids the disaster. Locals predict total failure of the grape harvest to come, but they are always imagining the worst.

We're allowed to pick the damaged cherries after the rain, the juicy, deep crimson Burlat that ripen early in the season. I decide to turn them into cherry jam, painstakingly removing the stones from 3.5 kilograms of cherries. Cherries are notoriously low in pectin and these ones are particularly watery, so I buy a packet of Gelvit jam sugar that already contains a small proportion of pectin. The recipe – equal quantities of fruit and sugar – comes from the little booklet that accompanies the sugar, but perhaps I'm too casual in following the instructions. They say quite clearly *respectez toujours les temps de cuisson indiqués*, always

adhere to the recommended cooking times, which in this case is 5 minutes once the jam comes to the boil. I leave mine simmering for about half an hour and the result is a deep, dark, rich mahogany colour, thick and syrupy and more like a Greek conserve spoon sweet than a jam for spreading on bread. Perhaps I should never have started with such a large quantity of fruit. Still, it tastes good, and Madame says *merci* when I give her a jar.

Madame's orchard has some 40 trees, and she knows all the varieties. Some are early season, some late. As May moves into June Madame moves from variety to variety, picking one tree at a time, the overlooked cherries getting bigger and darker and juicier. These are our secret treat. After lunch, when the children are asleep, we wander among the harvested trees in search of the forgotten fruit, the cherries that were passed over or perhaps were not properly ripe when the tree was picked. Now supersize and succulent, each has dimensions of sweetness and flavour I've never before encountered, and it's an effort to restrain myself, to leave some for the next day.

After the jam experiment I have more success with cherry tarts, the first one following Ginette Mathiot's recipe for *tartes aux fruits juteux*, tarts made with juicy fruit. It's very simple, just cherries without stones arranged on a shortcrust pastry base, sprinkled with sugar and baked. I prefer the slightly more refined variant from Elizabeth David's *Summer Cooking*, which has a thin layer of creamy custard poured over the cherries before baking. I always give a big slice to Madame, who says she likes the products of my baking, but I never know whether she eats it or gives it to the rabbits, nor whether there is ever any left over for Raymond.

The culinary triumph, however, is the *clafoutis*, especially when the firmer Montmorency cherries start in early June. Bright, clear red in colour, they are followed by the translucent and pale pink Napoleon, and the dainty, heart-shaped Cœur de Pigeon.

Clafoutis

Australian Gourmet, December 1979/January 1980

The children love the *clafoutis* — and I have no worries about accidentally swallowed cherry stones.

Serves 6

750 g cherries (about 2 cups stemmed and stoned cherries)
2 eggs
½ cup flour
3 tablespoons caster sugar (preferably vanilla sugar)
⅓ to ½ cup milk
butter

Preheat oven to 190°C (170°C fan-forced).

Butter a shallow ovenproof dish and arrange cherries over base (2 cups of cherries should form a single layer in a dish approximately 15 cm x 28 cm).

Break eggs into a bowl, beat lightly. Combine flour and sugar, pour over eggs and beat well to mix. Add enough milk to make a smooth batter (it should have the consistency of thick cream or pancake batter).

Pour batter over cherries, place in preheated oven and bake for about 35 to 40 minutes, covering surface with greaseproof paper if it browns too quickly.

Allow to cook slightly, before strewing more sugar over surface.

Some say *clafoutis* should be served cold, but I prefer it warm, or at least at room temperature.

These later varieties are better in cooking but lack the powerful punch of the succulent Burlat. We could probably manage to eat the whole *clafoutis* ourselves but I make sure there's some left for Madame, who scarcely has time to cook in cherry season.

But she must make time each year to do a batch of *cerises à l'eau de vie*, cherries in alcohol. This is just another of the simple cordials that locals make with fruit, sugar, and their entitlement from the *cave coopérative*. One evening, just before we leave at the end of June, Madame brings a tray with tiny glasses and her jar of preserved cherries as we sit under the big fig tree verifying accounts, making sure all rent is paid, the cost of electricity is covered, and there are no breakages or damages to report. She pours glasses of the blush pink liquid, adding a couple of pale alcohol-soaked cherries to eat with coffee spoons. It's a rare occasion that the liqueur is brought out and for us a singular honour, a silent compliment: perhaps we've been good tenants after all.

27 Progress

With the restoration of our finances, we are buoyant about the future. Where that future lies is less certain, our arrangements with Madame continuing only to the end of May. We consider the Luberon, somewhere around Gordes, but only half-heartedly. Caromb is very comfortable, and the cherry harvest is not yet finished. One evening, knowing both Madame and Raymond are at home, I approach them to enquire about extending for a month. *Nous sommes bien contents*, replies Madame; we're very happy for you to stay, though of course the rent will have to increase, she adds. It's getting near peak season. Beyond the end of June, we have no idea what we will do; all we know is that Madame's place is already booked.

The formalities of handing over the cash and receiving a receipt take place in the room that is normally closed. This is serious business and we sit at a big oak table, Madame and Raymond on one side, John and I on the other, facing the tall, glass-fronted bookcase. I'm intrigued by its contents – perhaps it is the library of the late husband? They're old books, mostly reference books – no novels that I can spy – and I ask if we can look at the two volumes of *Larousse Universel: Nouveau dictionnaire encyclopédique*, published in 1922. *Mais oui*, she replies. Madame now trusts us enough to offer them on loan, one volume at a time.

More encyclopedia than dictionary, this is a work Diderot himself would be proud of. After dinner each evening I reverently place the book on the cleared table and pore over its amply illustrated pages, drawn by the images more than the words: the machinery used in making chocolate; a 1920 map of Turkey and the Middle East; guides to trellising fruit trees and pruning grape vines; the different varieties of cabbage; and a palmistry how-to, a diagram showing the lines of destiny and the astrological associations. It is amazingly comprehensive, entries ranging from a list of all the fruits grown in France and the principal varieties of each to biographies of all the Kings Louis of France, from the first to the 18h. It even has a recipe for cherry jam. Madame's dictionary is an absolute treasure trove. I spend hours with these volumes and learn so much about France and the French.

More good news arrives in the mail. The first is a letter telling John the first examiner has approved his thesis, and the second is an unexpected invitation from the Université de Compiègne where the examiner's colleague is on sabbatical. It's possible, says the colleague, that there might be a short-term job on offer later in the year. It's encouraging but rather vague, and I'm not sure I really know where Compiègne is. In any case my sights are firmly fixed on Montpellier and Professor Jouanna.

For me, Monsieur Poste brings my first acceptance letter. *Australian Gourmet* will pay me $30 for my article on rabbit. I convert it into francs and am over the moon! Immediately I start planning more articles for both *Australian Gourmet* and its rival publication, *Epicurean*. Contemplating the ethics of writing for both, I decide a nom de plume is necessary. It has to hint at a French identity, though at the same time it should be equally plausible as an English name. My family name is found on the roofs of glasshouses on the outskirts of Carpentras. Bonnet is a long-established local family, and Denis Bonnet was a 19th-century artist

whose paintings I have seen in the Carpentras museum. Choosing a first name is easy; plenty of girls' names are the same in both languages, Claire or Jacqueline or Alice, but I choose the simple Anne, with an -e. For *Epicurean*, I am Anne Bonnet.

Lapin à la provençale
Rabbit, Provençal-style

(*Australian Gourmet*, July/August 1978)

Serves 6

1 rabbit, about 1 kg
2 tablespoons olive oil
salt and freshly ground pepper
½ cup dry white wine
½ cup chicken stock
1 cup peeled, seeded and roughly chopped tomatoes (or canned)
½ cup small black olives, stones removed
generous *bouquet garni* with plenty of thyme

Joint rabbit into 6 to 8 pieces (fore legs, back legs, saddle and ribs with backbone removed). Heat oil in a heavy pan, add rabbit pieces and cook over moderate heat until golden brown all over. Season to taste. Pour over wine, allow to sizzle for a few minutes then add stock, tomatoes, olives and *bouquet garni*. Cover and simmer gently until rabbit is tender, about 30 minutes for farmed rabbit, longer for wild rabbit.

Transfer rabbit pieces to heated serving dish. Remove *bouquet garni* from sauce and reduce sauce over high heat if necessary. Pour over rabbit and serve.

Christmas customs in Provence would make a good article, suggests the editor of *Australian Gourmet*. For months I have been fascinated by the displays of *santons* in the local shops and museums, these archetypal Provençal men and women who bring a heart-warming reality and familiarity to the Christmas crèche. Alongside Mary and Joseph and baby Jesus in the stable with the wise men and the oxen are all the characters of everyday Provençal life, or at least life in the 19th century when the *santons* became popular. There's the old lady with the bundle of sticks on her head, the shepherd with his sheep and goats, the red-scarved man with the hurdy-gurdy, the baker in his floury apron, the lavender seller with her basket of lavender, the old women with bunches of thyme, garlands of garlic, trays of figs, urns of oil, or a basket of sea urchins, and the street musicians with traditional flute and drum. All wear typical Provençal costumes from the previous century and their hand-painted terracotta faces are so lifelike you can see the weariness of the wood-carrier, the solicitude of the shepherd.

La Cuisine Provençale is my starting point. It tells me that Christmas traditions in Provence are not only particular to the region but also more faithfully followed than in other regions. The most important is the *gros souper*, the meal before the midnight mass, when an enormous log, the *bûche de Noël*, is ceremonially placed on the fire where it is to burn for three days. Everyone in the family takes his place at the table, set with three white tablecloths in honour of the holy trinity. The lady of the house lights a candle and hands it to the eldest of the family to blow out. From oldest to youngest, each member of the family lights and blows out the candle before the meal – a Lenten-style supper before Mass – can finally begin. It ends with *les treize desserts*, the thirteen desserts, which include dried figs and raisins, hazelnuts and almonds, dates, glazed fruits, fresh fruits from the

autumn harvest that have been stored in the cool of the cellar, white nougat and dark nougat, *calissons* and simple yeast-raised pastries made with olive oil.

Fascinated by the depth of meaning in these rituals, I decide that I need to do a lot more research. This kind of food writing, I realise, is not as simple as thinking up new ideas for school lunch boxes or choosing an appetising selection of recipes for summer salads or winter casseroles. The big municipal library in Carpentras will surely have scholarly works on Provençal folklore and customs, and I spend a whole afternoon there trying to discover the origins of these traditions and the history of the *treize desserts*. Perhaps I'm looking in the wrong places, since I don't get very far. I don't understand how to use the card catalogue, encyclopedias and dictionaries are no help, and the classic *La Cuisinière Provençale*, first published in 1897, has nothing about Christmas traditions. At home I find Waverley Root uncustomarily silent on the subject, and not even *Larousse Gastronomique* discusses Provençal Christmas specialities. If there's any information in Madame's *Larousse Universel* it's too well hidden.

How do you celebrate Christmas?, I ask Madame and Gilbert in turn. They shrug their shoulders. Neither is religious, and neither has a family to bring together for the festivities. Yes, of course we know about the *treize desserts*, they tell me, but it doesn't matter if you don't have thirteen, and you can put them on the table the next day, Christmas Day, after the roast turkey.

Madame and Gilbert might not be representative, I realise, but I suspect that the romantic images evoked by the description in *La Cuisine Provençale* might belong to another time, another world.

28 June at Caromb

With the period of self-imposed petrol rationing now behind us, we range freely in our explorations of Provence. Everywhere I see the imprint of Roman civilisation, from the imposing theatre and triumphal arch of Orange to the homely collection of artefacts in the small museum at Vaison-la-Romaine – fragments of pottery, fine-handled spoons, hairpins, jewellery, and a Roman balance that is essentially the same as the one Madame uses to weigh her rabbits. Most of this old Roman settlement on the banks of the Ouvèze is now buried beneath the modern town, but two small areas have been excavated. Walking along ancient streets, past small shops and private houses, I admire the remains of intricate mosaic floors and palely frescoed walls. In an arcaded garden ornamented with statues, I sense the swish of toga as the sound of my sandals on cobblestones awakens the ghosts of the past.

There are more reminders at Mazan, about five kilometres from Caromb, where we come across a series of Gallo-Roman sarcophagi laid along a wall of the cemetery. Once upon a time they lined the road from Carpentras to Sault, as do the sarcophagi along the Alyscamps at Arles. The paths we now walk, in and around Caromb, must surely have known Roman feet, and I keep my eyes peeled for any ancient coins that might have slipped out of a loose leather pouch or were buried for safe keeping. My

current dream is a house of our own in Provence, and a golden aureus would be a serious down payment.

It's impossible to ignore the past in this part of France. Everywhere it is inextricably entwined with the present. Though only one tower remains of the 14th-century summer palace of the Avignon Popes, its splendour can still be imagined, as can the sense of power the Pope must have felt as he gazed from this hilltop to his Avignon palace below, surrounded by the city walls. Buying a bottle of white and of red Châteauneuf-du-Pape wine to join the Bordeaux wines in our 'cellar', we are reminded that it was an Avignon Pope, Clément V, whose 14th-century vineyard near Châteauneuf-du-Pape reputedly lay the foundations for the region's current glory.

These June excursions provide early warning signs of the summer tourist invasion. At Vaison, German-registered cars outnumber all others. The foreign exchange teller in our bank at Carpentras, who normally has no customers, now has a queue in front of her desk. There is noticeably more traffic in the town and, like the locals, we get impatient with their slow driving, their unawareness of one-way streets, and their inability to read parking signs.

Not wanting to appear totally indolent we offer our services to Madame. I help her extract the seeds from last year's beans, now dry and brittle, first walking over the desiccated pods to crush them. The rose garden in front of the house needs weeding, and it's in a corner of this bed that I find the poppies. They are tall, almost as tall as me, with large pale flowers. As they die and drop their petals, they reveal a plump oval pod ballooning from the stem. Intrigued, I search for *pavot*, poppy, in the *Larousse Universel* and learn the proper name is *Papaver somniferum*. What are these flowers, I ask Madame. They've always grown there, she says, but I haven't seen them for the last couple of years – surprising, the

way they have popped up again. I query the bulbous swellings – surreptitiously, I have made a small slit and watched white sap ooze out. *C'est pour le mal aux dents*, she says, *ça donne sommeil*. An old Provençal remedy for toothache, it puts people to sleep. But Madame is no fool and quickly spots my feigned innocence. Next morning, before I stir, the tall stalk has been lopped off.

John offers to help with the scything; with all the late spring rain the grass in the orchard has grown very long. The *bonhomme* shows him how to hold the scythe and demonstrates the proper action, slowly twisting from the hips while keeping the scythe at a level height to get an even, clean cut. He also teaches John the tricks of sharpening the scythe. Returning for lunch Raymond comments to his mother, *Eh bien, tu t'as trouvé un faucheur!* So, you've found someone to cut the grass! This is possibly the most words we've heard him string together.

Scything is energetic work and John soon looks for a more congenial activity, offering to clear the large shed that houses the tractor as well as the discards and detritus of many decades, if not centuries. Among the genuine rubbish – old paint cans and disintegrating rags – he discovers many treasures: old coins, including one from 1856, old glasses, sheep and goat bells, a silver fob watch, iron drawer handles and a stamp with the name 'V. Nicolaud, Huissier, Beaucaire, Gard'. *Oui, c'était mon mari*, says Madame as we hand over the valuables, though she allows us to keep the worthless watch. Perhaps this explains the two Anduze pots, Anduze being only 80 kilometres from Beaucaire where her husband worked as a bailiff. For John, the final and most useful treasure is a pair of dusty old leather sandals, just his size. With a bit of cleaning and oiling they are perfect for summer.

Though I never dare address Madame in any but the most polite terms, we develop a mutually respectful relationship. Her affection for Stephanie extends to an offer to mind her one

morning so we have only one stroller to push up the hill. Her lined face softens when we give her some photos we have taken of her house, the two Anduze pots beside the door and the children playing in front. She runs out to show Raymond as soon as he returns, waving the photos in front of him and not even waiting for him to park his tractor. By now she doesn't hesitate to ask our assistance, such as driving her to her vineyard at Suzette when it's time to tie up the vines. From the way she says *'mon terrain'*, my own piece of land, we understand that this is part of her family inheritance and more precious to her than the marital estate at Caromb.

Suzette is a tiny hamlet, a tight cluster of houses at the top of a high point of the Dentelles de Montmirail, a razor range of jagged, sun-bleached rock above Beaumes-de-Venise. Madame's property lower down is breathtakingly beautiful, a peaceful valley amid hillsides of vines. Cherry and apricot and olive trees surround the low stone *mas*, and fresh, clear water flows from the spring nearby. The *mas* has been partly renovated and is now rented to a lawyer in Carpentras. While Madame works we walk to the crest of the ridge that marks the boundary of the commune of Suzette and separates the Côtes du Ventoux appellation, which applies to Madame's vines, from the much more valuable Côtes du Rhône. It seems so arbitrary that a line on a map can make such a difference to the price of a bottle of wine. The children enjoy the change of scenery and Madame approves. *L'air de campagne leur fait du bien*, she remarks as we return; country air does them good.

The flood of tourists with deeper pockets signals our time to leave. After three months of stability and starting to grow roots, we're about to become itinerants again. Regrets are almost overtaken by the thrill of anticipation and new discoveries. We've known for a long time that the first of the *estivants*, the

summer holidaymakers, would be taking over 'our' apartment at the beginning of July, and we have found a new rental in the village of Claret, north of Montpellier. As for August, the peak summer month, we have no idea, though September will see us back at Mas Laval, working the vintage with Jean-Pierre and Vivette. And then? Will there be a job for John in Montpellier? Or Compiègne?

Our last excursion is to the top of Mont Ventoux via the Col des Tempêtes. It's always been too windy, too cloudy, too hot, too misty, too hazy, too expensive, but at the end of our stay it's now or never. Madame comes with us; it's 20 years since she last went up the mountain. It's a clear afternoon and along the road from Malaucène cliff-sides are covered with yellow *genêt*, broom, massed against the brick red and brown of the earth and the rocks. On this side it's a more gradual climb; the shorter, steeper, more winding stretch on the eastern flank challenges Tour de France riders every few years.

Even before the summit, the vista is magnificent, through pine and fir forests to smaller hills and mountains below. At one point we look down on a passing cloud. The road is no problem for the DS but progress is slow and we have time to absorb the views and the gradual change in vegetation as we climb. Near the crest, the slopes are bare and the ski runs at the Mont Serein resort look dauntingly steep. A small patch of snow lingers on the summit, but the white mantle we view from Caromb is actually a rubble of greyish white stones. Changing into warm clothes at the summit, we brave a wind that almost rips our ears off, but the views more than compensate – to the right, the silver sliver of the mighty Rhône; to the left, the Alps melting into clouds; and below us, the towns of Caromb, Carpentras and Avignon merging into the landscape. Far beyond is the Mediterranean, according to the *table d'orientation*, but today it's lost in the horizon.

Although we've done it in the comfort of a car, this final adventure somehow assimilates us, as though it were – like a christening – a necessary rite of passage. We belong. All that's left is to say extended farewells to the friends we've made and to repack the tea chests. Our belongings have expanded: more books, more toys, more clothes for the children, the jars of cherry jam. After sorting essentials from non-essentials, we leave two tea chests at Caromb to be collected in a week. As we pack the car, scientifically filling each nook and cranny, Madame occupies the children downstairs. Even Madame, we think, might be sad to say goodbye, but we promise to see her again – and as we cram ourselves and the last bits and pieces into the car, she presents us with a basket of fresh young beans for our dinner.

29 Claret

It's an odd sort of village, I say to John as we take an evening stroll through the Claret on our first day. Not eerie, not sinister, neither bizarre nor mysterious, but different, discordant, puzzling, not like the other villages we know.

It's the first place we've rented sight unseen. Our upstairs apartment consists of two large rooms, one behind the other. On the other side of the stairs is a similar apartment and between the two a shared bathroom – shower and basin. At the other end of the hallway is the shared toilet. We have a proper stove and fridge, but only cold water over the sink. Because it's now summer, the rent is almost four times as much as at Nizas in winter. At any other time I would reject such accommodation but it's July, and half of France is looking for a place in the sun.

Our new landlady is Madame Commeiras. Madame Commeiras and her husband live above the Unico general store belonging to her nephew, Jean-Pierre. Its prime corner position – at the bottom of the main street, opposite the *place* – gives her an ideal vantage point to watch over all the comings and goings in the village, and I suspect she makes it her business to know what everyone is doing. Her daughter also has a shop, she tells us with pride, a kind of mixed business – household goods, haberdashery, gifts – run from her front parlour. The daughter's house is one of the newer ones

at the edge of the village and has a proper yard and clothes line. Magnanimously, Madame Commeiras offers us the use of the line to hang our washing. To me, her welcome rings false, but perhaps it's because I resent paying so much for such inferior accommodation.

Oeufs farcis à l'ail
Garlic-stuffed eggs

(*Epicurean*, February/March 1978)

The primitive kitchen facilities at Claret hardly encourage cooking, and in any case luscious melons are incredibly cheap. We eat them with slices of *jambon de campagne* (prosciutto-style ham) from Jean-Pierre at Unico. These stuffed eggs are also a favourite, the recipe from *La Cuisine Provençale*.

> 6 hard-boiled eggs
> 10 cloves of garlic
> 2 anchovies (4 fillets)
> 1 teaspoon capers (preserved in vinegar)
> about 6 tablespoons olive oil
> red wine vinegar
> freshly ground pepper

Shell eggs, halve and remove yolks and transfer them to a mortar (or small bowl). Peel garlic cloves, drop into boiling water and simmer 10 minutes. Drain.

Mash egg yolks with garlic, anchovies and capers, gradually incorporate olive oil as if making mayonnaise. Add a splash of vinegar and season with pepper to taste. Fill egg whites with this mixture. Serve chilled.

The Unico is a general store with a bit of everything except fresh meat, and also serves as a *dépôt de pain*. A butcher visits most days, sounding his train whistle horn as the van slowly makes its way up the main street. I learn to run downstairs as soon as I hear it; if I don't catch him until the end of the run there might be nothing but stewing steak left. One day I hear a different sound and, rushing to the window, see a tiny Citroën 2CV and a man calling, *Oignons de Lésignan, bien doux, bien doux, les bons oignons de Lésignan*. He stops near the *mairie*, and everywhere doors fly open as women rush to buy. Remembering the village of Lésignan, near Nizas, and the reputation of its onions, I join the queue. They're the biggest onions I've seen, somewhat flattened in shape, sweet and very juicy. In Nizas I was told they're eaten as *oignons farcis*, stuffed onions, and that's how I prepare them, following the recipe in *La Cuisine pour Tous*.

Avoiding Madame Commeiras, I ask Jean-Pierre about the doings of Claret. More aware of permissible limits now, I can be bolder with my questions. Who lives in Claret? What work do they do? Where? There's a Canadian, he says – or perhaps an American? – who has spent eight months alone in a hut in the wilds of Canada and is here to write up his observations. Intrigued, I make further enquiries of Madame Midi Libre, as we christen the lady who sells newspapers from her front room. *Mais oui*, she says, a Canadian, or perhaps he's American, who runs air charters in Borneo.

I need to find this mysterious stranger and hear his story first hand. On our ramblings through the village I try to identify his house, as if the colour of the door or the pattern on the lace curtains might somehow be a clue to the identity of the occupier. He must have left, I conclude sadly, unless he was a chimera in the first place, the product of amplified gossip. What I discover instead, nailed to a high arched garage door, is the hairy black

trotter of a freshly killed wild boar. As a hunter's trophy it's a symbol of masculine skill and courage but, for me, it's a reminder of what lies at the end of the path up into the hills that loom darkly over the village.

Perhaps knowing that I'm here for only a month, I don't form an attachment to Claret in the same way as I embraced Nizas and Caromb. I don't sense a history. The village seems to have developed as a straggle of dwellings along a narrow main street that veers and slews like a drunk taking a few steps at a time. The oldest houses are on this street; ours shows the year 1804 above the door, next door 1747. But it probably began as a medieval village, and indeed still has the medieval system of open drains running down both sides of the street. When I rinse the coffeepot in the sink the grounds wash directly into the gutter and flow gently down the stream. The *tout à l'égout*, a proper mains drainage system, is only just starting to be installed in some parts of Claret, but not where we are.

Living in an apartment in *centre ville* means there is nowhere for the children to play outdoors, except the little square outside the church, shaded by tall plane trees. We explore the roads and tracks leading out of the village looking for play sites but more often than not we are turned back by a foul smell that seems to come from the west of the village. *J'ai remarqué une odeur assez forte hier*, I mention to Madame Commeiras, who can't remember any unusual smell. Eventually she identifies it. *Ah oui, c'est l'huile de cade*, she replies. *Huile de cade? On s'en sert pour les shampooings et les savons*, she explains; it goes into medicinal shampoos and soaps. More like a tar than a clear flowing oil, it's distilled from the wood of the prickly juniper, a large bushy shrub that is native to the south of France. The inhabitants of Claret are inured to the acrid aroma, but I find it irritating and intolerable, and an excuse to escape.

So we go to the beach, just beyond Montpellier. The nearest two are Palavas and Carnon, two neighbouring seaside towns that bookend a continuous stretch of beach on a narrow strip of land between the Mediterranean and the *étangs*. These are a chain of saltwater lagoons, similar to the Coorong in South Australia, that stretch all the way from the mouth of the Rhône to Agde. The beaches are wide and sandy, though the sand is a dirty grey rather than golden or white, and the sea is a warm, calm, shallow pond. It's perfect for the children, who happily play naked in the sand puddles.

The friends we make in the village are transients, like us. A few doors away is the house of *les Parisiens*, and we pass it every day. Nods and *bonjours* lead to conversation, and we meet the large extended family: Monsieur and Madame Voillaume, Madame's sister, another friend and her husband, and all these children, exuberant, energetic Voillaume boys, and more cousins and friends in their late teens. I never work out who they all belong to. Monsieur is a senior manager at Elf and has some insight into the relevance of John's field of research. Outgoing and unpretentious, they are the opposite of the Parisian stereotype. They invite us for a drink and show us over the house they are renovating, still with its original outdoor sink, a shallow hollow chipped out of solid stone.

But we have old friends at Nizas and Caux, and we're eager to see them again, especially since Nizas is only an hour or so away. *Vous n'avez pas reçu ma lettre?*, asks Vivette when we visit, a couple of days after settling in Claret. Our *gîte* is available, she says. The previous booking was cancelled; I wrote to you to say you could have stayed here. My heart sinks. Filled with dismay and disappointment, I can only reply, in a small voice, No, we didn't receive a letter, when did you send it? Then I remember the strike at the mail sorting centre at Avignon and silently curse the

anonymous men and women whose arbitrary actions have meant we will spend the month of July in Claret. Bitterly, I reflect on what might have been.

30 Le Parti Socialiste

After six months in France, Australia is increasingly distant. Letters from family and friends give us some idea of what's happening at home but local news is more immediate and intriguing. It's an interesting time to be in France. There's been the novelty of electing a *maire de Paris*, the first since 1789. Jacques Chirac, the former Prime Minister, offered himself as a candidate and, to the surprise of many, won the second round and was appointed Lord Mayor of Paris toward the end of March. I'm with the many. I find him too sleek and suave to be completely honest, sincere and trustworthy.

No one who lived through the 'It's Time' campaign and the Whitlam victory could fail to be engaged by the current political scene in France, with a tired and out-of-date conservative government faced by an enthusiastic and energised opposition. Memories of the May '68 riots in Paris are still fresh, a revolt against the social, cultural and political establishment that saw students and workers battling with police in the narrow cobbled streets of the Latin Quarter. The impact of these events reverberated worldwide. In the years that followed, many counter-culturists retreated to peaceful self-sufficiency in rural France, especially in the south, sometimes raising a few goats and selling cheese at local markets. At Nizas we made friends with Jean-Patrick and

his partner, who had left Lyon for a simpler life, squatting in an old abandoned railway worker's house. It was solid enough but had only one room and a loft accessible by ladder – no kitchen, no bathroom, no running water. Romantic, perhaps, but not for me.

After the municipal elections in March produced a huge swing to the left, speculation immediately began about a possible change in government with the legislative elections to take place in 1978. Support for the Parti Socialiste has been steadily building over the past decade, Mitterand losing the 1974 presidential election by the slimmest and most heartbreaking of margins. An uneasy coalition of socialists and communists, the left has not had a majority in parliament since the beginning of the Fifth Republic in 1958. Its growing strength, post-elections, inspires a series of national strikes, *jours de grève national*.

I'm used to occasional strikes in Australia, but nothing so total as these, the first of which occurs when we are in Caromb. All public servants, including teachers and post office workers; all public transport workers; and all journalists and radio staff are on strike for 24 hours. Their action is effective; with no metro and no buses, Paris comes to a standstill. In Caromb all the shops are shut, even the *boulangeries*, but they have anticipated the strike and baked double quantities the previous day. With electricity and gas workers on strike there's no power. Yet these vital operatives are not so inflexible as to deny French families their right to a hot dinner. They acknowledge the sanctity of meals by providing power and gas for a couple of hours before midday and again in the evening.

It's impossible not to be caught up in the political drama, a David-and-Goliath battle, and to weigh the arguments of one side against the other. The left alliance favours shorter working hours and a reduction in unemployment, as well as nationalisation of key industries, including banking. Defending individual

liberty, the right warns that such policies can only lead to economic disaster. The radio broadcasts President Giscard d'Estaing's address at a major rally at Carpentras and I listen intently. Even if I don't understand every word, the message is clear. This is not a political address, begins Giscard, but who does he think he is fooling?, I mutter. Of course it's political. It's about France and its future, in particular its future in Europe, he says. In 1977 the EU is still many years away and a common currency is barely conceivable, but the decade to come is critical. Giscard outlines the benefits of a more unified France and the audience claps at all the right places while chanting 'Gis-card, Gis-card'. As a final patriotic gesture he asks the whole audience to join him in singing *la Marseillaise*.

After this blatant appeal on behalf of the right, there's no way I'm going to miss the inaugural meeting of a new branch of the Parti Socialiste in Claret. The village has had a socialist mayor for years but never a formal party organisation, and the party elders clearly believe the time is ripe to take advantage of popular sentiment. Around the *mairie* and at the Unico, posters go up announcing the time and place: 9 pm at the local school in the newer part of the village. I've never before been to a political meeting, never joined a political party and have no intention of ever doing so, but here, I can slip into my French persona and participate without implicating the Australian me. Outsider status gives me a kind of immunity.

At the advertised starting time, only about a dozen people, including me and John, are milling about outside the hall. I have time to slip home to check on the children, left asleep in the apartment. Half an hour later several large black cars arrive with the officials from Montpellier, and the crowd has swelled to a hundred or so, around one quarter of the village's population. Most are still in their working clothes, and most are men; I see

only four or five women in the audience. The party officials are all men, too, although I learn at the end that party rules require one of the office bearers of the new branch to be female.

The *maire* introduces the speakers, who include the local member and trade union heavies. The member speaks briefly, clearly and coherently, but all froth, nothing of substance, and immediately leaves to go elsewhere. A party secretary patiently explains why theirs is the people's party. He is followed by a passionate and idealistic union man who outlines, fervently and theatrically, the progressive principles of the Parti Socialiste and the virtues of its goals. I appreciate his rhetorical gifts but, regretfully, find his speech too rapid-fire and miss important chunks.

Next comes a quieter, more intense man whose hero, he leaves no room for doubt, is party leader François Mitterand. He preaches the gospel of the Parti Socialiste and what it can, and will, achieve for the workers. Experienced and shrewd, he knows how to attract the sympathies of the viticulturists in the audience, which means almost everyone. Everyone except me, and I take the opportunity to hurry back to check on Dylan and Stephanie. He's still talking when I return. The final speech is an anti-climax: the formalities of joining, the election of office bearers and committee rules are explained.

It's been a long evening but at last, it's time to toast the new branch. Unfortunately the celebratory champagne has travelled all the way from Montpellier in the back of a car in the middle of summer. It's now been sitting on the back seat, in the warm evening air, for over two hours. The celebration falls flat. Not one of the ideologues foresaw a practicality such as ice.

As a foreigner, voting is out of the question, but I have an interest in the future of this country that, for the time being, is my home. I sympathise with the Parti Socialiste cause but their alliance with the Parti Communiste Français, led by firebrand

Georges Marchais, fills me and many others with fear. I have glimpsed him on television, and he has the wild eyes and gestures of a demagogue. On the other hand, there's so much disillusionment with the right that the contest promises to be close. How can I not become involved?

31 Le quatorze juillet

July and August in France are the months for festivals, concerts, entertainments and festivities of all kinds, largely for the benefit of *les estivants*. I wish English had a word like this, with its connotations of warm carefree days and a life ruled by pleasure, instead of the bland and pedestrian 'summer holidaymakers'. Nîmes is welcoming Ella Fitzgerald and Count Basie to the magical space of its Roman amphitheatre, and Claret has a free open-air theatre performance in the *place*. It would be unsociable not to attend, along with everyone else from the village, and once the children are asleep and the evening is dark enough for the performance, we quietly join the crowd. It's *café-théâtre*, what the French call *théâtre des boulevards*, improvised by a young troupe of three women and four men and designed to entertain all audiences, from young boys to grandmothers. A blend of fantasy and myth, slapstick and satire, it gets plenty of laughs and, although some of the jokes and references sail way over my head, I happily contribute to the collection box.

But the big event for July, all over the country, is the French national day on 14 July, *le quatorze juillet* or Bastille Day. In Claret, everyone but us is familiar with the format of festivities but no one thinks to pass on this local knowledge. At last, with three days to go, a notice goes up in the window of Jean-Pierre's

store: there will be a *repas communal*, a community dinner, and a boules competition in the afternoon. Naturally we'll be there. I pay Jean-Pierre and he adds two more names to the list.

Bastille Day in Claret starts quietly. Apart from hurrying housewives who have to put dinner on the table, *jour de fête* or not, the only people in the streets are children: boys in their Sunday-best clean shirts and ironed pants, girls in long dresses with ribbons in their hair. Early morning business is brisk at Unico since the day deserves at least a few special treats, such as the best *jambon de pays* and a tray of enormous yellow peaches.

The men emerge later and congregate in the square. Their business is making teams for the afternoon's *concours de boules*, and they group themselves into threesomes according to individual skills. Toward midday the *maire* gathers together half a dozen men who sheepishly follow him to the *mairie* to unearth a few *drapeaux tricolores* and a dusty wreath. They file off to the *monument aux morts*, collecting a few more stragglers on the way, to get the official part of the day over and done with before festivities begin.

In a gesture of gallantry, the men have agreed to a parallel competition of boules for women so long as they can field at least four teams. While the men endlessly deliberate, trying to find the best combination of complementary skills, the women organise their teams efficiently and without fuss. The scale of the competition, with at least half a dozen games being played simultaneously, means that every level or almost level space in the village has been commandeered – the bare ground under the plane trees, the gravel around the church, even the bituminised road outside the *épicerie*, where due care has been taken to cover the hole at the end of the open drain.

The ladies' competition is just as serious as the men's, the participants just as committed, but success depends more on

chance than skill. Opposing each other in the final are the teams led by Jean-Pierre's wife and Madame Commeiras' daughter, who loudly directs her players as to where and how far the boules should be thrown. Ultimately her vociferous coaching is to no avail, and the other team takes the prize. The women all return home to prepare for the evening festivities.

The men employ both technique and tactics. Each team includes *pointeurs* who throw low and let the boule roll toward the jack, and a specialist thrower, *le tireur*, whose role is to lob his boule so that it lands close to, or on top of, an opponent's boule and sends it into oblivion. *Le tireur* is self-effacing, keeping to himself in the background until the moment his special talent is needed. Confidently and seemingly without effort, he launches his boule, and the sharp clang of metal on metal confirms his success. He walks away modestly, as if he knew this would be the result, leaving the rest of the team to show their jubilation.[1]

In the square, trestle tables are set up and an enormous pile of *sarments*, dried vine prunings, is ready to be lit. Having tucked the children into bed, we arrive for the dinner. *Asseyez-vous où vous voulez*, we're told, sit wherever you like. We avoid sitting with the Commeiras clan and find ourselves opposite a man we have christened 'the Fisherman', because several times we've seen him returning from the creek with his rod; we sat next to him at the Parti Socialiste meeting. Alongside him is Jean-Pierre's father-in-law from Béziers, a twinkle-eyed patriarch who gleefully tells us, over and over, how he's managed to leave his wife at home. Next to me is a family from Le Havre, renting a place for the summer; we've seen them in the village. As they all place their knives, forks and proper cloth serviettes on the table, we realise that this is a bring-your-own affair, and John quickly dashes home for implements, checking on the children at the same time.

There's an air of anticipation around the table. It's nearly nine o'clock, and the dinner should have started an hour ago. The manager of the *cave coopérative* takes over administration of the bonfire, now flaming high, and his acolytes prepare an enormous grid on which the dinner will cook. Everyone is anxiously awaiting the free *apéritif* – a double slug of *pastis* in a paper cup, topped up with cold water from a large garden watering can.

At last the first course arrives – paper plates of ham and sausage and *pâté* and olives and chunks of bread. Volunteers rake hot coals under the grids and throw on strings of fat pork sausages and spicy *merguez*. Wives are called in to help, handing out more bread, handfuls of potato chips, jars of mustard. The *cave coopérative* man wheels around a barrowful of bottles from the local vintage, one bottle for every two participants, and the assistant to the *maire* distributes the sausages and *merguez* equitably, one of each per person. The Fisherman thinks John did poorly in the distribution of chips and loudly calls them to return and give him more. Conversation subsides as everyone eats and drinks. After seconds of sausage, more wine arrives, then foil-wrapped triangles of La Vache Qui Rit cheese and fresh peaches, to be eaten with knife and fork. However makeshift, this dinner follows the standard French formula to the letter.

Around the table good humour and joviality reign. The square is filled with the sounds of eating and wine-amplified voices. More wine is broached and passed around. I listen, enthralled, to tales of the village, of the fish that got away and the wife who was left at home. The band starts up again and some young girls begin to dance. Eventually, everybody joins in. I find myself dancing with Monsieur Poste, lighter on his feet than I ever imagined him on his bicycle.

Midnight comes, the band is tired, and for some, such as Monsieur Poste, tomorrow is a normal day. Strolling back, we

exchange goodnights with the Parisians as we pass and, languidly climbing the stairs, reflect on the success of the *repas communal* in bringing the community together and celebrating *liberté, fraternité, égalité.*

32 *Courses de taureaux*

In Provence, *'les courses de taureaux sont passionemment suivies'*, notes my tattered Michelin guide. In summer, old Roman arenas become the setting for bullfights, either Spanish-style with picadors and toreadors, or the Provençal version, *la course de taureaux*, also known as *course libre* or *course camarguaise* or *course à la cocarde*. Michelin calls the latter *simples jeux tauromachiques*, mere games, but these bullfights are no simple frolic in the park, and the locals follow them *passionemment*.

I've admired the sturdy black bulls with their wide curved horns in the Camargue. I've read Laurence Durrell's account of a *course libre* bullfight, 'the heart and marrow of Provence'. But I've never been in the right place at the right time. At least, not until we decide to drive to Sommières – after all, it is only 30 minutes from Claret – and I discover that *courses de taureaux* are scheduled for the very same afternoon.

It's not because Sommières is close to Claret that we choose to visit, nor that it's a Roman town with a Roman bridge and Roman road. My reason is a personal one: Sommières is the town of Lawrence Durrell, and I need to make the pilgrimage. I have no idea if he's still there in 1977, and even if I did pass him in the street I probably wouldn't recognise him, but it's enough to know that I'm here, in his vicinity, and that the man with his back to me, sipping a *pastis* at noon, could well be him.

Durrell's *Spirit of Place* is part of our travelling library. As well as essays, it includes some of his letters from the late 1950s to the early 1960s. Introducing the collection, the editor describes how Durrell settled first on the outskirts of Sommières, then moved close to Nîmes, then returned to a different house just outside Sommières, 'a quite large 19th-century house, somewhat mysterious and romantic, hidden behind big walls, with a conservatory and overgrown garden'.

I search for clues in his letters and writings while poring over the Michelin map, but there's nothing to guide me, no hint that his house might be south of the town, or on the road to Villevieille. Disillusioned but not disheartened, I plan to be systematic and methodical in my search. From Sommières, we take every road out of the town and back again, my eyes darting from left to right looking for a large house behind a high wall. It's dispiriting; nothing seems remotely close. On the last road, a little-used lane, I see a modest, dusty house with a walled garden and deem it to be Durrell's. I'm satisfied.

Back in the town posters for the afternoon's bullfight are plastered around the square, and there's no question as to whether or not we will stay for the spectacle. This is not the Greek tragedy of a Spanish bullfight, whose ominous conclusion dulls the delight to be found in the skills of the toreador, the flashes of luminous colour beneath his cape. The *course de taureau* is a contest between man and beast, lively and spirited, the game always in balance as first the bull then the athletic *razeteurs* command the ring and take control. Often it's the bull who is victorious and who ends the season in triumph – for these bulls perform regularly from about May to September, in a variety of arenas throughout Provence. As Durrell writes, 'the bull is the darling, the hero of the crowd ... His is the name traditionally printed in scarlet poster-type on the placards, and his the applause when a *razeteur*

is sent sprawling over the barrier with a broken rib or tossed in a crumpled heap against the stockades'.

The Sommières arena is not big, perhaps only 50 metres in diameter, surrounded by tiers of narrow wooden benches. Loudspeakers broadcast scratchy selections from Bizet's *Carmen* as locals slowly filter in. Time is flexible here, especially in summer. I take my place, sensing Lawrence Durrell beside me as my virtual companion. Suddenly, *Carmen* gives way to a rousing trumpet rendition of the tune to 'Come to the cookhouse door, boys', and the big gates open. The first bull strolls out, looks around and, on cue, snorts and paws the ground. Native to the Camargue, the bulls are bred and raised in its marshes and grasslands and, even as seasoned performers, retain a free-spirited wildness. They are small in stature, black, with long legs for running, and curved, wide-set horns. Their keen, darting eyes could never be mistaken for a Jersey's.

The repeat of the tune brings forth the twelve *razeteurs* and five *tourneurs*, all dressed in white, with white sandshoes. The role of the *tourneurs* is to try to distract a charging bull or animate a lethargic one, but it's the *razeteurs* who provide the action. They are lithe and lean and supremely acrobatic. They are also fearless, or ostensibly so, since their role is to get very close to the bull and, using a kind of comb cupped in the palm of their hand, remove several decorations attached to the bull. There's the *cocarde*, a red ribbon pinned to the forehead; two white pompoms at the base of each horn; and, most valuable, the string wound around each of the horns. The object of the contest is to steal as many of these 'prizes' as possible within the allotted time, for rewards of both points and cash. If the bull is fast and fierce, cunning and clever, he might not lose any of his prizes.

Razeteurs have to be quick on their feet. If fleeing a bull they have to be able to leap fast and high, using the ledge of the wall

as a springboard to reach the safety of the inner circle. They have to watch the bull at all times, sometimes goading him, while anticipating his reaction. If he appears sulky and unwilling they have to coax him to perform for the sake of the crowd; no one appreciates a one-sided contest. If they manage to secure a prize, the audience applauds; if they manage to escape the point of the horns, a collective sigh of relief pervades the ground.

Our first bull is somewhat apathetic; he dutifully plays his part, allowing the *razeteurs* to remove all five prizes, then contentedly trots back to his pen. The second one is more hot-tempered. *Il est méchant*, people murmur to one another; mean and nasty, not a good sport. He repeatedly leaps over the stockade into the no-man's land between this wall and the first row of seats, where the *razeteurs* would normally take refuge. Spectators in the front row of seats immediately withdraw their dangerously dangling legs. As the bull takes their territory, so the *razeteurs* retreat to the bullring. This game is deemed unfinished, as only two of the prizes have been captured, and when the music signals its end the crowd jeers and boos. Bull number three is reasonably alert and fiery, but not skilful and loses all his decorations.

At interval the ground is watered to settle the dust and people leave their seats to buy icecreams and glasses of *pastis*. Then the music starts, and the action resumes. Number four bull is sprightly but not smart enough to outwit the *razeteurs*, who strip him of his prizes within 10 minutes. Number five is not much different. The programmers are keeping the best until last, for the final bull is Aiglon, a star performer; he knows what is expected and acts the part to the fullest.

It is soon apparent that this bull is more of a match than any of the earlier ones, and the *razeteurs* approach with caution. Inserting his horns between the planks that form the stockade, he tosses them menacingly aside as though they were matchsticks. He

leaps the wall into the no-man's land and chases *razeteurs* around this narrow circle, snorting and bellowing. He even mounts the inner wall, forcing the *razeteurs* to climb even higher for safety and some of the audience to hurriedly retreat. One *razeteur* is not quick enough, and the bull picks him up and throws him over his back. I imagine blood and broken bones, but the *razeteur* falls between the horns and, apart from a few cuts and bruises, is fine. Each time the bull is reckoned to score a trick, he is honoured by a snatch of the triumphal march from *Carmen*. Only three of the decorations are removed and the bull is declared the winner, to huge applause from the audience.

Next day's *Midi Libre* carries a full report under the headline *Aiglon termine en beauté*, 'Fantastic finish from Aiglon'. 'After three minutes he jumped over the boards, hot on the heels of Bailly, knocked a spectator in the corridor behind the stockade . . . He had the upper hand for the whole of the session and his leaps over the wall and bold, dramatic movements certainly pleased the audience,' gushes the local reporter.

In the 1950s Lawrence Durrell wrote about the legendary Gandar. On this afternoon, from his seat beside me, would he have found the feats of Aiglon equally memorable?

33 Where next?

Where next? This is the question hanging over us, and options are falling away.

September is settled: working a vintage with Jean-Pierre and Vivette. We'll live in their *gîte* and John will get paid as well as receiving a wine allowance, three litres a day. We assume I'll be working, too, though probably only half-days. The children will go to the local school. It's the custom, says Vivette, and Madame Molla confirms this. All the itinerant workers – Spanish, French, Portuguese – enrol their children at the local school for the month of vintage.

September is all well and good, but August? And after September?

Now we are near Montpellier again, Professor Jouanna has become elusive. All John can do is leave a message at the university asking the professor to phone Claret post office with a message. Days go by. Having arrived in France with no contacts, no prospects, to have hope of a job within a year has convinced me that miracles are possible. I caution myself that hope is as ephemeral as a waft of orange blossom, but still I am planning months, years, lifetimes, as if each possibility were as solidly rooted as the orange tree. As I get to know Montpellier the prospect of living there for a few years becomes even more appealing.

I like the old town with its cobbled streets, its elegant 17th-century gentleman's residences, its Arc de Triomphe, the statues and fountains in the Place de la Comédie. Most of all, I like the bookshops; never have I found so many bookshops in a French city outside Paris.

Eventually John manages to connect with Professor Jouanna and the news is dismal. He has heard nothing about the progress of the research contract, and at this stage it's unlikely he'll have word before September. Then again, it might be January. Or later. The rosy future I imagined is evaporating, vanishing into never-never land. He gently suggests that John should get a job to tide him over for six months. By March, he adds optimistically, all should be well.

Can we survive until March? *Australian Gourmet* and *Epicurean* are both paying me for my contributions but it's mere pocket money. Another letter from the Université de Compiègne arrives, redirected from Caromb, but it's now too late for John to travel to Compiègne to discuss what and how he could contribute. Instead he has to provide details in writing. Together we draft a letter summarising his thesis and describing his research interests, all very technical. I show it to the Parisians who carefully review every sentence and propose several modifications. It's delicate. He can't appear ungrateful for the offer, but at the same time he wants to let them know, in the most diplomatic of terms and without mentioning the anticipated offer from Professor Jouanna, that he's only interested in a six-month term.

For the present, all we can do is wait – and find somewhere to live for the next month. In desperation I read the classifieds in the *Midi Libre*, looking for possible rentals in this area. We visit real estate agents at Palavas, but the cheapest seaside apartment is 2,600 francs for the month, twice what we can afford. I write to all the departmental tourist offices in the south requesting

details of holiday accommodation. There's an address at Agde, but it costs 900 francs per week. The Syndicat d'Initiative at Carcassonne replies with details of a place for only 1000 francs for the whole month – but it's in the Montagne Noire, the Black Mountain region, and sounds rather too primitive as well as gloomy and isolated.

I seem to spend half my time at the post office. If I'm not buying stamps or searching in telephone directories I'm making phone calls, and I develop a kind of camaraderie with Monsieur and Madame Poste. I see him on his way up the hill every morning, on his old-fashioned bicycle. Round-faced and rosy-cheeked, Monsieur Poste always has a friendly word for everyone he meets. After asking the habitual question, *Ce sont des jumeaux?* he tells us that he has twin grandsons about the same age who live at Montpellier. If ever the national postal company, PTT, were searching for a happy face to feature on its posters above a slogan such as *Votre facteur sympa vous apporte de bonnes nouvelles* (Good news from your friendly postie), or *Le PTT vous apporte le bonheur* (PTT: bringing you happiness), they need go no further than Claret.

But for us there's no good news. Bastille Day comes and goes and still we have no plans for August. Spain is looking increasingly attractive after its recent devaluation, but horror stories about the roads to Spain becoming one gigantic traffic jam are something of a deterrent, only partly offset by the promise of beaches and living costs that are next to nothing.

By the third week of July, we reach the stage of buying a map of Spain and a French/Spanish phrase book, almost a badge of honour since we are now de facto French. I peruse tourist brochures of Spanish hotels, all way beyond our budget. I try the Touring Club de France, the French equivalent of the NRMA or RAA, but its cheaper places are fully booked. Hour after hour

I'm in the post office, ringing tourist offices up and down the Spanish coast, in and near Barcelona. Even at the end of a phone line I can hear the frenzy of the office in the background. Yes, of course you'll find something within 100 km of Barcelona, assures the English-speaking respondent, but the first two nights of the month could be difficult. This is enough to decide us. August will be Spain.

We have only a few days to make preparations for our Spanish adventure, most importantly concerning money. Travellers' cheques, we agree, but we also arrange for money to be transferred to the BNP branch in Barcelona. We also buy a cheap esky-type container to keep food and drinks cool, and limit ourselves to one book each – we want to keep luggage to a minimum.

Three tea chests are already in storage at Mas Laval but even so, the poor DS is more laden than when we left Caromb. Dylan and Stephanie are surrounded by bags and boxes piled on top of one another. The Parisians come to see us off and are amazed that I can find a place for my legs.

The phenomenon of the French *vacances d'été* is new to us. The radio has been predicting 10 million people – or is it 10 million cars? – on French roads on the first two days of August, the days that we will be travelling. The inconceivability of such numbers renders the warnings meaningless, and in any case they are completely outweighed by our excitement at the prospect of going to a foreign country!

34 Villanueva y Geltrú

Why the French insist on all starting their holidays on the same day is beyond my comprehension. Surely logic would point to the advantages of leaving a couple of days earlier, or later. Having relinquished Claret on the last day of July, we have little choice. The radio prophecies are realised: from Narbonne south, traffic on the *route nationale* is at a standstill. In one hour we progress less than 20 kilometres. From Perpignan we can take the autoroute, joining all the other French and German and Belgian and English cars heading for Spain. Nonchalant border guards wave us through as though we're just another French family *en vacances*.

The Pyrenees is a forbidding frontier. From a distance, they're just a gentle range of hills on the far horizon, softly blurred in the afternoon haze. Their immensity gradually reveals itself as they rise above the plain in all their bleak angularity, and it seems impossible that there could be a way through. Once on the Spanish side, however, the slopes are greener and gentler, and I see the familiar silhouette of the Veterano Osborne bull high on a hilltop. On my first visit to Spain, I imagined Osborne as a particularly famous bull, a veteran of the arena, a bull whose verve and valour are legendary. It's disappointing to discover he is merely a brand of sherry.

We have a Spanish map and a French–Spanish phrase book but no insider knowledge, no tips as to the region most likely to have plenty of cheap accommodation. I'm fixed on the coast. I feel as though this is a holiday, unlike the earlier months in France, and a summer holiday without sea, sand and sun is unimaginable. In any case, I remember the reassurances from the Barcelona tourist office.

Just over the border in Figueres I peruse the 'For rent' offers in real estate windows. Apartments are not quite so cheap as I anticipated. The least inexpensive on the Costa Brava is the equivalent of 2000 francs a month, far more than our budget can safely bear. Confidently following a naïve logic that assumes rents fall with latitude, we continue down the autoroute and find a hotel at Villafranca del Penedes, south of Barcelona and only 20 kilometres from the coast.

Villafranca is an unexceptional Spanish town but it's different to French villages, and I can't wait to explore. In a shop close to the hotel John finds new sandals for only 410 pesetas, about 24 francs, just as the old sandals that he rescued in Caromb start to fall apart. Wine is ridiculously cheap; a large glass of cold white wine costs just over half a franc. It's a measure of the extent of our naturalisation that in Spain, as earlier in England, the base for comparison is France. How much is it in francs?, I ask myself as I do a quick conversion. Not many, is the usual answer. The advantages of a summer in Spain are not difficult to appreciate.

Arriving at Sitges the next day I start to understand the pressure on coastal towns and their inhabitants from summer tourism. The town is teeming with foreigners. Even though I know it's a futile quest I ask about hotels and apartments, but the lady at the tourist office simply shakes her head. Continuing south we arrive at Villanueva y Geltrú, which seems less touched by the August influx. Directions in Spain, we notice, are nowhere near

as frequent nor as logical as in France, and finding the tourist office is not easy. Totally bamboozled, I ask directions from a small travel agency. It's blindingly obvious why I want to visit the tourist office and the man has an automatic response. You're looking for a hotel, a pension?, he asks, and starts rifling through a stack of cards, the names of people willing to rent out rooms for the summer. Immediately he makes a phone call, and from what I understand of Spanish it seems there's something suitable.

After a few minutes a woman arrives, and we follow her to a neighbour's house where we can possibly rent two small adjoining rooms for 600 pesetas a night, about 35 francs. It's time to be realistic: this is as good as we can hope to find, and we offer to stay for 10 nights, until 14 August. As for the second half of the month, I cross my fingers that by then apartments will be easier to rent. With negotiations all done in Spanish, of which I catch perhaps every fourth word, I'm not quite sure whether our landlady-to-be accepts us or has to talk to her husband before confirming. But with accommodation more-or-less settled, we head off to the beach. It's the same Mediterranean, but the sand is whiter and the water less shallow than at Palavas, and the children are happy to be out of the car.

Next morning our Señora is expecting us. She is concerned about the arrangements we have made for feeding the children, giving them proper meals. Communication is cumbersome, but at least this much I understand. Timorously I show her my own pan and ask if I might sometimes cook them some eggs in her kitchen. Impossible! She will have none of this and shows me the kitchen, indicating it is far too small for two people. I would like to say that I would only use her kitchen at times when she didn't need it but by this stage I have completely exhausted my vocabulary and need to consult the dictionary. I also recognise that people can be very proprietorial about their kitchens.

Later, with the help of the dictionary but more through guesswork and gestures, we agree on a mutually satisfactory solution: Señora will cook breakfast and dinner for the children. The kitchen, I understand, is out of bounds. I'm not entirely happy but for the sake of maintaining good relations I decide to go along with the arrangement and try to ask Señora what it will cost. Either she doesn't understand my rudimentary Spanish, or I don't understand her rapid reply, and we're at a stalemate until her daughter Mercedes arrives. She's a nurse, and has learned enough French for us to be able to converse. My mother acts as godmother to all the children in the neighbourhood, she explains, and that now includes your two. Money doesn't come into it, you're to treat this place as your own. Humbled, I thank Señora as best I can.

Señora's house is in the old part of the town, halfway between the medieval castle and the town centre with its *rambla* leading to the waterfront. A broad, tree-shaded boulevard, with shops and cafés and parks, the *rambla* is the heart of the town. By now we're thoroughly familiar with the logic and layout of French towns, where the *boulangerie* and the *charcuterie* and other food purveyors are clustered together, and with the customary range of each particular one, but in Spain there's a different paradigm. No *charcuteries*, no *crèmeries*, but we come across a *formatgeria*, a kind of *épicerie* with cheeses and sausages and canned goods, unexpectedly including IXL sliced pineapple. *Formatgeria* is not in the Français-Espagnol phrase book; I realise it's a Catalan word. After Franco's death at the end of 1975 the Catalan language is slowly reasserting itself. Villanueva will soon revert to its Catalan name of Vilanova i la Geltrú.

We fall into a gentle routine of breakfast, beach, lunch, home for siesta, late afternoon stroll, glass of wine, and home for the children's dinner for which Señora cooks an omelette,

what she calls *tortilla*. Lunch is a picnic from the *formatgeria*. The first time we cross the seafront esplanade to the shady park and lay out our spread, I am startled by a whistle. It's the Guardia Civil officer, and he's looking at me. Perhaps the lawn is out of bounds? No, I see others on the grass. The children, bare bottomed? He approaches us, points at me and wags a disapproving finger. Bikinis are not allowed in the town, he's telling me, and although we're less than a hundred metres from the beach I have clearly crossed the boundary between hedonism and civility. I quickly add a shirt. Villanueva is not Bondi.

Unlike resort towns such as Sitges, Villanueva has a life without tourists. It has a fishing industry, and sometimes our stroll takes us to the port area, full of fishing boats and surrounded by seafood retailers and restaurants. At the daily afternoon market fishermen stand in groups behind their day's catch, which is beautifully arranged in wooden boxes. The neatness of the fishermen's displays is testament to their efforts to provide this food and a mark of respect for their harvest: small fish, silvery and glistening, all of a size, the heads all facing the same way; miniscule, transparent squid with black beady eyes; giant red gambas and concentric circles of crabs on flat wicker trays.

Walking in a different direction one afternoon we stumble across the Museo Romantico Provincial and, since it's open and cool inside, we go in. We are perhaps the only visitors, and a kindly guide takes us from room to room, explaining the history of the house in heavily accented French mixed with Spanish and German. Built by a wealthy town merchant and landowner at the end of the 18th century, it was sold to the state in the 1950s totally intact, with all its furniture and art works, as if its inhabitants had just stepped out for the day.

More than just a house, this estate is almost a village, breathtaking in its splendour. No expense was spared in its furnishing.

The main bathroom boasts a bath sculpted out of a solid block of white marble, while Mademoiselle's bedroom has a four-poster bed of solid silver; elegant Sèvres porcelain sits on a magnificent secretaire inlaid with marble. Yet it's still a family home, a home for entertaining, for concerts in the music room, dancing in the vast ballroom; a home where men congregate in the billiard room with its marquetry table or in the arms room, hung with hunting trophies, boar's head and stag horns. All the rooms are heated by portable braziers, and I imagine the hard-working maid whose task it was to refill all the braziers with hot coals. On the ground floor are the working areas – the bakery; the oil room; the larder where hams and sausages, herbs and garlic were stored; the grain store and the wine cellar; the horse stables and carriage room; and then the peacock-studded gardens. Wandering from room to room I am transported back to the 19th-century and reminded of the pleasures of privilege.

In August Villanueva celebrates its *festa mayor* and the big parade passes near Señora's house. It begins with giants: first a dragon and two horses then enormous puppet figures, several metres tall, representing historical or legendary characters. Their immobile faces are astonishingly alive, with big, all-seeing black eyes. Bands of musicians alternate with groups of dancers, boys dancing with batons that they knock against one another to the beat of the music, and girls in embroidered white skirts circling around the boy who serves as maypole at their centre. Then come the acrobats, in dazzling white trousers with wide black sashes around their waists. Tension mounts as they start to perform, building a human pyramid: first a solid base of interlocking backs and shoulders, a second and then a third tier on top. I can see the strain in the legs and arms as the base steadies itself. Younger men, lithe and limber, clamber over the backs of the lower levels to form a fourth tier, and finally a little boy, no more

than seven, climbs to the very peak of the pyramid and stands tall, like the angel on a Christmas tree. I am spellbound; never have I seen such a demonstration of audacity and trust. The audience claps and whistles as the pyramid gradually dissolves and melts into the crowd.

We've fallen on our feet here, I say to John as we head off to the *rambla*, as we do every evening once the children are asleep. It's the centre of the festivities, the whole town congregating for the carnival. People are spilling out of cafés and snack vendors do a brisk trade in paper cornets of pumpkin seeds and salted broad beans, churros and wedges of fresh coconut. Bigger stalls festooned with hams and sausages sell their salty specialities on thick rounds of white bread while men of North African appearance grill spicy brochettes. We have a taste of everything with a glass of wine, finishing with some churros.

Perhaps it's just the combination of sea and sun, but it feels very much like a holiday. And we're only halfway through August.

35 Cambrils

Luck stays with us when we look for an apartment for the second half of August. At Tarragona all the real estate agents must be at lunch or having a siesta so we continue to Salou. It's touristy and flash and probably unaffordable. Cambrils, the next town south, appears to have plenty of apartments but none at the price we want. Then I spy, in an electrical and lighting shop, a sign for flats to rent and, despite a second sign with the word *completo*, I enter. The owners are French, and they tell me that just that morning a couple had come in, explaining that they had rented the apartment for the whole month but were now obliged to return to France on 15 August. Hallelujah! I write down the address and directions and we speed off. The French renters are expecting us and we agree on the spot. I am overjoyed, especially since a half-month rent, including gas, electricity and linen, is only 750 francs.

My elation is short-lived. When we go to Barcelona the next day to collect the additional money from the bank, BNP tells us it has no funds for us. How is that possible?, I remonstrate, we requested this transfer over two weeks ago. I should be accustomed to shrugged shoulders by now but I refuse to accept his response. Slowly and deliberately I narrate the whole story and plea with him to ring BNP Montpellier to investigate.

He's unconcerned. If you requested a money transfer then it will happen, ring us in a couple of days.

I reflect on my banking experiences in Australia. They've all been positive. As calm, efficient guardians of my money, banks provide funds when I need them and even reward my savings. I see them as symbols of prudence and stability, thanks to the Commonwealth Bank money boxes from primary school. How is it, then, that French banks can be so inefficient, so unresponsive, so incompetent? Of course I've never asked Australian banks to make international transfers so the comparison is unfair, but surely BNP should trust us, should realise that we need our money, and should offer every assistance in tracking the funds and handing them to us as soon as possible. Why does it all have to be so difficult?

The bank's responses don't appease but nor is it a complete catastrophe. Counting the remaining travellers' cheques we calculate we have enough for the rent and a modest standard of living until the funds arrive. Then we'll be able to spend up, taking advantage of Spanish prices. All will be well, I tell myself.

It's a relief to have our own place again. This outer part of Cambrils consists almost entirely of six-storey apartment blocks, each colonised for the summer by different nationalities. Ours has mostly French and Belgian tenants, others seem to be occupied almost exclusively by Germans. We're on the first floor with two bedrooms, a living room and a large balcony that is shaded from the sun until mid-afternoon. The apartment is quiet, reasonably cool, there's space outside for the children to play and it's an easy walk to the beach. Dylan is delighted by the trains he can see from the balcony.

The French renters told us about a farm on the other side of the railway line, about 10 minutes away, that sells fresh fruit and vegetables. Every couple of days we take the dirt path to their

shed to buy lettuce, cucumbers, and sweet, fleshy peppers and, my particular delight, tomatoes. Softer and juicier than the ones I'd been buying in France, they are perfect for gazpacho and *pan con tomate*, which becomes my daily lunch. After the beach, while the children and John have their siesta, I relax on the balcony with my bread and tomato and my holiday book, *La Condition Humaine*. At first it feels incongruous, my mind in 1920s China and my senses in Spain, but gradually they merge, and Malraux becomes permanently associated with tomatoes.

Like Villanueva, Cambrils has its own life and treats tourism as a temporary interruption – which is not to say that it doesn't provide for summer visitors. Clustered together in a bustling 'new town' near the sea are bars specialising in seafood tapas – fresh prawns, fried baby squid, grilled fresh sardines – together with restaurants, bodegas and interesting shops. I regret that we no longer have the services of a de facto godmother to allow us to explore the lively nightlife. The working centre is the sleepy 'old town' with banks and post office and municipal market. To get there from our apartment is a major excursion, since we have to cross the railway line dividing the town and the narrow road is always busy. Every couple of days we make the trek to telephone BNP Barcelona and check whether the additional money we requested has arrived. It's always the same disappointing response.

Fortunately, living is cheap, at least for basic food and wine. Manufactured products, on the other hand, are relatively expensive. Disposable nappies are sold only by the chemist and cost twice as much as in France. Cheap living comes at another cost; in its rush to modernise and industrialise, Spain has overlooked aesthetics and the environment. The new developments on the edges of towns, partly for tourists and partly for workers migrating from the country, are haphazard, crude and ugly.

Tomates farcies
Stuffed tomatoes

Australian Gourmet, March/April 1978

While the juicy Spanish tomatoes are perfect for *pan con tomate*, the large, firm French tomatoes are more suited to *tomates farcies*. Stuffed tomatoes feature in every charcuterie in France in summer, but once over the border in Spain are nowhere to be seen.

Serves 6 as an entrée or accompaniment

6 large ripe tomatoes
1 cup fresh white breadcrumbs
150 g minced pork, veal or beef, or leftover cooked meat
2 tablespoons chopped parsley
1 tablespoon finely chopped onion
1 clove garlic, finely chopped
salt and freshly ground pepper
olive oil

Preheat oven to 190°C (170°C fan-forced).

Cut a thick slice from the base of each tomato, and set aside. With a teaspoon, scoop out seeds and centre flesh, being careful not to break the skin. Discard seeds, finely chop flesh and add with juice to breadcrumbs. Mix in meat, parsley, onion and garlic, season to taste. Fill tomatoes with this mixture, top with reserved slices.

Oil a shallow ovenproof dish, arrange tomatoes in dish, drizzle over a little more olive oil. Cook in preheated oven for 30 to 35 minutes. Serve warm.

There is no integrated planning, no attempt to coordinate one large block of apartments with its neighbour, let alone harmonise it with the landscape. Infrastructure is arbitrary. Unlike France, where there's often a bypass road around towns and villages, main highways in Spain go through towns and villages, adding to traffic and noise and pollution.

Contrasts and contradictions abound. Bank offices are very sleek and modern, but staff are casual, with a couldn't-care-less attitude. Many towns boast new phone boxes that advertise direct dial international calls, but international extends only to the borders of Europe. Post offices are still living in the 19th century, their service slow and shambling with even the simplest transaction demanding plenty of patience. Postage rates seem to be arbitrary. I pass over a letter and say 'Australia' and without even weighing it the man says 20 pesetas. Compared with rates in France, this seems far too little and I query the price, adding the words *correo aereo*, whereupon the man asks for another 20 pesetas, slaps on more stamps, and drops the letter in his bag.

In the luxury of our own space we wind down. Time is at a standstill, the future too distant to contemplate. Decisions are postponed. The here and now is all that matters, and it all comes down to beach and tomatoes. There's no birthday cake, no fairy bread, no presents for Stephanie and Dylan on their second birthday.

As August progresses the weather starts to change, and overcast days and fierce winds replace the hot, still days that flowed in unbroken sequence earlier in the month. The sun has noticeably less force and this slightly milder weather is more comfortable, though it is still too hot to be at the beach in the middle of the day. There's a perceptible decrease in the population, and the traffic is definitely easier. The number of cars at our apartment block dwindles from 50 to about 20, then 10. Camping areas

now advertise vacancies, and the multilingual signs above hotels and apartment blocks near Salou that on our first visit all showed the word *Completo* now welcome guests. And darkness is looming at nine instead of ten pm.

Joining the summer deserters we leave Cambrils and head back to France, with a detour to Villanueva. Our international driver permits have expired, and at John's insistence I have asked my mother to send our renewed permits to Spain, to the address of Señora's daughter Mercedes. With visions of being stopped at the border, not allowed back into France because we lack valid permits, John is starting to panic. Relax, I tell him. No one has ever asked to see our licences, let alone the border guards, and why would they be interested anyway? I'm not surprised that there is no mail waiting for us in Villanueva, given the nonchalance of Spanish post offices.

In one final faint-hearted quest for the mislaid money we continue to Barcelona. We park the car at Plaza de Cataluña and once again I ring the bank. Surprise! The money we had requested is waiting for us, and has been for the past week. But why, day after day, have I been told that the funds had not arrived? The problem is in the translation. I've been telling the bank that I had asked for several hundred francs to be transferred from our French account, and they have looked for French currency. But of course there are no francs in Barcelona; our transfer is immediately converted into pesetas.

Cash in hand fortifies us, and we head for El Corte Inglès to get new winter shoes for the children. Every second Barcelonan is shopping in El Corte Inglès, and we have to fight our way to the children's shoes section, where we find ankle boots, strong and sturdy and practical, with a strap over the front instead of laces. At Figueres the next day John gets the guitar he's lusted after and the children get belated birthday presents.

From Figueres to Mas Laval, the trip is totally uneventful. Nobody takes any notice of a dusty old Citröen with two children sleeping in the back. The border guards barely bother with passports, let alone driving licences. Our foreign adventure is over and a new month beckons.

36 Home again!

Comme vous êtes bronzés!

Vivette is in her garden harvesting beans but she drops everything to greet us with a wide smile and effusive hugs. Jean-Pierre emerges beaming from the cellar. They're both tanned, too, though their tans come from outdoor work rather than seaside holidays. France and Vincent rush to the big iron gate and embrace Dylan and Stephanie. They are all as pleased to see us as we are to see them.

It's relief to be home, as it feels; to reconnect with friends and celebrate a homecoming. Vivette and I buy sausages and *merguez* from the butcher at Caux and pick tomatoes and lettuce from the garden. We set a table in the courtyard and Jean-Pierre puts a match to a huge pile of *sarments*, the dried vine prunings that burn so well and produce such good coals. It's the simplest of meals, all the more satisfying because of its familiarity. Relaxing with another jug of Jean-Pierre's wine we discuss the forthcoming vintage.

Mas Laval will provide about two weeks work, and Jean-Pierre and his team will then pick at other, larger vineyards in the region where vintage continues for three or four weeks longer. The wage is minimal but it should cover our rent, and even if we come out even we'll be satisfied. Vintage will be another

adventure, another new experience to add to the library of new adventures and experiences.

Our new *gîte* is on the northern side of the courtyard, between the rabbits and the turkeys. Kitchen, living area and bathroom are on the ground floor, with two bedrooms upstairs. No one can tell me what this part of the complex was originally used for, or who might have lived here, but the bread oven inside the enormous stone fireplace gives a clue. In her living room Vivette has shown me the old *pétrin* or dough trough, a low wooden tub with sloping sides whose size suggests an impressive baking. Its role today is to store tablecloths and serviettes.

The shoebox of letters that Vivette has kept for us contains news from family and friends and the long-awaited international driving permits. For John there's a letter from the University of Minnesota. Can you get over here by 1 October? asks the American thesis examiner. He's offering a research position in Minneapolis for a couple of years.

Minneapolis? It's the last place I want to go to. Nor is John enthralled by the prospect. We ponder the practicalities of going to America for a year and then returning to France but, however possible it might be in theory, we know in our hearts that it's unlikely to happen. On the other hand, it's already September. Winter is looming, and we can't afford to keep living off savings, however frugal our lifestyle. Nor can we remain drifters, flitting from place to place, each day waking up with the hope that a letter will arrive, that somewhere, someone else will make a decision that will determine our future, where we go next.

And yet . . . Minneapolis is so distant from the here and now that it could almost be on another planet. I have difficulty even imagining a life there. John agonises for a brief moment, but there can be only one response. Thank you for your offer, he writes, but I'd prefer not to interrupt my French studies, nor

impede the children's bilingual progress. Further, if you don't mind, there are certain aspects of the proposed research I'd rather not be involved with (a small white lie). It might be lacking in diplomacy but there's no ambiguity about his reply.

It is good to be back among old friends. In Nizas we call to see Madame Molla and catch up with Monsieur Molla, Poireau Sauvage and Joker. We drop in for an *apéritif* with Madame la Voisine who tells us she already knew we were back. News travels fast! The children are happy to be in familiar territory and they play with France and Vincent, either outside in the courtyard or in the main house. Stephanie shadows Vivette as she feeds the chickens, or picks vegetables in the garden, and we lose her for hours on end.

We're among friends In Pézenas, too, recognised by the burly butcher and even the manager of the Washmatic. At the market the friendly cheesemonger and his wife remember us and give the children a big slice of emmenthal each. Apart from cheese, our market requirements are minimal. Vivette gives us vegetables – tomatoes, superb melons, leeks, celery, lettuce – and Jean-Pierre offers chickens and eggs. I realise now why all great chefs insist on fresh eggs for omelettes.

Before vintage proper it's time to pick the table grapes, black *oeillade* and white *chasselas*, the latter traditionally eaten with fresh *cantal* cheese in the Languedoc. Jean-Pierre has only a few rows, and he picks in the morning so that the women can prepare the grapes for market in the afternoon. Armed with a pair of scissors I join Vivette, Mamie and Vivette's mother in the filtered light near the entrance to the *cave* and trim the bunches, removing any hard, shrivelled and damaged grapes. It's not difficult work, and it's conducive to gossip. This is where I learn about the Nizas *boulangère* and the Fontès doctor, almost down to the how and the when and the where. It is like listening to

Under Milk Wood in French. The women are unashamedly candid, their stories intruding into the most intimate details of people's private lives. I almost blush to hear some of the tales, at the same time realising that here in the country your business is everyone else's business.

Meanwhile, John is helping Jean-Pierre with the preparations for vintage, cleaning out the vats and sorting out all the equipment. Overjoyed to have male company in what is normally a female-dominated household, Jean-Pierre is in his element as he explains to John the role and purpose of every tool and implement, every step in the winemaking process.

And then an invitation arrives from the professor at Compiègne. My heart is still firmly fixed on Montpellier but Compiègne does at least have the benefit of being near Paris, and we cannot wait forever. John catches the overnight train from Montpellier to go to Compiègne and discuss the offer. It's the first time he has been away from the children for more than an afternoon, and they are old enough now to recognise the absence. Stephanie sheds many tears, but seems to understand. John gone Paris, she says over dinner; and then, as if to reassure herself, John coming back.

It's amazing how easily things fall into place. Professor Touzot's job pays 6000 francs per month but without the *treizième mois*, the 13th month, which many employers offer as a kind of bonus. John is happy with the organisation at the university and the work he'll be engaged in. From his preliminary enquiries it seems we'll have no difficulty finding a house to rent. And we agree that to experience Paris – I conveniently overlook Compiègne – is far more important than experiencing Minnesota.

After the months of agonising over if-this, if-not-that, it's almost an anti-climax, the decision made for us. There's no sense

of relief in accepting it, more a feeling of resignation, of coming to terms with the fact that although it's not our first choice it's our only one. Only gradually is this replaced by the excitement of anticipation.

37 *La vendange*

The harvest of table grapes is a mere *amuse-bouche* compared with the serious business of vintage proper. The climax of the year's efforts – from winter pruning to first bud burst in March, through flowering and setting and the long, slow ripening – it involves the whole community, for just about every family has its patch of vines passed down from one generation to the next. Women who happily stay at home for 11 months of the year go out to the vineyards and contribute their labour, and even sprightly 70-year-olds do their share. No one gets married during vintage, and anyone who is unlucky enough to die then is buried quickly, without the usual at-home ceremony and funeral procession. During vintage there's no time for such frivolities.

Like every other vigneron in the district, Jean-Pierre keeps a close watch on his grapes, tasting the berries and checking their sweetness. Nevertheless, it's not for him to decide when to start picking; it's the commune that sets the date. And one day, after the first fresh, crisp morning of autumn, he returns from Caux with the news: *la vendange commence lundi*, vintage begins on Monday.

This is the signal for the butcher to keep his shop open seven days a week, for the *boulangerie* to bake an extra batch of bread every day. Schools open an hour early and provide a hot midday

meal for the children, instead of sending them home for lunch. Clothing stalls at the weekly market display outfits for vintage, though most people simply wear their oldest clothes. Students and hitchhiking travellers make their way here to earn a little cash to fund further travels, and families, sometimes whole villages, arrive from Spain to add themselves to the work force.

It's a boisterous, joyful, exuberant month. The countryside suddenly changes from a tranquil, never-ending sea of green to a series of vivid, animated scenes reminiscent of Breughel as brightly coloured headscarves and bold t-shirts bob up and down along the rows. Quiet lanes that normally see only the yellow van of Monsieur Poste become major thoroughfares for the busy trucks and tractors laden and overflowing with the harvest. In the village *la vendange* is the only topic of conversation and even the *vendangeurs* speak knowledgeably about *carignan* and *aramon* and *oeillade*, and the quality of the harvest; the higher the sugar content (as measured in degrees Baumé) the better. On a Saturday night, the Spanish contingent organises a Spanish-style ball at the *salle des fêtes*.

On his first day John returns exhausted after four hours picking. He barely has energy to eat a quick snack before grabbing an hour's sleep, and it's time to return to the vineyard for another four hours. At the end of the day he helps Jean-Pierre in the *cave* for an hour or so, but he's in bed before nine. It's exhausting work, especially after a month of lazing on the beach.

Sometimes I take the afternoon shift, but I have other duties. There's the morning run to Caux, taking France to school and Mamie to do her daily shopping. With Vivette working in the vineyard, it's now Mamie's job to cook the midday meal. I assume the role of family chauffeur, driving Mamie to the doctor when she has a heavy fall and taking clean clothes to Vincent who has been offloaded to live with his grandparents in Fontès for the month.

The idea of Dylan and Stephanie attending the local school during vintage is abandoned after less than two days. Despite Vivette's repeated assurances I'm not totally convinced that all French children begin school at two years – though *école maternelle* is really only nursery school. And Dylan and Stephanie have never even been to playgroup. Nevertheless, the first morning seems encouraging and I manage to slip away without them noticing. I return at noon to pick them up and hear Dylan's plaintive sobbing as soon as I get near the door. They'll soon settle, I tell myself. Stephanie seems happy enough. *Dylan va à l'école*, she announces to Vivette that afternoon. But the next day they both start crying as soon as we arrive in Caux, and when I leave them at the school I hear Stephanie at the gate calling me and saying, Want go outside. It is more distressing for me than for them, so I gather them up and take them home. *Ecole maternelle* will have to wait.

At Mas Laval I also have the turkeys to manage. With Christmas on the horizon Jean-Pierre has expanded his poultry flock with a couple of hundred turkey poults. It's the first time he's raised turkeys, and he calls them *bête*, stupid, since they can't even find their way out to the green grass in the old orchard outside their barn. He has to place a few wily old hens in with them to lead them out when the shutters are opened. When they do make it outside, they fly up into the low branches of the fruit trees but lack the sense to jump or fly back to earth. I have to patrol every so often and rescue the adolescent birds from their adventurous perches or toss them back if their wings have taken them beyond the fence.

Grape-picking is hard, back-breaking work, for eight hours a day, six days a week. These are bush vines, around a metre high, and the bunches hide beneath the foliage. You have to bend over to cut them, and after half a row your back is suffering from

the unaccustomed movement, so you change to a squatting position – until your knees start to complain, and you return to standing and bending. After less than an hour your back is aching, somewhere in the middle between shoulders and waist, and however you twist and turn the pain does not subside and you're longing to hear the church bells that announce midday and the end of the morning's work.

Jean-Pierre's vines are laden and the buckets fill quickly. Every 10 minutes you straighten up and, if you're near the end of a row, carry your 10-kilogram load to the large plastic *comportes*. Or a *videur* collects your full bucket and hands you an empty one. Grape pickers here are called *coupeurs*, and each *coupeur* is given two rows of vines at a time, working from start to end and back again. There's usually one *videur* to every six *coupeurs*, and the *videur* is kept busy the whole day, collecting and emptying buckets and tamping down the grapes in the *comporte* with a large wooden pestle-like implement that Jean-Pierre calls *une masse*.

The ancient Roman vignerons have left their legacy in word and deed. Jean-Pierre tells me the team of pickers is called *un colh*, a term that recalls the old Provençal *colhir*, to pick or harvest, itself derived from the Latin *colligere*. But for the fact that he uses concrete vats instead of terracotta amphorae, Jean-Pierre's winemaking scarcely differs from Roman practices. He relies on the natural yeasts on the skin of the grapes for fermentation, although he admits to adding a little *levure de Bourgogne* – Burgundy yeast – to get things going. Fermentation takes four to five days and each evening he does the *remontage*, opening the tap at the bottom of the vat and transferring the juice to a holding tank, then pumping it back through the top opening of the vat. Winemaking is the task Jean-Pierre likes best, and he grins and beams as the foaming crimson liquid gushes out, spraying him all over and causing dusty rivulets to trickle down his legs.

With fermentation finished, the residue is pressed. Jean-Pierre hires a press for the day – or evening, since much of the labour is provided by mates after finishing their own work. He pumps the free juice to a separate tank then climbs into the vat and forks out the marc – skin and pips – through a small trapdoor, while his mates transfer it to the press. It's a very gentle press. Two plates at either end of the perforated drum slowly rotate, advancing toward the centre and squeezing the marc of its remaining juices, which trickle into a big tray underneath. The first pressing juices join the wine in the tank but the second, third and possibly fourth pressings go to the distillery, along with the marc.

By October *vendange* is finished. Jean-Pierre is reasonably satisfied with the result, despite a few days of rain, and the last pick comes in at about 12 degrees Baumé, promising a very good wine. After the final pressing everyone assembles around the big table to celebrate another year's harvest. The dish Vivette always cooks for the occasion is *soupe aux choux*, a misleading name since its main ingredient is bread. Stale bread is arranged in alternate layers with a few blanched cabbage leaves and grated *cantal* cheese, the whole then covered with broth – though Vivette uses only water – and baked in the oven. Filling and economical, it satisfies hearty appetites before the grilled sausages and salad and cheese.

I feel that I've been extraordinarily privileged to share the whole experience of vintage with Jean-Pierre and Vivette, to have made new friends, to imagine my muscles and hard work contributing to a joyous drink that previously, when all I had to do was turn on a tap and fill the enamel jug, I had taken for granted.

These six weeks at Mas Laval have been the best of the past six years, says John.

38 Partridge

You've never eaten partridge?

I'm used to these questions by now. No, we don't have partridges in Australia. I've never seen one, never had the opportunity to eat one.

Once the grapes are harvested, crude handwritten signs go up in every vineyard: *grappillage interdit*, no gleaning. There might be a few missed bunches left on the vine or spilled on the soil, but no one is allowed to scavenge them. These sweet berries are for the game birds, pheasants and quail, woodcock and grouse, some native but many of them raised on farms then released in the countryside. On the way to Caux we have to stop the car as Mother Pheasant and her brood of chicks cross the road, and occasionally I catch a flash of brilliant bronze and turquoise plumage between the rows in the vineyard. Jean-Pierre sees it, too, and curses that they are still off limits, totally protected until the hunting season officially starts.

Good-natured Alain, one of Jean-Pierre's mates who helped with the pressing and is a peerless hunter, offers to get us a partridge before we leave. He's as good as his word, presenting us with a small, plump bird, beautifully plucked and dressed. It's a red-legged partridge, a variety native to this southern corner of the country and generally considered far superior to the more common grey variety. It looks as innocent as a baby.

How will you cook it? asks Vivette. Never having eaten one, let alone cooked one, I have no idea, and I resort to Elizabeth David for advice. For young partridge in good condition, she recommends roasting in the oven, as does Ginette Mathiot who adds, in her no-nonsense voice, '*Un perdreau à deux personnes*', one partridge serves two. Not wanting to ruin possibly the one and only partridge I'll ever eat, I ask Vivette what she would do. *Comme un lapin*, says Vivette. She would pot-roast it as she does rabbit, on top of the stove in a heavy iron pan, perhaps with some garlic cloves and thyme. This sounds good enough to me, especially since the stove top in the *gîte* is more reliable than the oven.

It's a special meal for just the two of us; this is not something I want to share with the children. And, unlike the experiment with snails, this ingredient comes with a high commendation. Any caution I might have had about eating a new food, and especially a wild one, vanishes with the first taste. The meat is firm and white with a delicate but distinct flavour, and I understand why the simplest way of cooking is the best. If the wonga wonga pigeons that 19th-century Australian colonists praised to the heavens were as good as this, I can understand why they were almost eaten out of existence.

With an abundance of grapes at the door I trial different recipes to include in my article on vintage for *Australian Gourmet*. White grapes become grape jam. Vanilla-scented and intensely sweet, it has a consistency like a slightly jellied honey and is best eaten spooned over *fromage frais*. With the black grapes I make a *gâteau aux raisins*, following a recipe that uses grapeseed oil rather than butter. John ate a similar cake at a restaurant he was taken to in Compiègne and requested the recipe for me.

Most memorable of all is the salad of autumn fruits – pears, grapes and figs – that my *Larousse Gastronomique* calls *fruits rafraîchis à l'occitanienne*. Wandering in the vineyard beyond

the vegetable garden – the part of the property that belongs to Jean-Pierre's uncle where the vines have been all but abandoned – I discover a short, stocky vine with enormous golden-bronze grapes, translucent amber orbs that sparkle in the sun. I have never before seen grapes like this, so large, so beautiful. I taste one; it is like no grape I have ever eaten, sweet and suave and musky and deeply perfumed. I ask Jean-Pierre about this extraordinary vine. He remembers it always being there but has no idea of its name, except that it's probably one of the muscat family. For me it is the grape of grapes.

At the close of vintage the landscape changes, the vines giving their custodians one final reward as the rippling green hillsides become an impressionist's canvas of crimson and yellow, russet and burnished copper. They'll return to life next year, as we promise Jean-Pierre and Vivette: yes, we will return for a visit. Our gift of an evergreen mimosa tree, the nearest we can find to a wattle, seals our promise, together with some passionfruit seeds sent from Australia.

We are as sad to leave as they are to say *au revoir*. Yet while we have the excitement of a new town and new friends to look forward to, for Vivette and Jean-Pierre the cycle of work continues. Next month it will be time to kill and dress the ducks, then the 200 turkeys. You'll come back for Christmas? urges Vivette. January means pruning the vines, Vivette's job being to collect the cuttings and tie them in neat bundles. There are the rabbits to look after, and the kids to be born. Next spring Vivette will be making goat cheese.

Our tasks are to collect and sort our possessions and work out how all of it will get to Compiègne. In between packing and cleaning we do the round of farewells in Nizas, in Caux, to Vivette's parents, to Professor Jouanna. Everyone is delighted that John eventually has a job. Beneath their acceptance of our

vagabond lifestyle was always an underlying disapproval. In their philosophy, it is not natural not to work.

Having sent the tea chests to Compiègne by rail, we leave Mas Laval with enough wine to keep alive memories of the Midi: one 10-litre and one 20-litre *cubitainer* of last year's wine and a small oak barrel with 30 litres of this year's vintage, for aging. These are in addition to two suitcases, two rugs, a box of books, a duffel bag of sheets and towels, another bag of clothes, the red bag of odds and ends, a box of food and an esky, a bucket and a rubbish bin. Getting everything to fit in the DS is nothing short of a miracle.

39 'The cold, dark north'

Sombre stone churches with lofty spires, dreary grey roofs of slate and thatch, gloomy villages with closed shutters: these are my first impressions of the north as we approach Compiègne. There are no vineyards. People are wrapped in raincoats. Faces in the street are pale and wan and downcast. The 'cold, dark north', Laurence Durrell calls it, in contrast to the sun-dazzled Mediterranean. It's a far cry from the warm pink stone and terracotta tiles I've become accustomed to. I am struck by its dourness, its silence, in contrast to the exuberance and boisterousness of the Midi which, in so many ways reminiscent of Australia, now feels like home.

Heading north past Avignon on the autoroute, the Rhône sparkles in the distance below. My last glimpse is a curve of the river below Châteauneuf-du-Pape that is indelibly etched in my memory as the place where Hannibal and his elephants traversed the river on their monumental voyage from Africa. When Gilbert told us the story and drew a mud map, there was no question of not seeing the site with my own eyes, and we made the pilgrimage from Caromb, traversing vineyards to reach this particular stretch of the Rhône. I ignore my suspicion that it's simply local legend. To me, this spot represents Hannibal's crossing, and this is what remains in my mind, my last view of the Midi before we cross the invisible border between Oc and Oil.

After Nizas, hardly bigger than a hamlet, and Caromb, a simple village, Compiègne comes as a shock. Boasting connections to such eminent figures as Joan of Arc and Napoleon, it's a town proud of its part in French history. It has a proper *château*, a royal *château* no less, built for the pleasure-loving Louis XV. Stretching behind it is the vast royal domain of hunting grounds, merging into the even more vast Forêt de Compiègne that, were it not for the river Oise blocking its advance, would completely encircle the town. It's a potent reminder of the absolute power of the monarchy in pre-Revolution times.

As the principal town of its *département*, Compiègne is too grand for a simple *mairie* and glories in a flamboyantly gothic *hôtel de ville* complete with clock tower and pointy turrets. Orderly, polite and well-heeled, it quietly goes about its business with the same self-assurance that it has shown for centuries. Its fortunes have been built on agriculture and trade and the river highway still carries plenty of traffic. Barges, the gentle giants of the French waterways, moor at the banks of the Oise or glide solemnly beneath the bridge with their loads of sand or coal or wheat.

It is nothing like the dusty towns and villages of the Midi. This dissimilarity is evident not only in its colours and character but also its smells. Everywhere is the pervasive smell of dampness, but in the heart of town the unmistakeable aroma of Normandy and its cheeses wafts from the *crèmeries* and the warm fragrance of just-baked *pains au chocolat* fills the afternoon air, just in time for the final school bell.

Compiègne is still France, but food here is different. Bread is lighter, *pâtisseries* creamier, more buttery, more varied. The goat cheeses of Provence give way to a vast diversity of soft, white mould cheeses made from cow's milk. Alongside the classics of camembert, brie and *coulommiers* are the more localised varieties

such as heart-shaped *neufchâtel* and square *carré de l'est*, large rounds of *chaource* and *saint-andré*. Instead of peppery *saucissons*, *charcuteries* sell soft *pâtés* and terrines and rillettes. Fish come from the Channel and the Atlantic, many of them flat. Unlike fish from the Mediterranean, I find most unrecognisable.

Compiègne's food shops also reveal subtle distinctions in its society. Sophisticated *traiteurs* sell expensive delicacies such as *pâté de foie gras truffée* and pheasant terrine, and offer to cater for receptions, large and small. There must be half a dozen or so *traiteurs* in the centre of town, all with exquisite window displays to advertise their skills, which suggests a level of refinement and wealth here, a degree of formality, that was generally absent from towns and villages encountered in the Midi. Yet there are no *caves* offering wine in bulk, no liquor store, not even Nicolas, the Dan Murphy's of France. As yet another illustration of the deep chasm between south and north: here beer is the standard drink.

In this royal town nuances of class seem to assume greater significance. I become aware of the symbolism of the *particule* – the *de* in such names as General de Gaulle, Antoine de Saint-Exupéry, Henri de Toulouse-Lautrec – that hints at high birth and the possibility of ancestral domains. Where one went to school or university, where one lives, all influence one's place in the social hierarchy, as does the way one speaks. When I talk to people here, and listen to their replies, I notice a difference in accent. And it's not because my native tongue is English. Living in Nizas and Caromb I unconsciously picked up the lilt and twang of the *accent du Midi*; here in the north, it marks me as low-born and uncultured.

My initial impressions of Compiègne might be coloured by the fact that I'm viewing the town through the lens of the university, where John will be working. Until now most of the people I've met in France, the people I've talked to, have been country

folk, farmers and vignerons, shopkeepers and housewives, all smart and knowledgeable in their own way but happy to lead a life of simple certainties: if it's February then it's the season for wild leeks. Now in Compiègne I realise that, however much I've learned about living in France so far, I am still a novice.

40 A house in the forest

Plenty of houses to rent at Compiègne, John was assured. And an accommodation officer at the university to help you.

On arrival there's only one house. It's in Saint-Jean-aux-Bois, a charming little village in the middle of the forest, full of romance and stories. The house looks as though it might once have been the stables of the hostelry, adding a patina of history. But apart from a fully equipped bathroom and a kitchen sink, it is completely empty. I'm expecting something like the furnished *gîtes* we're rented previously but there's no such accommodation here. Compiègne is not a holiday destination.

Optimistically I look through the local *Trading Post* equivalent and do the rounds of the real estate agents, one by one. At the sixth I have a strike. The accommodation person from the university has already done the same thing, and arranged for us to inspect a house at Sempigny, near Noyon. It's about 18 kilometres from the university but as soon as I see the neat little house and garden my mind is decided. It is perfect.

From the outside the house is plain and unprepossessing but it's spacious, with large rooms and high ceilings and lovely tiled floors in the kitchen and dining room. Beneath the stairs is the entrance to a proper cellar. It's surrounded by lawn and weeping willows and a bed of strawberries. Oblivious to the risks posed

by a running stream beyond the back gate, I see myself in the warm-smelling kitchen, children happily playing in the sunny back room. Like the restored stables, the house has not a stick of furniture, except for an enormous cupboard in the kitchen. Undeterred by the additional costs – 10 per cent of each month's rent to the agent, the cost of an initial inspection and inventory, reconnection fees for water and electricity – we offer to sign the contract immediately.

The owners live at Noyon, so we wait for them to come to the house to meet us. We shake hands and exchange pleasantries, and politely they ask about our furniture. We don't have any, I reply gaily. We'll buy everything, I add, probably second hand, but all we need to move in is a couple of mattresses to sleep on. Shaking hands again, we agree to return to Compiègne for the signing.

Back at Compiègne, we wait in the agent's office – but the owners mysteriously fail to appear. Instead, the agent gets a message to say that they are having second thoughts. In other words, they don't consider us the right kind of tenants. Cautious, prudent and conservative, they are looking for people with similar values to whom to entrust their house. Birds of passage with no furniture, who have had five different addresses in the past 10 months, are, in their eyes, hardly better than gypsies. How dare they, I fume. The cheek, implying that we are not good enough, not trustworthy enough, to occupy their precious house. It takes me a day to calm down.

Outside of an apartment, there is only one other possibility. John's new boss, Professor Touzot, thinks he knows a house for rent at Rimberlieu, a newish subdivision with large houses on large blocks surrounded by the forest it was carved from. It's where he lives, along with many other university academics. An exclusive *lotissement*, it has its own club for the benefit of residents, with tennis courts, restaurant and swimming pool. It is

not at all appealing and I am reluctant to inspect. Fairytales have taught me that forests are dark, menacing and ill-omened, and I imagine all sorts of dangers for the children, from poisonous mushrooms to wicked wolves.

My stubborn refusal to consider an apartment in Compiègne itself finally leaves me no choice. Are you sure it is for rent?, I ask Madame Petitpoisson, the agent, when we arrive. On the table are the remains of a meal, clothes are strewn all over the floor and in the kitchen a pile of dirty dishes is waiting to be washed. At least it has some furniture. Anyone less desperate would refuse to rent it in such condition. *Vous aurez du travail*, comments Madame Petitpoisson. Ever practical, she arranges for someone to check *le chauffage*. *Le chauffage*: it's not something I've ever had to deal with. The equivalent term, central heating, exists in my vocabulary but it's an abstract concept. Now it takes concrete form, the first of many new word–object associations I learn in the north for things outside my Australian experience.

It's a simple, basic house. Beneath ground is the garage and the boiler and tank for the *chauffage*; at ground level is a compact kitchen, bathroom, living area and a small bedroom that is destined for the children's play area. Upstairs is the loft, one large area under the eaves, where we will all sleep. Once I restore a semblance of order I survey the furniture: a large, solid dining table and eight chairs, a sideboard, a double and a single bed, a shabby sofa. Not generous, but we'll manage. I buy a small cupboard for the kitchen that gives me a little more benchtop space and second-hand single beds for the children. With the Dick Bruna friezes around the wall, their corner of the loft is almost a bedroom.

The satisfaction of being in our own place after a week in a hotel room overrides the lack of heating, the general lack of lights and the fact that only one hotplate on the stove seems to

work. But the *chauffage* man gets the system working, we buy new globes and work out which switches work which lights, our new fridge and washing machine are delivered, and I start to unpack the tea chests that were sent by train. By the time I've cleaned the kitchen and everything in it, done several loads of washing and stacked books on the new bookshelves, I'm dusting off my hands and wondering what to do next.

I don't wonder for too long. A dodgy stove with only one reliable element quickly becomes *insupportable*, as the French would say. I imagine that it will be impossible to get spare parts for a large American range in Compiègne, but replacement knobs and oven shelves are surprisingly easy to find. The resourceful local electrician checks the wiring, connects the knobs to the appropriate hotplates and fits new elements to the oven. I now have a fully functioning stove with two ovens and two warmer drawers, and once I reaccustom myself to cooking with electricity I revel in the luxury.

A house that's been abruptly abandoned has forgotten treasures. Our landlord says we can do what we like with everything that's left, including a television set that makes noises and tries, unsuccessfully, to show pictures. This is as exciting as sorting through Raymond's shed in Caromb. In the garage is a lawnmower, stiff and decrepit, and a children's swing that we hope to erect in summer. John discovers a bike beneath the stairs, pumps up the tyres and takes it for a ride. We supplement our winter wardrobe: I now have a windproof, waterproof jacket at least two sizes too large, but it's exactly what I need when I have to run to the roadside at the sound of Monsieur Boulanger, and John is proud of his new jumper that looks quite smart once I cover the worn elbows with leather patches.

The real treasure is in the cupboard upstairs: a couple of boxes of books, mainly children's books, plus a set of Michelin

maps and guides from the 1950s. I read the French books to the children in French, adding an English version in parallel for each page. I'm not sure if this helps their bilingual development; I suspect it produces instead a garbled childish franglais. But Dylan and Stephanie enjoy their new books and remember enough of the story to be able to do the narrative as they turn the pages of *Les Trois Petits Cochons* and *Blanche-Neige*. I hear their voices filtering down the stairs when they're supposed to be having an afternoon nap.

It's through this inherited library of children's books, especially the *Petit Tom* series, that my natural history education begins and my vocabulary expands. The forests of the north house a completely different and foreign menagerie of animals – squirrels and badgers, moles and hedgehogs. I learn the sounds that French animals make; ducks go *coin, coin,* cows *meuh, meuh* and roosters *cocorico*. Saying them out loud as I'm reading to the children, I realise they're much closer to the actual animal noise than the English approximations. *Petit Tom* introduces me to the life of the forest, and I discover that the slimy, repulsive, bright orange creature that I see among dead leaves on the forest floor is a *limace*, a slug, and a delicacy for Monsieur Hérisson the hedgehog.

I know I'll get used to this new environment but for the moment it's impossible to escape the feeling of isolation, of being hemmed in by the forest. The streets of Rimberlieu are as still and silent as the barren trees. The only interruptions to the day are Monsieur Poste in his yellow van and the *boulanger* from Coudun. It's a cause for rejoicing that Paris is just down the autoroute. We escape as often as possible.

44 Work – and flying

Almost immediately John starts work at the Université de Compiègne where he quickly becomes known as l'Australien. He has an office with a telephone, a luxury we've done without until now. After 10 happy-go-lucky months he settles surprisingly easily into a work routine that seems merely to require of him that he turn up most days.

Blithely putting behind him money troubles of the past, John decides that it's time to take up flying. Having discovered that Compiègne has a fully functioning aero club, he makes sure that his regular route to the university takes him past the small airstrip and the headquarters of the Aéroclub de Compiègne. He's convinced that it's the quickest way to get to work but I suspect wishful thinking. I prefer my route down the hill to the river and the sugar beet refinery where warning signs show a diagram of a car skidding, and below it the menacing word *'Betteraves'* (sugar beets).

It's fortunate for John that the vice-chancellor of the university is also president of the *aéroclub*. Claude is passionate about flying and is building a light plane in one of the university workshops. Before long he and John are best mates and lengthily discuss the finer points of *Premiers Pas vers le Pilotage*. I call it *My First Book of Flying*. Actually, taking the first steps is not

so easy since the club has only two planes and instructors are usually fully booked on Saturdays and Sundays, but John is not deterred. I'm only five minutes away at the university, he tells his instructor, an ex-UTA pilot. Here's my phone number. Give me a ring any weekday and I'll pop over immediately.

There's a small flaw in John's plan. We have only one car, and some days I need the DS. There's no village to walk to at Rimberlieu. The *charcuterie* at Villers-sur-Coudun is a kilometre away and the tiny *épicerie* at Coudun several kilometres further. The essential services – bank, post office, market, supermarket, *crèmerie* – are at Compiègne, which means a car trip. The only answer is to become a two-car family. When John spies an ad for a 1961 Citröen 2CV for only 650 francs, he is the first to inspect it. He snaps it up.

A French classic it might be, but the Deux Chevaux is an idiosyncratic little car. With its flap-out windows and canvas fold-up roof, it's as primitive as a vehicle can be. The gear mechanism, a peculiar push-pull lever that protrudes from the dashboard, has a trick to it that I never quite master. Designed to be practical and utilitarian, its nod to comfort is minimal; its reputation is for simplicity and economy. John calculates that savings in fuel consumption, compared with using the DS, should more than compensate for the initial outlay, and after a few more months will also cover registration and insurance. He is convinced it's a good buy, an absolute bargain.

The 2CV behaves beautifully until one evening when John is returning home after midnight at the end of a long computer session. Crossing the disused railway track near Bienville, the little car shudders and comes to a complete stop. All John's efforts to coax it back to life are in vain. It's December, nights are freezing and he has no option but to dash to the nearest phone box and ring Professor Touzot, who left university just minutes

earlier. Together they manage to get the car to the local garage and eventually he arrives home. According to the garage it's not a serious problem, but repairs cost half as much as the initial outlay on the car itself. A month later, when it suffers the indignity of being run into by a motorbike, John decides its days are numbered. For all its reputed feats of endurance, for all its workhorse tenacity, the 2CV is not invulnerable. Someone else can have the thrill of owning this antique.

While John is working and flying, I am trying to investigate possible work opportunities, another reason why I need the car. Our long-term visas have now been traded for *cartes de séjour*, green cards valid to 1981, and a *carte de séjour* allows me to look for paid employment. I have the addresses of two *garderies* (crèches) that look after children on a casual basis – for an hour, a morning, a day. I'm hoping I might be able to work as an English language tutor, and the helpful man at the Syndicat d'Initiative suggests I contact the *lycée technique* or the two private high schools, and even the university.

I'm not sure I really want a job but I feel a sense of obligation, that if John is working and earning then I, too, should be making an effort, contributing to the maintenance of the household and support of the family. Perhaps I have unconsciously absorbed the norms of my environment. In France, it's taken for granted that wives will have a paid job; four out of every ten married women work, and this statistic takes no account of the unpaid labour provided by wives like Vivette. Which is why the state and local governments subsidise childcare.

In Compiègne it's provided by Maison de la Famille, a casual *garderie* that looks after children for about the same as it costs me to park the car in *centre ville*. My first visit, without the children, leaves a good impression. There are plenty of toys and activities, no more than 20 children at any time, from babies to

four-year-olds, and two sympathetic carers. They'll like this one, I tell myself, tired of negotiating shops and bank and post office and cobbled streets with two children in a double stroller, especially when the temperature is near zero.

How would you like to go to Compiègne to play with other boys and girls?, I ask them sweetly. Stay here, replies Stephanie bluntly. Choosing to ignore her preferences, I go to Compiègne and park in front of Maison de la Famille. Stay here in car, pleads Stephanie. They're clearly unwilling to be left and I explain to the carer that they're not used to being looked after. Back soon, I say, then turn and run. I hear them both screaming at the tops of their lungs. When I return, less than an hour later, Stephanie has calmed down and is lying on the floor. Dylan is still crying. It takes a few more weeks for them to accept that I'm not abandoning them like the wicked stepmother in Hansel and Gretel, and gradually they are happy to stay for longer periods. *Stéphanie est impeccable*, says one of the carers. *Elle parle très bien français.* Is she equally proficient in English?

The work scenario is less easily realised. The *lycée technique* and the other two *lycées* are both fully staffed and cannot use my services. The English professor at the university is vaguely interested in my offer of help but certainly not before the new year. John comes up with the idea of enrolling for a *doctorat de troisième cycle*, the equivalent of a masters degree, in *génie biologique*, biological engineering. At least you'd get a student allowance, he adds. It hardly fits with my career plans but I'm willing to go along with his suggestion – until I discover that the research project involves testing toxic substances on white mice. My idea of paid employment is starting to recede.

I make one last bid, asking if the local paper if there are any possibilities for freelancers, although I have no idea what I might freelance about and even less about journalistic practices

in France. The answer is ambivalent, but I'm pretty sure it's a polite way of saying no.

At least I can keep myself occupied with regular articles for *Australian Gourmet* and *Epicurean*. And there is so much around me to inspire more articles for other Australian newspapers and magazines. Having worked as a writer at *Choice* magazine, I'm interested in consumer movements in France; the French equivalent, *Que Choisir?*, began publication one year later than *Choice*, in 1961. I want to investigate how the provision of child-care facilities, like the municipal *garderies* at Compiègne, benefit the lives of working mothers. I'd also love to write a story on the lives of the people in the barges I see chugging up and down the Oise.

I almost have to hide my relief when the English professor finally tells me, ever so regretfully, that he can't offer me any work as an English tutor.

 42 Potatoes

I prefer to think it's not my blind prejudice, but the clear skies of Paris contrast strikingly with the gloom of Rimberlieu. Most mornings we wake to fog or frost. Days are overcast, grey and damp, and if the sun appears at all it might only be for an hour or two in the early afternoon. By the time its faint rays reach the earth, all their warmth has already evaporated. Remembering what my mother said about fresh air and linen I persist with old habits, pegging sheets on the makeshift line I've rigged between the trees. A couple of hours later, I find them frozen stiff.

Winter in northern France is depressing and hibernation seems the only sensible option. In December and January darkness falls before five in the afternoon. On many days headlights are necessary in early afternoon as mist and cloud invade the streets. Maximum temperatures hover around one degree. A winter snowstorm covers the roads and at Rimberlieu it is almost impossible to know where the sealed road finishes and the muddy verges begin. Visiting Péronne and Amiens, to the north of Compiègne, I see lumps of ice floating in the Somme canal and a shallow pond is frozen solid. This is not my kind of climate. I do not understand it.

I do understand, nonetheless, that central heating is an absolute necessity. And I quickly realise that it's not cheap. Our

chauffage is thirsty, and a full tank of fuel lasts only a month. John gets an advance on his salary but by the time we have paid three months rent in advance plus 10 per cent of the annual rent to the agent, then paid for the electrical appliances, the first tank of heating fuel, the electricity bill, another tank of fuel, the second-hand beds for the children, the 2CV and its expenses, and the necessary car service for the DS, we are penniless. And then there are John's flying lessons, another fuel bill in January, and the car insurance due for renewal. Once again we draw on the Sydney account.

It's back to our standard solution to the problem of over-stretched resources: no red meat. Economising on butter and cheese is unthinkable, and a boiling hen and *charcuterie* products are still affordable. Nearby Villers-sur-Coudun has an honest, homely *charcuterie* with all the standard products of the *charcutier*'s craft, and I know I can achieve wonders with a few slices of *petit salé* or *poitrine fumée*.

One of John's new mates at the *aéroclub* tells him about a local farm that sells rich, creamy milk, fresh rabbits and other farm produce. It's on our route home so we call in and talk to the farmer. When he offers 50 kilograms of potatoes for five francs, the equivalent of 10 centimes a kilogram, it's a deal I can't refuse. This winter there's a glut of potatoes, farmers having responded to the high prices of the previous season when potatoes were in short supply, and increased their plantings. Our bargain potatoes are in fact sold as animal food, but the farmer's family eats them, as does John's friend. They're seconds, with some imperfections, but after sorting them and rejecting any that are split or bruised, we still have about 40 kilograms of potatoes. Even by my most enthusiastic calculations, they will last until spring.

The potatoes offer a challenge, and I'm determined to show-case them to best advantage as the centrepiece of our meals. At

least four evenings a week our dinner is potatoes in one form or another, and I discover how versatile they can be. Elizabeth David and Madame Mathiot, together with a feature in *Elle* magazine, '*Leçons de pomme de terre*', give me some inspiration but mostly I improvise.

Pommes de terre au lard
Sauté potatoes with smoked speck

Though new to me, this is a standard way of cooking potatoes in France, my inspiration coming from a feature in *Elle* magazine, '*Leçons de pommes de terre*'. The recipe specifies the yellow-fleshed Belle de Fontenay variety but failing these, try Kipfler, Nicola or, as a fallback, Desiree.

Serves 6–8

1 kg potatoes
200 g smoked speck
2 tablespoons lard (or oil, or butter)
salt and freshly ground pepper

Peel potatoes, cut into small cubes, wash in hot water and dry in a clean tea-towel.

Having removed rind from speck, cut it into small pieces about 1 cm wide. Blanch in boiling water for 1 minute, drain.

Heat lard in a large frying pan, add potatoes and speck and cook over low-moderate heat, stirring and tossing from time to time, for about 35 minutes until potatoes are golden brown. Season to taste.

Gratin dauphinois
Potato gratin

Epicurean, 'Listener's Choice', August/September 1979

Adding grated cheese is not traditional but when your gratin represents both meat and potatoes for your dinner, then surely a little liberty is allowed.

Serves 4 as a main or 8 as an accompaniment

750 g firm, waxy potatoes
salt and freshly ground white pepper
1 clove garlic
45 g butter
2 to 3 tablespoons grated comté cheese (optional, see page 217)
about 2 cups milk
½ cup cream

Preheat oven to 180°C (160°C fan-forced).

Peel potatoes and slice thinly, pat dry with paper towels. Season lightly with salt and pepper, toss to mix. Rub a shallow fireproof gratin dish with cut clove garlic, butter liberally. Arrange potato in layers in dish. Add milk to almost level with top. Bring slowly to boil on top of stove, pour over cream and dot with remaining butter. Transfer to moderate oven and cook for 30 to 40 minutes until potatoes are tender and surface is golden.

If necessary, gratin may be left in warm oven for 15 to 20 minutes or longer, covered loosely, before serving. Dot surface with a little more butter to prevent drying out.

Over the next weeks and months we eat *gratin dauphinois*, grating some of my favourite *comté* and adding it between the layers of potatoes; potatoes sautéed with *poitriné fumée*; potatoes sautéed with *poitriné fumée* and chestnuts; Spanish omelettes with cubes of potato; galettes made with grated potatoes; potatoes baked in their jackets and filled with grated *comté*; *gratin au jambon*, with small chunks of ham between the layers of potato; potato and spinach gratin.

And of course potato goes into the basic vegetable soup that warms us on cold winter days. I can almost make it with my eyes shut, though it's always slightly different, depending on the proportions of each ingredient: diced leek, carrots, celery, turnip, potato, all softened in butter and cooked in chicken stock, then puréed in the *mouli*, enriched with *crème fraîche* and sprinkled with parsley. Compiègne is cream country, where *crème fraîche* comes in half-litre tubs. It swirls so beautifully into thick vegetable soups that it is now one of my favourite ingredients.

I store the sack of potatoes in the wheelbarrow in the basement garage. By the end of April only a few kilograms are left in the bag and they're starting to sprout. Reaching into the sack in the dark – we keep forgetting to replace the blown light globe – is like plunging my hand into a nest of spiders, sending shivers up my arm. I call it a day. We have had more than our money's worth from our five-franc bargain. It is time to return the remainder to the environment.

43 Christmas

Christmas in France means foie gras rather than fresh prawns. And oysters and champagne and truffles and game: all the gastronomic luxuries that, by sheer coincidence, happen to be in season and at their best in the middle of winter. Outside one of the Compiègne *charcuteries* I see a *sanglier*, a wild pig from the forest, all black and hairy, hanging in the chill air, a fine rivulet of blood from his mouth congealing across the footpath. The Marché Saint-Germain has little *marcassins*, baby wild pigs, almost like cuddly puppies in their caramel-and-cream striped coats. *Pâtés* of hare and pheasant and wild boar take pride of place in window displays, along with another Christmas speciality, *boudin blanc aux truffes*, truffled white pudding. I suspect my supermarket *boudins blancs* from Carrefour are probably less than authentic but the specks of black persuade me that I'm eating something special.

The mangoes of my Christmasses past would never resonate with the French. Instead, the seasonal treat here is chestnuts. Roasted chestnuts epitomise the winter aroma of Paris as much as the sugar-laden air around fairy floss sellers represents spring. Coming up from the metro or turning a street corner you find the chestnut man, capped and coated and scarfed, behind a three-legged brazier of glowing coals, a sack of chestnuts at his side.

The scent alone is enough to warm you. From December through to February, French markets sell chestnuts in their shell, the best quality coming from the Ardèche region west of the Rhône. Spanish and Italian imports are cheaper but typically smaller and, as I discover, more likely to disintegrate in cooking.

Chestnuts are a revelation. I have never eaten them and at first I'm ambivalent, wondering what all the fuss is about. But they gradually win me over, and I learn how to score and boil and peel them, making sure I remove every trace of the hairy, bitter, interior skin while burning my fingers at the same time. 'It is all a question of how much heat your hands can stand', warns Elizabeth David, 'and it is well known that women are better at this than men'.

Patience and dexterity eventually bring their rewards, in this instance soft-textured, crumbly and slightly sweet chestnuts that happily consort with either sweet or salty partners. Ginette Mathiot gives a recipe for braised chestnuts, to be eaten on their own or combined with braised onions or, even better, brussels sprouts. My favourite combination is braised chestnuts tossed with tiny crisp strips of *poitrine fumée*, with or without a few potatoes from the wheelbarrow, the floury sweetness of the chestnuts a perfect foil for the smoky, salty, fatty pork.

It is as *marrons glacés* that chestnuts reach the pinnacle of perfection. A triumph of French *confiserie*, they are *bonbons de luxe* and one of the indulgences of Christmas – an expensive indulgence, since so many of the steps in the long and complicated candying process are done by hand. *Marrons glacés* are not part of my Christmas tradition so my introduction has to wait until the riot of post-Christmas sales, when all perishable luxuries are marked down and become affordable. Many *confiseries* sell them loose, and this is where I find *marrons glacés brisés*, imperfect or broken *marrons glacés* that are offered at bargain prices. From first

taste I am seduced. Though almost indecently calorific, they are irresistible. For a few weeks, *marrons glacés brisés* are the first and most important item on my weekly shopping list. Discovering a supply, by chance, brings the same sense of triumph and elation that I felt as a child when the bag of broken biscuits from the bottom of the grocer's tins contained mostly pieces of scotch finger.

The children have not yet grasped the concept of Christmas, though they visit the *arbre de Noël* erected in front of the *hôtel de ville* and see *sapins de Noël*, Christmas fir trees, for sale outside shops in the town. Maison de la Famille puts on a special *goûter de Noël* with lots of chocolate. Stephanie becomes entranced by the *bûche de Noël* on the cover of my *La Table et Ma Cuisine* magazine, and I decide this will be our Christmas treat, a sponge roll filled and covered with chocolate cream. As the recipe instructs, I enhance its likeness to a log by making rough lines with a fork in the chocolate cream coating and adding offcuts to resemble sawn-off branches. Less interested in eating than in embellishing it, Stephanie is allowed to decorate the cake with the collection of miniature plastic dwarfs inherited with the house, sticking them on and around the cake and beneath the cocoa-dusted meringue mushrooms, exactly as the children pictured on the magazine cover have done.

But the customary traditions of Christmas are outside their experience – fortunately, since our budget makes no provision for presents. They won't miss presents, we tell one another; we'll buy them toys when we can afford it. But in honour of the occasion we buy a large sheet of plyboard and a can of green paint labelled '*Pour les tableaux verts*' to make the children a big blackboard for their playroom wall.

We haven't counted on the benevolence of the university, which gives us, and all other parents on the staff, a gift voucher:

120 francs to spend at a toy shop in Compiègne. This sum translates into a wigwam-style tent for their playroom, a toy telephone set with batteries that actually works, a plastic biplane for Dylan and a lotto-style game with the same animals that feature in their library of French books. Another unexpected bonus is money from my parents, which we spend on two small Christofle silver forks and six new books for the children. Our present to each other is membership of Les Amis du Louvre, entitling us to free entry to the Louvre and half-price admission to many other museums as well as a subscription to the glossy magazine, *Revue des Amis du Louvre*.

Christmas dinner is turkey rather than duck. A small one is not too expensive and it reminds us of Jean-Pierre and Vivette. I roast it, serving it with brussels sprouts and yet another variation on potatoes, one of Ginette Mathiot's recipes in *La Cuisine pour Tous*. Christmas dinner merits a little extra care, and *pommes de terre farcies*, parboiled potatoes hollowed out, filled with a onion-mushroom-parsley stuffing and baked, could have been invented for the occasion. We uncork our special Châteauneuf-du-Pape wine and plan visits to Paris. With the new Amis du Louvre cards, Paris is all ours.

44 Parisian weekends

If Compiègne represents the Monday-to-Friday working world, weekends are synonymous with Paris, especially once flying lessons are scheduled for weekdays. The autoroute is a magic carpet that whisks us from dark forest to sparkling city in what feels like an instant.

We escape to Paris on our first weekend in Compiègne. On a Sunday morning the city is vibrant and alive, the air redolent of leisurely lunches not yet on the table. There's a joyful bustle in the streets. This is the Paris I remember. I want to stand in the middle of the square, raise my arms above my head and breathe in its very essence. People move around me, nonchalant, not looking up, interested only on reaching their destinations. Do they take their city for granted? Are they oblivious to its beauty and its stories, its massive medieval walls and Art Nouveau metro entrances? Do they ever stop to imagine the lives behind attic windows high on arched roofs? Never, I vow, will I be so ungrateful. Paris might now be close enough to be part of my own everyday but I will never lose my sense of awe and admiration of this magical city.

I create my personal Paris, a collage of the sites and sights that resonate with me. The Place Vendôme where I window-shop for a necklace from Van Cleef & Arpels, a watch from Jaeger le Coultre.

The Pont du Change, which leads toward the Conciergerie and reminds me of poor Marie-Antoinette imprisoned in her dark dungeon. Cézanne's bold bathers and Manet's audacious nudity in the impressionist collection of the Jeu de Paume museum. Monet's *nymphéas* in the Orangerie next door, a kaleidoscope of turquoise and mauve and deep, dark green that is almost hallucinatory. Most of all, this personal Paris includes Maillol's sensual and seductive sculptures in the Jardin du Carousel – Pomone, la Méditerranée, Vénus – these sturdy and yet sublimely graceful Mediterranean women who remind me of *la gitane* at Nizas, so admired by Madame Molla.

With Paris within our grasp, and the offer of a house just outside the *périphérique* while the family is away after Christmas, we take our fill of its museums and galleries. Tourists are few in winter and we can wander at will, admiring Greek antiquities in the Louvre, Rodin's garden of sculptures, delicate porcelain teacups in the Musée des Arts Decoratifs, and Picasso and Matisse in the new Musée d'Art Moderne in the Centre Pompidou. Barely a year old, the Centre Pompidou is an incongruous assembly of glass and multicoloured pipes and raw scaffolding, or what appears to be scaffolding, and it's hard to reconcile it with the graceful elegance of its surrounds. Parisians are still divided on its merit. If not beautiful, in the classic sense, it is certainly arresting, challenging preconceptions of both architecture and museums. Here everyone is welcome, even the youngest, since Pompidou includes a *bibliothèque des enfants*, strictly for children only.

'I don't want to *aller au musée*.' After several visits to the Louvre, Stephanie openly rebels. She might not understand the individual words, but she knows what '*aller au musée*' involves. It can't be much fun watching a passing parade of knees and legs, especially when constrained in a stroller. Dylan would much rather be watching the *bateaux-mouches* taking tourists up and

down the Seine, and the hard-working *péniches* with their loads of sand or timber. To placate them we add animals to the list of sights. Sometimes it's the zoo at Vincennes with its sleepy panda but more often, because it's closer and free, we go to the children's zoo at the Jardin d'Acclimatation in the Bois de Boulogne. Now it's my turn to sit back as the children run after the poultry – hens and ducks and pheasants and swans – and pat the farm animals – cows and sheep and pigs, rabbits and donkeys. Stephanie decides she wants *un petit lapin* for a pet while Dylan prefers a squirrel. We see plenty of these, scurrying up trees, as well as a hibernating badger and a hedgehog, some rugged bison and a real-life wild boar. I learn that the French word for shaving brush is *un blaireau*, the same word as badger, because the brushes were originally made out of badger hair – and the best, the most expensive ones, still are.

Paris also has bookshops, including specialist English bookshops, and these become another focus of our visits. While John falls over the flying magazines, I head for the children's books at Librairie Galignani, which calls itself 'the first English bookshop in Paris' and dates back to the beginning of the 19th century. I could lose myself here and would buy them all if I could, but restrain myself to just two per visit. Between their sessions at Maison de la Famille and the books I read to them, Dylan and Stephanie are well on the way to being fluent in French.

Sometimes we stroll randomly, by now well aware of what to wear in a Parisian winter: hats, coats, gloves and sturdy shoes with thick soles. Around Saint-Germain, memories from a summer of study resurface as for Proust at the taste of the madeleine: the *crèmerie* where I used to pause and marvel at the sheer variety of cheeses; the venerable dome of the Institut de France guarding the nation's intellectual reputation; the aroma of chocolates from Debauve & Gallais, isolated in its 19th-century splendour; the

austere simplicity of the church of Saint-Germain-des-Prés; the historic Pâtisserie Viennoise that I frequented while studying and the nearby Sorbonne.

It might be the arty, bohemian *quartier*, but it is also well-heeled, and the Saint-Germain market has foods that never reach Compiègne. I am amazed at the variety of wild mushrooms – frilly orange *girolles*, sombre *pleurotes* and black *trompettes*. From China come winter persimmons and fresh lychees. Some stalls resemble a hunter's pantry, stocked with furry hares and feathered pheasant, partridges, quail and woodcock. *Charcuteries* display trays of wild boar cutlets with dark red meat, legs of wild boar for roasting and delicate lard-wrapped fillets of deer. These are luxuries that, for now, I can only dream of.

Vous êtes rive gauche ou rive droite?, ask Parisians. The river divides personalities as effectively as it divides the city. I am most definitely *rive gauche*, left bank. This is where my heart is, where I feel most at home. If ever I could afford to live in Paris, this is where I would choose to be.

It's probably no coincidence that friends in Paris are also *rive gauche*. Claudie, a colleague of John's at the university studying for her doctorate, shows us another aspect of the city by inviting us to an exhibition of *artisanat* – pottery, weaving, silkscreen printing, jewellery – near Pont Neuf. Dominique, who gave us so much help in Strasbourg and now works in Paris, invites us to lunch at Le Commerce, a Parisian institution that has been operating for over 50 years. I am expecting a small, family-run dining room but this is completely beyond my concept of a restaurant: three levels of dining beneath an arched skylight, tables to seat nearly 1000 people, energetic waiters in the classic uniform of long white apron, black waistcoat over white shirt, and acrobatic serving staff juggling a dozen dishes at a time. If I shut my eyes I can almost imagine myself back in the 19th century.

Its vast and inexpensive menu lists all the simple, timeless dishes of a typical working class Parisian bistro, from *céleri remoulade* and *betterave en salade* to *coq au vin* and *tête de veau vinaigrette*. While it would never draw the attention of a Michelin inspector, the food is unpretentious and honest, the service speedily efficient and the presence of two young children at lunch is accepted as normal. For Stephanie the real treat is icecream. Ever since seeing a picture of one in a book, she has been wanting *une glace*.

The Voillaumes from Claret also live on the *rive gauche*. I bring them up to date with our news and they invite us to drop in for *apéritifs* one evening. The following week we have dinner with them. All the family we knew at Claret join us around the table, and we hear what has happened in the village since we left. Parisians have a reputation for stand-offishness, for not welcoming strangers. The Voillaumes couldn't be further from this stereotype. Easy-going, unpretentious – the coffee is instant, but the *digestifs*, *framboise* and *mirabelle*, are superb – they want to know all about our experiences, our triumphs and our frustrations.

It's hard to believe that we have now lived in France for a year! Twelve months ago we were strangers, unsure of the city, ignorant of our future, timidly searching an opening that would lead to a new world of possibilities. Today we can stride confidently through the city, bolstered by the security of a job and a home and a network of friends and colleagues. Never in my wildest dreams could I have imagined such a fairytale ending.

45 Geese

January and February are the coldest months, dark and dismal. Snow falls on several occasions. At Rimberlieu it gets up to the bottom of the door shutters and stays on the ground for a week. Snow is a novelty, but it quickly wears out its welcome. On the news there is talk of the birds who will die because of the snow and people are encouraged to feed them. We scatter breadcrumbs, a habit Stephanie continues even when the snow has gone.

Though I dream of a return to Montpellier before the next winter, I am reluctantly coming to terms with the northern weather. I now wear a knitted hat outside the house, and wrap a thick woollen scarf around my neck. I tape over the keyholes of the French doors to stop the drafts and close the shutters each evening, sometimes as early as four o'clock. Why would anyone choose to live here?, I ask myself. Jobs, education opportunities? No wonder the Midi is the choice of residence for retirees, heading for more benign climates as soon as their working life is over.

I'm also trying to come to terms with our immediate environment, including the Forêt de Compiègne, which is large enough to have a Michelin map all to itself. It's far too cold to go for walks in the forest but we can drive through it. They're alien to me, these dark trees and shrubs and creepers, but the cheery

sight of red-berried holly and deep green ivy is vividly familiar from Christmas cards. Yet my primitive fears of the forest persist. It's a constant looming presence on my horizon, and I begin to understand its metaphoric power in folk tales and fairy stories, the edge of the forest a liminal space between light and darkness, clarity and obscurity, safety and danger. Visiting the Clairière de l'Armistice – a clearing in the middle of the forest where the armistice ending the First World War was signed – I realise the symbolism of the site, the light of peace overcoming the darkness of war. In this part of France it is difficult to escape the latent presence of war. Solemn white-crossed war cemeteries are all too frequent and war-shattered buildings, like the abbey at Ourscamp, near Noyon, still stand in ruins.

Nearer to home, we explore the Compiègne countryside, flat and bare, the roads lined with muddy piles of sugar beets waiting to go to the refinery. Green paddocks dotted with enormous black-and-white Hollandais cows alternate with bare brown fields covered with mounds of humus to be returned to the soil. In the distance the regularity of this pattern is interrupted by a splash of white. As we get nearer I see geese, hundreds or even thousands of them, being herded from one paddock to another like a mob of merinos. Some run, some walk, some stretch their wings as though to fly. And beyond them are even more geese paddling in a pond and wandering among the dry stalks of summer maize. This must be worth a story, I tell myself. As the crow flies, the farm is just over the hill from our house, near enough for me to hear the honking if I open the windows in early morning. I plan a visit.

It turns out that this is the biggest goose-raising enterprise in France. When I call on the farm and introduce myself, Monsieur and Madame tell me they have nearly 7000 birds. *Pas pour la foie*, Madame reassures me. These are not the grey-brown Toulouse

variety of geese destined to produce foie gras, but instead a bird for the Sunday roast, their plumage almost pure white. Voracious eaters, they are ready for table only 14 weeks after hatching. Madame sells them, plucked and dressed and weighing four to five kilograms, for 18 francs a kilogram, which compares quite favourably with chicken, priced anywhere between 8 francs (industrial chicken) and 21 francs (for a top-range *poulet de Bresse*) per kilogram. Standard free-range birds, like Jean-Pierre's, here cost around 15 francs per kilo.

In his working clothes, Monsieur is a rough and ready farmer, though clearly a very prosperous one. Looking around, I realise that this is a very large farm, bigger perhaps than the whole village of Nizas, and in addition to geese they have several hundred Charolais cattle and racehorses. Invited into his office for an *apéritif* I'm slightly uncomfortable, just the two of us, but a goose farm is so far outside my experience that I need to ask questions. Monsieur points to a photo of a horse on the wall. Top prizewinner in France this year, he tells me. I approach closer to the photo and read the name: Demester. *Oui, Daniel Demester*, he confirms. At last I know his name.

He has no problem with me taking photos, though not today. It's been snowing, and the birds are all but invisible. A couple of weeks later a reasonable day arrives, and this time I take Dylan and Stephanie with me. While I try to capture the most photogenic of the birds the children happily sit in the car looking at all the farm animals, chickens and geese and a young foal with its mother. When I return to the car Stephanie asks for a baby horse. What would you do with it? She pauses, perhaps searching for the right response. Eat it, she says.

It's not the answer I'm expecting. There's no *boucherie chevaline* specialising in horsemeat in Compiègne and I'm pretty sure she hasn't noticed the horse imagery decorating the Paris ones. Then

I remember the animals she's grown up with in France, the hens and ducks and rabbits at Mas Laval, Madame Nicolaud's rabbits, all of which ended up in someone's pot. It must seem logical that animals are destined to be eaten. Horses aren't for eating, I gently explain, we don't eat horses. Unfazed, she changes her mind. Look at it, she decides.

I order a goose from Madame and return to collect it a few days later. It seems large, but it's all skeleton and empty space inside; the quantity of meat is surprisingly little for a four-kilogram bird. Even though it is young it has managed to accumulate a good layer of fat. Roasted in accordance with Madame's advice, it yields just enough for four adults and another dish based on leftovers. I can't help feeling disappointed. The goose is tender enough, with a flavour reminiscent of duck or young lamb, but it's nowhere near as memorable on the plate as it was among its friends in the paddock.

My story gets written, but it's not really right for *Australian Gourmet*, nor for *Epicurean*, and in any case I've already written pieces for the next two issues. If it were in French and more reporter-like, perhaps I'd have a chance with the local newspaper, but that would involve another interview with Monsieur Demester. It becomes all too difficult, and the article is filed away with other drafts and ideas.

46 Television and politics

When we've had enough of twiddling the knobs and getting nothing but static, we decide to call in the television repairman. Whatever he does, it's an easy fix, and for only 130 francs we get a working television set. It is actually the first television we have had in all our married life and such a novelty I'm perfectly content with black-and-white images, though France has had colour television for the past 10 years. There are only three channels, all government-owned, and to my astonishment they all show advertisements. It takes little time to settle on the ABC-like Antenne 2 as our favourite.

The children are still too young to understand television. In any case most of the dedicated children's programs are aimed at older children. Occasionally a show about animals will interest them, but not for too long. We take to it with avidity. For us, it's another means of understanding France and the French, especially their politics. I'm also a devotee of Michel Guérard's cooking show, despite its inconvenient timing around lunchtime on Saturdays. He's a generous teacher, patiently explaining his little tricks and *tours de main*, always with a twinkle in his eye. Having watched him prepare a dish of boned chicken winglets with white wine and cucumbers, and fascinated by the way they puff up into plump and succulent little cushions, I immediately

write to the television station for the recipe. *Ailerons de volaille au Meursault et aux concombres* is on our table the following week.

The nightly news, 8.00 pm on Antenne 2, is not the bland, one-directional experience I'm used to, where a calm, smiling face in suit and tie dispassionately recites the day's events. Here the presenters are not simply newsreaders but rather interrogative journalists who also debate with their guests. I enjoy the combative style of the top Antenne 2 presenters, Jean-Pierre Elkabbach and Patrick Poivre d'Arvor, who take command of the interview and dismiss glib deflections, all with a steely charm that disguises the savagery of their questioning.

Especially with the general election looming, news and current affairs programs grab our attention. A month in Spain, followed by the long days of vintage and the business of moving and settling, briefly distracted us from the political scene but here, so much closer to the seat of power, it is impossible not to be engrossed by the daily goings-on. After *la rentrée* in September, which signals the start of the school year, the revival of the cultural calendar and the return of parliament, workers resume their strike actions. We are almost near enough to Paris to feel the pain of Parisians when *boulangers* go on strike, protesting against the refusal of their request for a price rise. There's terror and panic in the streets and Paris goes without bread for two whole days. Driving school instructors stage Operation Escargot on one of the autoroutes leading into Paris, slowing traffic for the right to charge higher fees. Railway workers lead a four-day go-slow campaign. EDF goes on strike, which means we have no electricity and no heating from seven in the morning until four in the afternoon, apart for the two hours around midday. From time to time in the succeeding months there are lightning strikes, without notice. The workers are certainly making their presence felt.

Watching the news and listening to morning commentaries

on the radio, I am fascinated by the shifts and slides in popularity, the gibes and counter-gibes as both left and right gear up for the elections. It's the mythical aspects of the contest that appeal to me, the brash outsider pitted against the establishment. The right has held power for so long it has developed a self-justified sense of entitlement, vigorously challenged by the left, whose passion has been fuelled by victories in the previous year's municipal elections.

Equally intriguing are the internal politics of both sides as they try to present an impression of unity. The right is an amalgam of five conservative groups who try to keep their infighting in-house, though there's no doubting the ill-feeling between the conservative RPR party of Jacques Chirac and the more moderate UDF, representing the ideas and policies of President Giscard d'Estaing. Giscard's manifesto, *Démocratie Française*, has been strategically reissued as a five-franc paperback, and I decide I can afford five francs to discover his philosophy and aspirations for *la France*.

He might be on the conservative side but Giscard nonetheless seems to have some sound ideas. French society, he writes, should be organised for the good of the people as its goal and with the people themselves as the starting point. The France he envisages will be more egalitarian, offer more individual liberties and, at the same time, be more competitive. It will require political and social reforms that cannot be achieved by either the communist or socialist models. This New France, Giscard seems to suggest, can be a beacon of light for the whole world. I can't be sure I grasp all the complexities of his vision, and my understanding might be less than perfect, but I sympathise with his principles and his ideals. The reasonableness of his rhetoric is persuasive. Chirac, in contrast, is all bombast and braggadocio and naked ambition.

After my attendance at the party meeting in Claret I have continued to follow the progress of the left, the Parti Socialiste under the charismatic François Mitterand and the Parti Communiste led by rabblerouser Georges Marchais. Tall, imperious and a powerful orator, Mitterand reminds me of Gough Whitlam; Marchais, in contrast, is a swaggerer, a tub-thumper. There's no doubting the fire in his belly, and in his eyes, but it's a wild, dangerous fire. In recent months cracks have been appearing in their uneasy alliance. Most disagreements concern nationalisation, the idealist communists favouring state ownership, the more pragmatic socialists lukewarm to the idea.

This is the background to the long-awaited elections. They have all the elements of a Greek tragedy, or perhaps an update of *Julius Caesar*. And in March the climax of all the debates, all the polling and politicking of the past 12 months, finally arrives. As the results come in I am glued to the television, buoyed with excitement and cheering for the underdog. Voting is voluntary but the turnout is an exceptional 84%, and the left is a clear winner with 50% of the votes, the right 46%. But this is only the first round. The French voting system always involves two rounds, the first as a kind of popularity contest to rank the candidates, the second pitting the candidate who received the greatest number of votes against the runner up, unless one candidate gains an absolute majority in the first round. So the first round, which might include candidates from all of the right-leaning and left-leaning parties, is effectively a culling of the least popular, and its results don't necessarily indicate voting patterns in the second round.

Not that this matters to tonight's political commentators, especially the exuberant left sympathisers who are jumping up and down, talking over everyone else and waving wildly while Jean-Pierre Elkabbach and Patrick Poivre d'Arvor try vainly to

maintain decorum. After 20 years, the left at last see government within their grasp and internal feuds are, if not forgotten, at least swept under the carpet. We have a sense of déjà vu, the euphoria oddly reminiscent of the 1972 Australian election when Whitlam came to power.

A week later voters are in a more sober mood. The second round bursts the balloon of optimism as the right is returned. The socialists improve their share of the vote and, for the first time since 1936, secure a higher percentage than the communists, but this is bitter consolation. Perhaps they still need to temper idealism with practicality – which includes remembering to chill the champagne.

47 'Yes, we live in Europe'

Here at Rimberlieu we are nearly in Belgium; the border is only an hour or so to the north. This part of France, Picardy, shares much with its northern neighbour, including a beer-drinking tradition. *Epiceries* sell beer in litre bottles, and it's a litre of beer that workmen drink with their midday meal, not wine. In Australia I'd never associated brussels sprouts with the Belgian capital but at Compiègne's wintry market they are plentiful and cheap, a seasonal staple. Strangely, I don't remember ever seeing them in Pézenas. Pearly white witlof, which the French call *endive*, is also of Belgian origin. It's new to me, but the crunchy, yellow-tipped leaves with an intriguing contrast of sweetness and bitterness become the basis of our winter salads.

Despite its proximity, we might never have visited Belgium were it not for an invitation from Chris, John's old IBM colleague. Chris is moving back to Sydney to open an office for another computer firm but before he leaves he invites John to the opening of their Brussels office at the beginning of March. It's so close we can hardly refuse, especially when it promises the novelty of a different country.

The Hay plain is flat, but Belgium is flatter. It is also considerably more populated. Every square metre of land is settled or cultivated. There are no woods or forests, no wildernesses, no

secluded picnic spots beneath the trees off a dusty lane. It is often more reminiscent of England than of France, especially in the north, the Flemish-speaking part of the country where English is almost an alternative language. In Ghent and Bruges, as in England, people ride bicycles everywhere, and ads for Watney's and Double Diamond Pale Ale are plastered on walls. With their white and brown loaves, square or high top, their currant buns and raisin loaves, bakeries in Bruges could almost be mistaken for their English cousins.

I expected Belgium to be more like an extension of France, more like this northern region of Picardy where we live. And it is – but only in the French-speaking part and in bilingual Brussels. Brussels is an elegant, sophisticated city and we arrive early enough to wander around its Grand-Place and to make the pilgrimage to the popular statue of the boy playfully weeing into the pond, the Mannekin-Pis. After John returns from the reception we leave the hotel and find a nearby bar for a glass of wine. All around I hear familiar French sounds, the rhythm of a language that carries a sense of home. In Brussels I have little awareness of being in a foreign country.

Once again, I'm reminded how culture is related to language, how linguistic boundaries are also cultural boundaries and how intrinsic to culture is food. The north and the south of France could be separate nations, each lacking in understanding of the other. Jean-Pierre won't eat eggs cooked in butter, and the neighbours of Australian friends, diehard Parisians who have never ventured as far south as Provence, look suspiciously at the *anchoïade* croutons I offer them when they're invited for drinks one afternoon. It's unimaginable to me that they have never heard of this savoury paste of anchovies, garlic and olive oil. Only later do I realise that they might be wary of a food they don't recognise, especially when it's murky grey in colour and

distinctly oily, even more especially when it's been made by foreigners. *Goûtez l'anchoïade*, I encourage them. Timidly, so as not to appear impolite, they take a bite. Only when I reassure them that it's patriotically French, a speciality of Provence, do they start to enjoy it. It's ironic that it should be an Australian who introduces them to *anchoïade*.

Anchoïade
Anchovy spread

Once I discover *anchoïade* in the pages of *La Cuisine Provençale*, I make this lovely salty, garlicky spread quite often and soon can dispense with the recipe. Anchovies are a pivotal ingredient in Provençal cuisine. At Caromb we would buy whole anchovies in bulk at Leclerc, then fillet them and store them in grapeseed oil.

6 to 7 anchovies (12 to 14 fillets)
3 tablespoons olive oil
2 cloves garlic
red wine vinegar
freshly ground pepper
thick slices of bread, to serve

If using whole anchovies, soak in cold water for a few minutes to release some salt, then separate each into two boneless fillets.

Crush anchovy fillets with olive oil and garlic to make a relatively smooth paste. Season with a splash of vinegar and a little pepper to taste.

Spread on thick slices of bread, pressing down to ensure the mixture penetrates. Lightly brown under oven grill. Serve hot.

At our Brussels hotel the next morning, arriving late for breakfast, we are obliged to share a table with another guest. He introduces himself: English, and a regular visitor to Brussels for business. I chat briefly with him while trying to interest the children in eating. Polite and affable, he tries to engage Stephanie, an outwardly charming little girl, in conversation. She is silent, stony-faced, refusing to open her mouth. Perhaps she's shy, frightened of strangers?, he suggests. I suspect she's just being contrary but I can hardly admit this. No, I reply, she's not used to talking to people who speak English.

You live in Europe, then?, he asks.

He says this in such a matter-of-fact way that momentarily I am shocked. We have lived at so many different addresses, like butterflies darting from plant to plant, but I had never considered the larger perspective.

Yes, we live in Europe.

It gives me a strange thrill to hear myself say this. The words roll so easily off my lips that it takes a few seconds to grasp their import. No longer floating, we are anchored, however temporarily. For now, Europe is my point of reference, though my nationality has not changed, nor my allegiance. It's as though I've stepped out of an Australian frame and found a new place in a French one. Living in France, in Europe, brings with it a deeper understanding of civilisations and cultures, introduces me to new ideas, new ways of thinking. I am awed by the privilege.

48

Spring and salons

Mars envoie ses giboulées, March heralds April showers. I discover the rhyme in *Comptes et Comptines*, one of the children's books that came with the house. Just when the chill of winter seems interminable, an endless sequence of damp, bleak days, the weather begins to change. I become aware that the days are lengthening. No longer do I have to draw the curtains and close the shutters at five. The sun makes an occasional appearance and even offers a promise of warmth. The children can play outside, especially after we erect the swing structure, complete with climbing ropes, that we found in the garage. At Rimberlieu, outdoor furniture suddenly appears on the south-facing terraces of houses that have been in hibernation for months.

By April, the forest reveals unmistakable signs of spring, little white anemones and pale yellow primroses responding to more hours of daylight and a rise in temperature. Clumps of crocuses pop up and flower in front lawns. The slender shoots of green that poke through the leaves of the forest floor and beneath the trees at the back of the house are, I discover, lilies of the valley, or *muguet*. Until now I have known lily of the valley only as a scent, as in the Roger & Gallet soap my mother occasionally uses, but here it is a wildflower and at Compiègne the first weekend of May is celebrated as the Fête du Muguet. In Paris, too, spring

makes its presence felt. Trees blossom in the Jardin des Plantes, their low boughs covered in palest pink. The winter snow, now melted, swells the Seine which floods over its banks and rises so high that barges and *bateaux-mouches* cannot pass underneath the bridges.

With the weather more propitious for flying John buys a second second-car. This time it's a Simca station wagon, dark blue. Simone de Beauvoir's first car was a blue Simca, I recall, but hers was a Simca Aronde, an earlier model. Compared to the glamorous but temperamental DS, the plain, unpretentious Simca is practical and reliable. With these virtues it gradually usurps the role of the DS and becomes the family car.

Warmer days draw people out of their houses, and gardens are resurrected at Rimberlieu. Stands selling Vilmorin and Caillard seeds appear in the most unlikely of places – the village *boulangerie*, the corner *tabac*. I dig a patch at the back of the house, facing south-east for the sun, and sow 18-day radishes, chervil, cucumbers and lettuce. In the pots outside the French doors I plant multicoloured nasturtiums, and the nigella seeds I find in the garage are scattered over a narrow bed near the driveway.

Meanwhile the moles, roused from their winter slumber, start tunnelling beneath our lawn. Telltale piles of dirt indicate their meandering nightly progress. I have never seen a mole, not even at the Jardin d'Acclimatation. When he hears this, our neighbour Jean-Pierre Kernavez offers to lend us a trap, but we set it only one night; curiosity is outweighed by sympathy, and I prefer that they remain enigmatic and unseen. Our affection for moles is not shared by the *aéroclub*, where flying has to be cancelled for a week *à cause des taupinières*; the moles have burrowed under the airstrip and their molehills make it too dangerous for take-off and landing.

Spring brings the *salons*, trade shows. There's one almost every

week in Paris, some devoted to industry and manufacturing, such as the Salon de l'Automobile and Salon International de l'Aéronautique, others appealing to a more free-wheeling audience such as the Salon de Vivre Autrement, celebrating natural and organic foods and alternative lifestyles.

One of the first of the spring season is the Salon International de l'Agriculture, held in the Parc des Expositions, a vast exhibition centre just outside the Périphérique at the Porte de Versailles. A French counterpart to Sydney's Royal Easter Show but without the sideshows and ring events, it brings to Paris thousands of farmers, their animals and their produce. *On sait toujours quand c'est la semaine du Salon de l'Agriculture*, says Claudie. *On voit tous ces paysans dans le métro.* She seems to resent sharing her metro with country bumpkins. I think it might be worth a visit.

The Royal Easter Show is big, but this is immense beyond my imagining. There's no way I can see everything, so I focus on the animals, breeds unheard of in Australia with poetic names like Bleu de Maine, Rouge de l'Ouest, Charmoise and Berrichon du Cher, all of which are sheep. Their owners are unmistakably non-Parisian and comfortably at home among the rural smells of straw and hay and manure. With the pragmatic earthiness that characterises people of the land, they see no need to segregate the edible product from the animal that produced it. Fresh goat milk and goat cheeses are on sale right next to the goats, ham and *charcuterie* alongside a pen of lumbering Landrace pigs. Beribboned cattle quietly ruminate in full view of a refrigerated window displaying prize-winning carcases, and their owner proudly sells packets of succulent steaks along with advice on how to cook them.

It's leisurely viewing in the animal pavilion but the gastronomic pavilion is very different. The Vins/Provinces de France hall is packed. It is impossible to penetrate the traffic, to see

what delicacy has everyone crowded around a particular stall. The methodical plan I had formulated goes out the window and I resign myself to a catch-as-catch-can strategy. It's obvious where the priorities of Parisians lie as they bypass the paddock and go straight to the plate. Or the glass. Tastings and samplings are offered from all sides, from all the regions of France, all with their distinctive foods and wines, from Jura to Jurançon, Bordeaux to Bourgueil.

To my disappointment there are no free samples of Brittany oysters, but Auvergnats in broad-brimmed black hats hold trays with cubes from an enormous 45-kilogram round of *laguiole* cheese. Their Provençal compatriots, red kerchiefs knotted around sweaty necks, compete for custom with thin slivers of *saucisson d'Arles*. With the taste of salty pork still on my palate I pass up on chestnut honey from the Cévennes but try the *pain d'épices* from Reims, persuaded by the stallholder who assures me that his fine-textured gingerbread, made with honey and rye flour, is totally authentic and absolutely the best. A small cup of vanilla-scented coffee from La Réunion is a perfect complement to a piece of Breton madeleine. But my stomach rebels before I complete the gastronomic *tour de France*. The tumult of the crowd and the cacophony of sounds and smells and tastes defeat me.

I find more leisurely pleasure in the local market. I abandoned the market in Compiègne in December when it was so cold that even the carrots froze, but now I can return. With the first of the new potatoes and the first *petits pois*, admittedly from Spain, spring is so much more inspirational than dull winter. Radishes shyly show their scrubbed pink-and-white virtue, spring onions are transparently honest. Spinach leaves are vivid green and beautifully young and tender. Salad greens increase in variety, and lettuce is no longer watery and insipid. The butcher retires his trays of *bourguignon* and *pot-au-feu* and gives the foreground to

platters of pale pink veal and lamb. Spring lamb is juicy, surprisingly lean – and now, affordable.

Spring in the north of France is a real awakening. Seasonal transitions in Australia are more subtle, less dramatic. I could, if I chose the days carefully, swim every month of the year in Sydney. Here it's as though I have at last been released from a dark, dank prison.

49 'Our correspondent in France'

If the dearth of jobs in Compiègne put a damper on my half-hearted quest, the government's generosity added the final full stop. Thanks to John's new status as an employee in a French enterprise, the children are eligible for child endowment, *allocation familiale*, of 167 francs per month. On top of this, the government gives me 230 francs a month as a *mère au foyer*, at-home mother. The unexpected bonus is even sweeter when the first payment includes two months in arrears. I spend it on a toaster so we can enjoy hot toast and butter and my new marmalade for breakfast. The French do excellent jams, rich in fruit – the labels actually tell you the proportions of fruit and sugar – but they don't understand marmalade. After a year of jam for breakfast I've completely lost my taste for Vegemite.

It's no loss, not finding work. Domestic stability and financial security give me time to think and I can concentrate on writing my now-regular features for *Australian Gourmet* and *Epicurean*. More and more they reflect my life in France, what is happening around me, and because I delight in all the little moments that make up the days and the weeks, the words flow more easily. I write about my breakfast companions on radio France-Inter, Jacques and Dominique, and how they exhort me to celebrate Breton artichokes and cauliflowers; remind me of

the hundred-and-one variations on the *routier*'s truck-stop staple, *côtelettes de porc*; and invite me to honour *la journée des petits pois* with a feast of peas. I write about making mayonnaise with a wire whisk as the French do, rather than a wooden spoon, and how the French phrase, *monter une mayonnaise*, somehow encapsulates the magic of coaxing two seemingly incompatible ingredients to unite as a glorious, golden pool.

Australian Gourmet now refers to me as 'our correspondent in France'. To the editor of *Epicurean* I remain Anne Bonnet. I've signed a statutory statement confirming that Anne Bonnet and I are one and the same and had it properly witnessed and certified by the *maire* at Caux, so that her cheques can go into my bank account. With the proceeds of my first cheque from *Australian Gourmet* I buy the children a collection of model animals, small but lifelike, so they can create their own farm, their own Jardin d'Acclimatation. For myself, I head to the specialist cookware shop in Compiègne where I've been eying off the copper saucepans. A copper frying pan and a medium-size saucepan with a flat multipurpose lid are the start of my collection.

So much about living in France inspires me to write, or at least to investigate and research. With John taking care of the children for an afternoon, I go to the Paris offices of the Comité du Travail Féminin to get more information on working women in France. Its library is daunting but, with the help of a friendly librarian, I discover a vast treasure of statistics and reports. In France, I learn, almost one in every two women aged between 15 and 65 are in the workforce – and this excludes women like Madame la Charcutière at Caromb, whose contribution to her husband's business is taken for granted. Further, over two-thirds of women with one child have a job, mostly full-time. This level of participation far exceeds what I would expect of Australia.

In my enthusiasm for the subject I remember Simone de

Beauvoir's classic, *The Second Sex*. I can't claim to have read and understood it all, and most of what I remember relates to the history and myth sections of the first volume, but I'm convinced it must be relevant. And the author lives practically at my doorstep. She will be the ideal person to help me understand French affairs.

Simone de Beauvoir's memoirs form part of our travelling library and the third volume describes the apartment she bought, overlooking the Montparnasse cemetery and Rue Froidevaux. It's not a long street and French posties are very resourceful, so I put on my best, most polite French and write to her at Rue Froidevaux, humbly requesting an interview. It's a long shot, I know, but meeting Simone de Beauvoir would be the equivalent of reaching the summit of Everest. For day after day, week after week, ever hopeful, I await a reply. But nothing arrives, not even a *Je vous remercie, mais je regrette*... I never know whether my letter arrived at its destination, though later I learn that her actual address is Rue Schoelcher, just around the corner from Froidevaux. Still, if Monsieur Poste had any compassion he would have forgiven my mistake.

While Maison de la Famille offers an invaluable childminding service I can only take advantage for a morning or afternoon, not a full day. If I want to spend a day in Paris then I need someone to come to the house to look after the children. I ask the man at the goose farm if he knows someone local, but he can't help. So I post an ad in the Villers-sur-Coudun *charcuterie*: *Cherche jeune fille pour garder enfants, Rimberlieu, un jour par semaine.*

My notice gets absolutely no response, but Professor Touzot's wife Michèle offers us the *jeune fille* who cleans and keeps an eye on her children after school. On Tuesdays Evelyne has little to do at the Touzots, since the children go to a dancing class after school. It's not the ideal day; many museums in Paris closed on Tuesdays.

What I don't envisage is that libraries might follow suit, and on my first Tuesday in Paris I arrive at the Centre Pompidou to find the whole building, including the public library, very sternly *fermé*.

After this setback I plan my Tuesdays more carefully. The Bibliothèque Forney at the 14th-century Hôtel de Sens is open Tuesday afternoons, and here I read about old Paris, its streets and its monuments. Climbing the spiral stone staircase to the reading room, I feel a sense of wonder: so many generations have walked these steps, so many hands have stroked the same wall. In Sydney my grandfather would point out landmarks, tell me the history of Hyde Park Barracks, explain the names of streets and suburbs, but none of those aroused the same veneration, none of those resonated with history as this does. Perhaps I was too young.

When April school holidays arrive, Evelyne takes a break – and never returns. My days in Paris are fewer and less regular, but at last I manage to get to the Centre Pompidou library. It's one of the few libraries in Paris that encourages proper browsing, with rows of bookshelves on several levels, the books within easy reach. This is the kind of library I was looking for but never found in Béziers and Pézenas, and I can't prevent the smile spreading across my face as I breathe in the comforting aroma of paper and leather and bindings. In the cookbook section, which contains mostly 20th-century publications, I happily flit from book to book like a bee in a bed of borage.

Disciplining myself to research the history of mustard, the theme I've chosen for my next article, I come across the *Almanach des Gourmands* for 1804, written by someone who calls himself '*un vieil amateur*', and read that Russians eat Monsieur Bordin's mustard as though it were jam. Unaware at this time that the *vieil amateur* is in fact Grimod de la Reynière, whom I later come

to admire as the father of gastronomic writing, I assume he means that Russians spread the mustard thickly. It's years later, when I better understand the savagery of his acerbic wit, that I wonder if he is referring rather to a lack of gastronomic savoir-faire. The mustards of Monsieur Maille, he writes, are better known in the north of the country than the verses of Racine, perhaps a snide criticism of the 17th-century dramatist; Grimod, I discover, was also a theatre critic. Delighted as I am to discover these snippets of history, what warms me even more is the knowledge that Maille mustards still exist, and I can savour history with my sausages.

Still, there's always the library at Compiègne and I have a free subscription, another of the perks of John's job at the university. The French, normally so pedantically logical, are oddly reluctant to embrace the Dewey system and I am constantly bewildered and frustrated by the variable systems of classification. Consulting the catalogue I hear the echo of the two old ladies in Béziers (Why would anyone want to borrow a *livre de cuisine?*) but this collection, although limited, includes some real treasures, forgotten classics of the 19th and early 20th centuries. There's Alexandre Dumas's *Grand Dictionnaire de Cuisine*, which includes a whole essay on mustard, and Escoffier's *Aide-mémoire Culinaire*. And for local food I can turn to *La Vraie Cuisine de l'Artois, de la Flandre et de la Picardie*.

One of my favourites is Curnonsky's *Cuisine et Vins de France*. Curnonsky – a pseudonym – was a food writer and gastronomic journalist, a 20th-century successor to Grimod de la Reynière. Like Grimod, he founded a magazine and, like Grimod, he recognised and rewarded the best restaurants, the best chefs, though he dismissed the pretentious, the needlessly complicated. His 'best' was sometimes the most simple. In *Cuisine et Vins de France* he elaborates his theory of *les quatre cuisines françaises: la haute cuisine,*

la cuisine bourgeoise, la cuisine régionale et la cuisine impromptue. I wonder what he would have made of Australia. The roast leg of lamb would surely epitomise *cuisine bourgeoise*, the barbecue possibly *cuisine impromptue*, but I am hard pressed to find counterparts to the others, as I understand them in France.

All this reading informs my articles – I discuss Curnonsky's categories in an article for *Epicurean* – but I learn even more when I start to frequent the kitchen of La Belle Epoque and talk *cuisine* with Madame Mourichon.

50 La Belle Epoque

La Belle Epoque is a small private restaurant, the choice of university researchers when they want to impress potential partners. John regales me with accounts of his lunches, especially when they involve SNIAS or SNECMA and he can talk flying. The French have an inordinate love of acronyms; SNIAS is Société Nationale Industrielle Aérospatiale, still based in an old building in Neuilly with the faded letters of *Blériot Aviation* visible on the facade. SNECMA refers to Société Nationale d'Etudes et de Construction des Moteurs d'Aviation. Both companies are involved in research projects at the university.

Tell her she's welcome to drop in one morning, says Madame Mourichon, when John mentions my interest in food and cooking. Standing forlornly on the outside step, I ring the bell and wonder what on earth I can say to justify my intrusion. But Madame Mourichon remembers her invitation and graciously welcomes me, and my awkwardness begins to fade. I perch myself in a corner of the kitchen and observe, occasionally venturing to ask questions. On this day, with a booking for only one table, the kitchen is not busy and she has time to talk. Does she need any help, casual, unpaid, I ask? She doesn't, but invites me to visit whenever I want, and offers to lend me cookbooks.

Madame Mourichon's speciality is *pâtisserie* and desserts. Her

partner in the kitchen, in charge of meat and sauces and *garniture*, the vegetable accompaniment, is a practical, no-nonsense woman who tells me she learnt her skills under a chef in a *maison bourgeoise*. She says this with some pride, as though it gives her credibility and authority, especially in comparison with Madame Mourichon who is apparently self-taught. I note, though, that whenever they have a slight difference of opinion it's Madame Mourichon who has the last word. And it's Madame Mourichon who composes the menu, a simple, traditional menu that usually starts with one of the standard basic hors d'œuvres – *carottes rapées*, a few slices of *saucisson, œufs mayonnaise* – followed by a main course, perhaps roast pork or roast beef or chicken in a cream sauce, then cheese or dessert. Nothing extravagant, nothing that diners would not recognise. The elegant, light-filled dining room opens on to spacious lawns and a formal French garden. Unostentatious and discreet, it's a perfect choice for university staff wanting to be seen as responsible, prudent and *bienséant*, a lovely French word that, with its associations of good manners and good taste, encompasses so much more than the English 'proper'.

Madame Mourichon's gâteau aux poires (ou prunes ou pêches ou abricots ou raisins)
Madame Mourichon's pear cake (or plum or peach or apricot or grape)

Australian Gourmet, April/May 1979

Madame Mourichon's handwritten recipe calls for '*4 tasses à thé de farine, 3 tasses à thé sucre, 1 tasse à thé fromage blanc and 1 tasse à thé huile*', but half quantities work well, yogurt replacing *fromage blanc*. The fruit should be reasonably firm and not too juicy.

2 cups flour
1½ teaspoons baking powder
1¼ cups caster sugar
½ cup natural yogurt
½ cup oil (such as grapeseed or safflower oil)
grated rind ½ lemon
2 eggs
1 cup seeded grapes, or 2 to 3 firm pears, peeled and cubed,
or equivalent other fruit

Preheat oven to 180°C (160°C fan-forced).

Sift flour and baking powder, add sugar. If desired, reserve 2 tablespoons of sugar to sprinkle over fruit. Make a well in the centre and add yogurt, oil, lemon rind and eggs, mix thoroughly. (Alternatively, combine all ingredients in a mixer.)

Grease, or line with baking paper, a cake tin 24 to 26 cm diameter or 22 to 24 cm square. Pour cake mixture into tin, top with fruit, and sprinkle with reserved sugar if desired. Bake in preheated oven for about 45 minutes or until cake tests done. Turn out of tin immediately and cool on rack. Serve slightly warm, with cream if desired.

I sometimes glimpse Monsieur Mourichon in his study. Although we are formally introduced there's no small talk and I have no idea what he does all day. As the only son of a notable Compiègne family, he has inherited the large and solidly bourgeois residence just below the *château*. Perhaps, in agreeing to allow his residence become a restaurant, he was indulging his wife's fondness for cooking and entertaining, but I suspect the idea was Madame's, the reasons were financial and it's her energy that sustains it.

Talking food and cooking with Madame Mourichon becomes the highlight of my week. It seems so long since I could indulge this passion, and with a better understanding of French ingredients and techniques I am even more eager to learn. The children now play happily with other children at the *garderie*, and at least once a week I leave them for an hour or two while I drop into La Belle Epoque. Gradually I am entrusted with small tasks – trimming radishes, shelling eggs. I must pass the test, since Madame asks if I can help for a big reception, 80 people to lunch, and I spend three hours washing and hulling strawberries, washing and preparing the salads, finishing the strawberry tarts.

In return for my help, Madame Mourichon invites me to accompany her to Rungis, the big new wholesale market south of Paris. I always regret never having seen the elegant iron-and-glass structures of Les Halles, the legendary market site; when I was in Paris in 1972 all that was left were a few skeletal fragments. Today there's just an empty space that I traverse on my way from the library at the Centre Pompidou to the Gare du Nord to catch the 4.15 to Compiègne. I try to imagine it as it once was, a site of incredible hustle and bustle, the sound of barrows mingling with the calls of the sellers, and marvel that, despite the crowds and the chaos, the market managed to collect and distribute foods as efficiently as it did.

The vastness of Rungis is overwhelming. It's not one large space but many individual pavilions, each the size of an aircraft hangar capable of accommodating a fleet of Concordes and each housing a specialised trade – fishmongers, butchers, grocers and greengrocers. These halls are reserved exclusively for professionals, restaurants and retailers. Occasional customers, like Madame Mourichon, are directed to a separate hall that is more like a traditional covered market with numerous specialised shops – cheese merchants, commercial *pâtisseries*, shops

specialising in spices or Italian *salumi* or kitchen equipment. Compared with the usual street markets it's significantly cheaper, with prices about 15% less. Madame buys a side of pork, several chickens, a round of brie and a bounty of summer fruits – cherries, strawberries, apricots – some of which she offers to me. On the way out I spy Monsieur Lenôtre's van.

Gaston Lenôtre is a highly successful *pâtissier*, a brilliant star in the gastronomic firmament with several shops in Paris, all in the most prestigious *arrondissements*, and the author of *Faîtes Votre Pâtisserie Comme Lenôtre*. It's the cookbook Madame Mourichon currently favours. Lenôtre intended his book to introduce ordinary cooks, like me, to his *nouvelle pâtisserie française*. Unlike *nouvelle cuisine*, it hardly seems revolutionary, though among the classic recipes are several new ones of his own invention, such as *la concorde*. As befits a lad from Normandy, butter features in almost all the recipes. Never, he says as he shakes a metaphorical finger, never substitute any old fat for the 450 grams of butter when you make a brioche. I wouldn't dare.

After Madame Mourichon lends me her copy of Lenôtre for a couple of days I am immediately inspired to cook. The recipes are methodically presented and quite straightforward, at least to read; what takes them out of the ordinary is the emphasis on presentation. My first choice, as I turn the pages, is pear tart – *tarte aux poires aux amandes*, the pears arranged on a buttery almond paste. Next I embark on the *brioche aux raisins*. So enamoured am I with the results that I immediately write to the book's publisher, Flammarion, offering to translate the book into English. I am surprised to get no reply. Perhaps they think that an audience across the Channel will never be attracted to such extravagances.

In thrall to Lenôtre, I embark on a baking spree. I go to the specialist culinary supplier at Compiègne and equip myself with

a *cul-de-poule* (a large stainless steel bowl, literally translated as a hen's backside), a *moule à manqué* cake tin with slightly sloping sides, six tartlet tins and 65 sheets of *papier sulfurisé* for lining cake tins and baking in general. A long rolling pin without handles, like Madame Mourichon's, and a pastry brush complete the purchase. I am starting to feel like a professional.

I start with *génoise*, a kind of sponge that takes advantage of the power of heat to augment volume. Next is a classic *quatre-quarts*, this time following a Tante Marthe recipe I have saved from the *Midi Libre*. Cakes, I realise, don't necessarily have to start with the standard formula I've grown up with, of creaming butter and sugar. French cakes take advantage of the aerating power of eggs and egg whites. Self-raising flour is unknown, although some recipes call for *levure chimique*, baking powder, sold in small individual sachets. And cakes here are made with honest, natural ingredients: butter, fresh eggs, sugar, flour, ensuring cakes are axiomatically good. The French are pragmatic about cake, as they are with chocolate. While it might be an indulgence relegated to Sundays, eaten then and only then – a daily croissant doesn't count as cake – there's no hint that it should be a guilty pleasure.

Through Madame Mourichon I am introduced to a little-known *pâtisserie, tarte au sucre*. Soft and spongy, deliciously caramelised, it's a speciality of this sugar beet-growing north and so obscure, so specifically localised, that neither Waverley Root nor Elizabeth David mentions it. Even the normally authoritative *Guide Gourmand de la France* passes over *tarte au sucre*. I rarely see one in the Compiègne *pâtisseries*, though our *boulanger* from Coudun occasionally has one in his van on Sundays. It's essentially a brioche dough sprinkled with brown or raw sugar, covered with cream and baked, its prime ingredients being flour, butter, cream and sugar. Having mastered the brioche, I'm not fazed by *tarte au sucre* and develop my own recipe to include in one of my articles.

Quatre-quarts
Simple butter cake

Australian Gourmet, February/March 1979

Counterpart to the Victoria sponge of English baking, the fine-textured *quatre-quarts* is the quintessential French cake, all genuine goodness.

>250 g softened butter
>1 cup caster sugar
>grated rind 1 lemon
>4 extra-large (60 g) eggs
>2 cups flour
>pinch salt
>1 teaspoon baking powder

Preheat oven to 190°C (170°C fan-forced).

Using an electric mixer, beat butter, sugar and lemon rind until light and creamy. Separate eggs, add yolks one at a time, beating well after each addition. Sift flour with salt and baking powder and fold into mixture. Beat egg whites until very stiff, carefully fold about one-quarter into cake mixture then fold in remainder.

Grease and lightly flour a 23 cm round cake tin (or line with baking paper). Pour mixture into tin, bake in preheated oven for 30 to 35 minutes or until cake tests done. Cool on a wire rack.

Taking inspiration from the *far breton* that I like to buy at Breton stalls at the Parisian markets, I sometimes arrange softened, seedless prunes over the surface before baking.

Tarte au sucre
Sugar tart

Epicurean, 'Listener's Choice', August/September 1979

If anything could endear me to the north of France, it would be this simple tart, its pairing of cream and sugar epitomising the region.

Serves 4–6

225 g flour
pinch salt
1 tablespoon sugar
1 teaspoon instant dried yeast (10 g compressed yeast)
½ cup warm milk
1 egg
30 g softened butter
about ½ cup sugar, brown or white
3 to 4 tablespoons cream

Sift flour and salt, add sugar. Dissolve yeast in half of the milk. Beat egg with remaining milk. Add egg and milk to flour mixture, mix well, then mix in dissolved yeast, milk and softened butter. Beat well with wooden spoon until mixture no longer sticks to base of bowl – it should have consistency of a very thick, solid batter. Sprinkle lightly with flour, cover and leave to rise in a warm place for about 30 minutes. (It is possible to make the dough mixture several hours before you want to cook the tart, leaving it in the refrigerator to rise very slowly. Remove from refrigerator about 1 hour before it is to be cooked.)

Butter a large cake tin or tart tin (at least 26 cm diameter) and spread mixture evenly over base. (Alternatively, trace a large circle on baking paper, line a baking tray and pat dough to shape.) Leave

to rise for a further 15 to 30 minutes (if dough has been in refrigerator, it will need about 1 hour in a warm place).

Preheat oven to hot (210°C, 190°C fan-forced). Using fingers, make deep dimples over surface of dough. Strew tart surface fairly thickly with sugar – you may need more than half a cup – then dot with cream. Bake in hot oven for about 20 minutes. If the tart browns too quickly, reduce heat.

The surface should be slightly caramelised, the texture light and spongy.

When I discover that Carrefour has added cookbooks to its range, I immediately buy my own copy of *Faîtes Votre Pâtisserie Comme Lenôtre*. Next to fall into my shopping trolley are Paul Bocuse's *La Cuisine du Marché* and *La Pâtisserie pour Tous*, a companion volume to *La Cuisine pour Tous*. My library expands even further when, on a remainders table in Paris, I happen upon more volumes in the same series as *Cuisine Provençale*, for other regions of France: *La Cuisine Occitane*, *La Cuisine Lyonnaise*, and *La Cuisine des Trois B.*, covering the south-west corner of France.

My culinary capabilities and knowledge increase every day. With my new boning knife I painstakingly bone a whole chicken to be stuffed and poached for *poulet en gelée*. Undaunted by its complicated construction, I embark on a *pâté en croûte*, complete with a decorative arrangement of chicken livers through its centre. After these feats I reason that *coq au vin* should be child's play, and order a genuine rooster from the Compiègne market. Do you want me to joint it?, asks the poulterer. Breezily I decline his offer; I know how to cut up a chicken, and a rooster is essentially the same but bigger. I forget that a rooster is also much older, and that the reason for long, slow cooking is to make its tough

flesh edible. Roosters, I discover, have sinewy, unyielding wing and leg joints. I almost need a hacksaw to get through them and rue my misplaced confidence. But once the rooster is in pieces, cooking the dish is simplicity itself, and after three hours the flesh is soft and tender, bathed in a rich dark sauce.

The most important lessons I take home from La Belle Epoque concern the virtues of simplicity and seasonality and the importance of quality. You can't make good cakes with second-rate ingredients, warns Lenôtre. Even the most simple of dishes, such as delicate pink radishes with good Normandy butter, sea salt and crusty bread, deserves the same care and attention as Lenôtre's sophisticated *marquise au chocolat*. When Madame Mourichon tells me her lunch menu will begin with scrambled eggs with chives I am dumbfounded; in my universe, scrambled eggs belong to breakfast. Then I realise that these are the first chives of the season, and that their fresh green sharpness on creamy eggs announces spring as surely as the songs of birds in the forest.

54 Wild strawberries

Warmer days and longer evenings coax Rimberlieu residents outdoors, some tending their gardens, others taking a leisurely stroll. No longer secluded behind curtained and shuttered windows, neighbours become more neighbourly. But it's through Yorick, a large floppy black poodle who often wanders from his backyard to ours, that I make friends with Madame Kernavez three houses away.

Madame Kernavez is an enthusiastic cook and knows all the nearby farms and orchards that sell fresh produce. She also tells me there are wild strawberries here. I never imagined finding wild strawberries practically on my doorstep, but there they are. I stumble on them accidentally, growing beside a cleared strip that runs from the crest of the hill down to the sports club. Inconspicuous among the weeds and wild grasses, the low, spreading plants are clearly related to the garden strawberry but the fruits, hiding under the leaves, are minuscule, hardly bigger than a redcurrant. You need sharp eyes to find them. Even at their most prolific, I'm lucky to harvest a cupful in half an hour. Stephanie is keen on picking them but more interested in eating them. At least three out of every four find their way to her mouth.

What these unassuming little fruits lack in size they make up in punch. Deep crimson outside, pearly white within, they have an incomparable intensity of flavour, a three-dimensional flavour

that takes time to make its presence felt then lingers, persists, and imprints itself on your memory. And such perfume! Even just a spoonful of the wild fruit transforms a bowl of garden-grown strawberries.

I never imagined that summer would soften the menacing, malevolent forest, cajole it into revealing a kinder side. Now welcoming, with dappled sunshine filtering through the leaves, it surprises me with its gifts. More wild strawberries show their shy faces at the edge of the forest opposite our house, but I'm not going to fight with the blackberries to retrieve them. Venturing a little further I have the thrill of seeing my first wild raspberry and my first wild cherry, a tiny fruit barely bigger than an olive stone. *Fruits de la forêt* instantly makes sense. It's also the children's favourite flavour of yogurt.

Strawberries, raspberries and cherries are the leaders of *les fruits rouges*, a group of berry fruits that, somewhat paradoxically, also includes green gooseberries and the deep purple-blue blackcurrants, blackberries, elderberries and bilberries (*myrtilles*). Together and individually they're emblematic of summer, but the most ubiquitous are the strawberries. French strawberries are powerfully aromatic, especially the large, luscious Périgord strawberries, and you can smell them in the market well before you see them. In Australia strawberries come in small punnets as if they were rationed, but here there is such a profusion that you buy them by the kilo and eat them like apples, one bite at a time.

From early June I take it for granted that there will be strawberries in the market and on our table. Stephanie adores them, especially the strawberry purée that I pour over her *petit-suisse*. When I see a program on making sorbets on television I know I need an electric *sorbetière* whose small rotating paddle churns the mixture during the freezing process. With this new device I make *sorbet aux fraises* and *mousse glacée de fraises*, and am all prepared to

move on to *glace aux fraises et à la crème* when suddenly, in mid-July, strawberries inexplicably disappear. Stalls that, a week earlier, were overflowing with perfumed strawberries now display other fruit. *Pas de fraises après le quatorze juillet*, the market lady tells me, shaking her head; she offers no explanation for the abrupt conclusion to the strawberry season, as if this is common knowledge. I turn to other *fruits rouges*. Raspberries are transformed into a spectacularly successful *sorbet de framboises*; blackcurrants and redcurrants prove an inspired flavour for my experimental frozen yogurt.

Eventually, at the end of July, the local cherries are ready. The varieties here are different to those of Provence, some pure creamy white with barely a blush of pink, very fleshy and sweet. At last I can attempt the complicated Lenôtre recipe for *tartelettes aux cerises* that requires me to prepare, first of all, a shortcrust pastry, then a *crème patissière* and an almond cream to blend with it. I have just taken my tartlets out of the oven when the children wake from an afternoon sleep. Dylan takes one look at them, the cherries pinkly translucent, and exclaims, 'Nipple tarts!' He's right; the fruit takes on a dark, deep pink that is exactly the colour of nipples.

In France, *les fruits rouges* often find their way into preserves, not only homely jams but also more exotic alcoholic confections. From the beginning of summer supermarkets start stocking *eau-de-vie blanche pour fruits*, 40% or 60% strength, an inexpensive neutral alcohol specifically destined for homemade liqueurs. I use it to make *liqueur de fraises des bois* – essentially, wild strawberries, sugar and alcohol. The colour of the strawberries gradually permeates the liquid and the fruits rise to the surface. I leave the jar on the little landing halfway down the stairs to the garage, and whenever I pass it I can't help lifting the lid to inhale the intoxicating fragrance. I'm never tempted to take a sip; the aroma alone would awaken the souls of the dead.

Sorbet aux fraises
Strawberry sorbet

This is the first recipe I try in my newly acquired *sorbetière* – and naturally I add some of the tiny, intensely flavoured wild strawberries from the edge of our lawn.

Serves 4–6

750 g strawberries
150 g sugar
1 cup water
juice ½ orange and ½ lemon

Set freezer at coldest setting.

Set aside about 150 g of the best strawberries. Wash remainder, dry and hull, then puree in blender.

Over gentle heat, gradually dissolve sugar in water, cool.

Add orange and lemon juice to strawberries, then chilled syrup. Pour mixture into *sorbetière*, place in freezer and switch on. Remove paddles when they stop churning. (Alternatively, use an icecream maker.)

If the sorbet is made in advance transfer it to bottom of refrigerator to soften for at least 30 minutes before serving. Garnish with reserved strawberries.

The *eau-de-vie* also goes into large jars of *confiture du vieux garçon*, bachelor's jam, which is not a jam in the traditional sense but a heady confection that, in the depths of winter, brings back all the warmth and perfumes of summer. It's served in tiny glasses, with a spoon for the fruit. Did it earn its name because it's a sweet and highly alcoholic liqueur, the sort of drink presented in a pretty glass and offered to women, I wonder? Or because it's a lazy gentleman's 'jam', no cooking involved, simply equal weights of fruit and sugar plus alcohol to cover? It's a serial preserve, beginning with strawberries and wild strawberries with sugar and alcohol to cover. As they ripen, other summer fruits are added with more sugar and alcohol, each sacrificing its individuality to create a liqueur that is far greater than the simple sum of its parts, a triumphal harmony that inspires ecstasy at first sip.

The magic ingredient is time. Jean-Pierre's cellar at Mas Laval offers ideal conditions for my alcoholic experiments to mature, so I leave them there and look forward to sharing with our friends the culmination of the mingling of flavours. Alas! In our absence, the teenage son of a family renting the *gîte* discovers the hidden treasure. One sip leads to another, and then another . . . By the time his guilty pleasure is discovered, three-quarters of the *confiture* has disappeared, and most of the *liqueur des fraises*. However resentful I am, however reproachful, I can hardly blame him; the liqueurs and the fruits are irresistible. The dregs that remain are even more precious and memorable.

Confiture de vieux garçon
Bachelor's jam

Australian Gourmet, December 1979/January 1980

Some tastes make such a vivid and lasting impression that they can be retrieved from the memory and enjoyed all over again. Writing this recipe brings it all back, the sensuous, heady perfume, the concentrated perfection of ripe summer fruit.

Rum, vodka or brandy is the best substitute for the French *eau-de-vie*.

>   Berries (strawberries, cherries, raspberries, redcurrants, blackcurrants)
>   Stone fruit (peaches, nectarines, apricots, plums)
>   Sugar
>   Alcohol

First, sterilise a very large, wide preserving jar. Strawberries will probably be the first layer, followed by cherries and raspberries. Wash fruit, dry and remove stems – for cherries cut the stalks to about 0.5 cm. Weigh the fruit, and for each variety add the same weight of sugar and cover with alcohol. If you're lucky you might find redcurrants and blackcurrants for the next layer. Then stone fruit, probably peaches and nectarines followed by apricots and plums. Choose the most highly perfumed fruits; aroma is far more important than appearance. Make sure the alcohol covers all the fruit.

Seal well and find a good hiding place where the *confiture* can mature in cool, dark conditions for at least three months.

52 Summer

The official start of summer is 21 June, and on that date the Oise changes from a working highway to a Renoir-like site of pleasure as barges offer *promenades en péniche*, leisurely cruises. Stephanie likes to call the barges *bâteaux-mouches*, because these are what she has seen on the Seine in Paris, but Dylan knows they are *péniches*, dressed up perhaps, but essentially the same as the working barges we see whenever we cross the Oise. Two children, same upbringing, different sexes, genes at work. They're excited to go on an afternoon promenade, and rush from side to side of the boat. I'm surprised by the different side of Compiègne that the river reveals, tranquil and bucolic.

Social activities intensify in the weeks before holidays empty the town. Although I've lived here now for over eight months, long enough to feel properly grounded, the ladies of the Compiègne Accueille committee consider me a new resident; I have not yet been officially welcomed. Everyone who has recently arrived in the town, or at least everyone considered respectable enough, is invited to a formal afternoon tea in the house where Madame de Pompadour used to entertain her female friends. We eat strawberry tarts and make polite conversation and the Compiègne ladies offer their *cartes de visite*. My lack of reciprocity must mark me as uncouth, unless my newcomer status can pass for an excuse.

The academic year draws to a close and the university organises a party for the group of graduating masters students. The North African students respond by inviting the whole faculty to a *méchoui*, a whole spit-roast lamb, Algerian style, crisp-skinned and spicily aromatic. The *aéroclub* decides on an impromptu summer soirée and I find myself volunteered to make desserts for 12. Sometimes Stephanie and Dylan come with us to these events – they realise very quickly that parties often mean potato chips – but often they stay at home. I'm grateful the Kernavez girls live so close and want to earn pocket money.

In July my mother comes to visit and stays until the children's birthday in late August. She takes the adventurous route, flight to Athens, overnight coach to Brussels, train to Compiègne. I have no idea which train and wait expectantly while three trains from Brussels arrive at Compiègne station, set down passengers and continue on their way to Paris. It's 18 months since we left, and although letters have been frequent we've spoken by phone only two or three times. Will she recognise me, I ask myself. Will she discern that I'm not the girl she farewelled at the airport? But the changes are interior and invisible, and only I am privileged to sense their subtleties. If I looked carefully into the recesses of my mind I would probably find a corner that represented an enhanced awareness of the way the world functions, and how the people who make up the world each play their individual parts in maintaining and sustaining it, from morning to evening and then all over again.

It's Stephanie who first spots 'Ganma', immediately recognising her stepping from the carriage. What processes are happening in their young brains?, I wonder. Have I lost clarity by overthinking, needlessly complicating things? Instinctively, without hesitation, the children understand the grandmother-

grandchild relationship and accept her into their lives. It's as if she had been a constant presence, as if she had rocked them, comforted them, changed their nappies and played with them every day since they were born.

I love watching the three of them together, although I still feel guilt at having removed the children from their grandparents for my own selfish benefit. And the children love being around Grandma, which means I can spend time at my typewriter or in the kitchen. I embark on a frenzy of entertaining, returning previous hospitality and having neighbours in for dinner. Jacques, the ex-air force pilot from the *aéroclub*, entertains my mother with tales of his exploits during the war, such as the time he was returning to France across the Mediterranean when his engine stalled. It could have been curtains but, looking down, he spotted a handy aircraft carrier and brought his plane in for a perfect landing. I never know if it's a true story, though I'm sure it has been embellished along the way.

I want to immerse my mother into my world, directing her gaze so that she sees things from my perspective and perhaps starts to understand why, why France. She loves the greenness of Rimberlieu and its gardens, but I'm anxious to introduce her to Compiègne's best *pâtisserie* and *charcuterie* before they shut down for August. I take pride in showing her 'my' Paris, especially the Centre Pompidou and Musée d'Art Moderne. I'm used to a quiet Paris, the winter-spring Paris, and peak tourist season is a revelation. The exterior escalators at Pompidou are so crowded that staff have difficulty controlling numbers; the square outside is full of lively activity with a Greek folkdance group, bare-chested fire-eaters, impromptu street theatre and everywhere people and more people, all carefree and happy and on holiday.

It's a blissful, idyllic time. The children have long sleeps in the afternoon and then happily play outside until the light starts to fade around ten. With the swing, a new sandpit and a small blow-up wading pool, there's plenty to keep them occupied. It's warm enough for them to spend most of their time naked, and they revel in this freedom.

But I want also to show my mother other aspects of France. The Midi is a too far away, and I know all about the problems of accommodation in August, but Normandy is practically on our doorstep. I have another reason, a secret reason for choosing Normandy. I want to find the little hotel where I stayed for a night when I returned to France, on my way to the Sorbonne, after a month in England. It was this night, this hotel, that finally and definitively convinced me that France was where I belonged, or where I wanted to belong. England represented the safety and comfort of familiarity but France dared me with challenges and rewarded me with the thrill of new discoveries within myself.

Meandering along the smallest of D roads, even the children appreciate this lush, peaceful countryside with its contented chocolate-and-cream Normandy cows and horse-drawn carts for transporting the milk. I can't remember the name of the village I'm searching for but some landmarks are fixed in my brain: a tiny watercourse, a right turn, a copse at the top of the hill. And I've pinpointed some possible candidates, thanks to the detail of the Michelin map. The first village is not the one I am looking for; I can tell immediately that the approach is all wrong. With the second, I know as soon I turn off the main road toward a group of poplars and a low rise that I have found it: the hotel is called l'Orée du Bois, the edge of the woods. I point out to my mother the balcony of the attic room where I stayed, waking to a calm and gentle landscape, green as far as the eye could see. A

feeling of exquisite contentment floods over me as I remember breakfasting in the garden with a pot of coffee, fresh baguette, creamy Normandy butter and homemade strawberry jam.

I have no intention of staying there this time; my plan is to find a hotel in a seaside village where the children can play on the beach and perhaps paddle, though I have my doubts about swimming in the cold waters of the Atlantic. By now I should have learned my lesson but once again, I underestimate the force of August in France. From Fécamp through Yport to Etretat every hotel is full. We can only admire the jagged cliffs so often painted by Monet and other impressionist artists, before retreating inland and at last finding a room at Bolbec.

Next day we have our day at the seaside, or at least by the sea at Honfleur, where we explore the picturesque *vieux port*. Stephanie spies a *boulangerie* with a window full of bread in animal shapes and insists on buying a 'duck bread', though I think it's meant to be a seagull. Even in August it's hardly seaside weather. The French laud the benefits of the ozone-rich air, of brisk walks along the flat, broad expanses of sand, and perhaps that's the appeal of these Normandy beaches. The listless grey sea tempts only the most audacious. This environment, and the fashionable resort of Deauville, was Proust's inspiration for Balbec, where the narrator meets and falls in love with the sporty Albertine. Would his novel have been different, I wonder, if he had holidayed at one of the sunny Mediterranean beaches instead?

Poulet farci en gelée
Stuffed chicken in aspic

Epicurean, October/November 1978

During my mother's visit I invite Monsieur and Madame Kernavez to dinner and serve this chicken with a salad of fresh green beans.

Serves 8

1 large plump (but not fat) chicken
300 g very finely minced pork and veal
1 small onion, finely chopped
1 clove garlic, crushed
grated rind ½ lemon
1 tablespoon very finely chopped parsley
salt and freshly ground pepper
1 egg
½ cup dry white wine
1 tablespoon brandy
2 onions
2 carrots
1 calf's foot, split
2 cups chicken stock (from carcass, after boning)
bouquet garni

First, bone chicken. Lay chicken on its breast and make a long cut from neck opening to tip of the parson's nose. Using a small, sharp knife, its edge always next to the bone, carefully pull and scrape flesh from backbone. Cut through joint where thigh attaches to body, and similarly where wing attaches to body. Continue detaching flesh from bones as far as the ridge of bone that runs down centre of breast. Do the same for both sides, then turn on to its back and carefully lift

and cut to separate skin and flesh from breastbone. Next, scrape meat from thighs and cut through joint between thigh and drumstick. Do the same for first wing section. Spread chicken out flat, and season lightly with salt and pepper.

For stuffing, combine pork and veal, onion, garlic, lemon rind, parsley and seasonings, bind with egg then stir in wine and brandy. Mound this mixture along centre of boned chicken, wrap and sew together with fine string. Secure wings and drumsticks to body, and tie into a neat shape.

Peel and slice onions, scrape carrots and cut into quarters, then arrange on base of deep, oval, ovenproof casserole. Place chicken on top, add calf's foot and stock – and water if necessary – to just cover. Add *bouquet garni*. Cover with foil or baking paper then lid. Cook in a slow (160°C) oven for 2 to 2½ hours. Leave chicken to cool in liquid then transfer to a plate and place in refrigerator.

Allow cooking liquid to simmer another hour on stovetop, before cooling and straining through fine sieve. Take out 1 to 2 cups and strain again though a sieve lined with fine cloth or paper towelling. (The remaining stock can be saved for soup.) Refrigerate, removing all traces of fat when thoroughly cold. If not sufficiently jelled (or if you can't get a calf's foot), add some gelatine softened in cold water, warmed over gentle heat and stirred until dissolved. Place in refrigerator to chill. When set the jelly should be firm but not hard, not quite as hard as dessert jellies made from packeted crystals.

Remove strings and thread from chicken, separate wings and drumsticks from body. Slice meat and arrange slices on serving dish, slightly overlapping, the whole supported by wings or drumsticks. Gently warm jelly then carefully spoon over chicken. Chill until ready to serve. Any remaining jelly can be set in a shallow dish then cut into small cubes and arranged around edge of chicken. Serve with a salad of your choice.

53 *Au revoir*

Just as I feel settled and comfortable in France, it is time to uproot. For some months John has been casting eyes toward America. Even though his boss at the Université de Compiègne would like him to stay, the Minneapolis professor who was so affronted when John refused his job offer eight months ago has overcome his indignation and repeated his invitation. Moving to Midwest America was never on my radar. The idea appals me, but with Professor Jouanna still not in a position to offer John a contract, my dream of a return to the Midi remains that, a distant dream. The career advantages of working in America tip the scale.

The weeks close in. John puts in 11-hour days in order to finish off his work – but also to give him time for more flying lessons. He is determined to complete the first part of his pilot's licence in France, which means getting as much practice as money and weather permit. He's more nervous about the navigation test and theoretical exam, and studies long into the night. Three days after the tests his instructor arrives to congratulate him on graduating to the status of pilot.

I, too, have work that I want to finish: at least three articles to write. And a visit to make, to the editorial offices in Paris of *La Table et Ma Cuisine*, a new monthly magazine I've been buying that takes a contemporary, less traditional approach to food and

photography. I want to sound out the possibility of *Australian Gourmet* using some of its images. It's a measure of my acclimatisation that I'm confident enough to telephone, to explain who I am and what I'd like to discuss. As it happens, the cost of images is prohibitive but I enjoy meeting journalists with the same passion for food and cooking. I leave with a parcel of back issues plus a free subscription.

This might be my last chance to spend a day in Paris by myself, so I take the opportunity to browse the bookstores on the Boulevard Saint-Michel. I want to get a French thesaurus and book of quotations before we leave, and choose *Larousse Analogique* and *Larousse de Citations*. My mother's leftover francs buy the Hachette *Dictionnaire des Synonymes*, more than a thesaurus in that it explains nuances of meaning. I know the word *méchant* typically translates as naughty, but it can also mean savage, as in the sign *Attention – chien méchant*. In this book I discover other interpretations; for example, it can also mean wicked or depraved. It all depends on the context. Dipping into this book as one might an encyclopedia is a delight, and it deepens my understanding of the French language.

Just around the corner, off Rue Saint André des Arts, is the Occitan bookstore. Ever since I encountered the Nizas shepherd speaking words I could not understand, I have become fascinated by the lost language of the Midi. In the *Midi-Libre* I read of attempts in Toulouse to promote it, to teach Occitan, and I write to L'Institut d'Etudes Occitanes for more information. Delighted to welcome a new disciple, they respond with details of correspondence classes, of summer schools, and this specialised shop in Paris. It's the tiniest bookstore I've ever entered, and though most of the books are far too complicated and advanced for me, there's one simple guide, *La Langue Occitane*. At last I start to comprehend the force of the linguistic boundary that

divided France for many centuries, effectively separating south from north.

I make enquiries about flights and transporting our belongings to America. The cheapest option, it seems, is to fly Icelandic Airlines from Luxembourg to Chicago, via Reykjavik. But before I can make a booking I have to present valid American visas, and we're still waiting on these. Organising the tea chests is easier. All we will have to do is deliver them to the Paris offices of the transport company, from where they will be shipped to Chicago – at three times the cost of freight from Sydney to Marseille!

There are so many goodbyes to say, so many hopeful *au revoirs*. And a farewell party to organise – as Australians, we have an obligation to put on a farewell party. We invite neighbours from Rimberlieu, colleagues from the university and a few *aéroclub* friends. Madame Kernavez lends me additional plates and glasses and cutlery. In the finest spirit of Curnonsky's *cuisine à l'improviste* I bake *tartes aux herbes* with the bounty of my garden: tarragon, chervil and parsley. I cook chicken and rabbit terrines and a big bowl of ratatouille. I buy enough cheeses for two large platters, and douse fresh sliced peaches with alcohol for dessert. On the day of the party John assesses the menu and decides 'not enough', so I make another quiche and two almond cakes and two grape tarts. He buys 10 baguettes from the *boulangerie*. With luck, we'll have just enough wine; we can't take it with us. We are not going out with a whimper.

The party is a great success. It's a warm evening and guests wander in and out through the French doors. My herb tarts are a hit and people ask for the recipe; I have to confess that I made it up as I went, but I'm not sure they believe me. Aimé Esperandieu's Provençal rosé, the last half dozen bottles from our purchases last year, en route for Claret, goes down a treat, and Jacques from the *aéroclub* asks for the address so he can make an

order. At the end of the evening we have five baguettes to spare and but a mere dozen assorted bottles of wine.

Once more it is time to shrink our life into four tea chests. The threads attaching us to our life here have to be loosened and severed. The garden-loving neighbour is grateful for my gift of leftover seeds and garden fertiliser. The children's car seats, beds, little table and the lovely Provençal chairs we bought in Caromb go to new homes after I pin an *A Vendre*, For Sale, notice on the board at the *garderie*. Madame Mourichon's cook offers to buy our refrigerator and washing machine. On our last day we jam everything left into the Simca; four cases, three soft bags, the strollers and car seats, the clothes basket full of odds and ends, a box of wine plus a few bulging plastic bags. Somehow we fit ourselves on top.

Impossible to leave France without one last encounter with of the south of France, the region closest to my heart. By the time we reach Caromb and take over 'our' apartment, thanks to Madame, I am starting to relax. I lean over the thick sill and take a deep breath as I gaze over the peaceful orchard. The air is warm and welcoming, and I think how wonderful it is to be back in the Midi where it's still blue-skied and sunny, where people are tanned and carefree, where the second-harvest figs are rich and sweet and the tomatoes full-flavoured and intense. Memories of our earlier stay here flood back: finding sand for the children's sandpit, looking for Roman coins, confronting the ferocity of the mistral, and I compare our tentative steps then with our confident strides today.

It's vintage time again, and Madame Molla has let l'Escoute to Spanish grape pickers; there is almost as much Spanish as French being spoken in the streets of Nizas. We move back to Mas Laval and as I accompany Vivette on the daily shopping round of butcher, baker, *épicerie*, I am surprised and gratified that

I am recognised. Here everyone talks to you, there is always a conversation happening. You calmly wait until the conversation of the shopper before you ends before it's your turn to buy your bread or your sausages, or else you join in, and since it's usually about the weather, today's and yesterday's and tomorrow's and last year's, anyone can contribute.

We are just settling in, regrowing old roots, when the telegram arrives confirming our visas. On our last evening we take Jean-Pierre and Vivette to dinner in Pézenas, at Le Beffroi, and afterwards stroll in the deserted streets of the old town. In the soft yellowish light, it's like walking through a stage set. There's an eerie calm, and I half expect to see a bewigged Molière emerge from one of the 17th-century doorways.

A year ago, when we arrived in Compiègne, I was struck by the chasm between Midi and north. These profound, irreconcilable differences hit me again as I move in the opposite direction. The mild climate – *doux*, gentle, the French would say; the people, open and friendly; the food, essentially local, natural, seasonal, with more garlic and less cream, green salads dressed in plenty of oil instead of beetroot and *carottes rapées*. This is my kind of food, my part of France.

In Paris everything falls into place. After collecting visas from the American Embassy and booking air tickets for four days hence, we are frantically busy in our final days. John goes to Compiègne to sign off on completed projects. We lunch with the Voillaumes, giving them a book on Aboriginal bark paintings. We have a final drink with Claudie in the shadow of the Bastille. I spend an afternoon in the Place de la Madeleine, making notes for an article for *Australian Gourmet*. Michel Guérard has just opened a shop in this ultimate foodie destination that already boasts luxury *épiceries* Hédiard and Fauchon, as well as La Maison des Truffes and Caviar Kaspia.

All too quickly *Jour J* (D-Day) is here and it's over, the whole experiment. I don't even have time to say proper goodbyes – to the Tuileries gardens, the Centre Pompidou and its library, the Marché Saint-Germain, to the park near the Sorbonne and the elegant arches that span the Seine, to the squares and the crooked streets that I return to and see afresh time after time.

Twenty-one months ago we arrived in France with the simple goal of sampling life in a different country and, despite the frustrations and hardships, despite money problems, despite all the uncertainties and ups and downs, we made it. I might not have become a different person, but the experience of living in France leaves an indelible imprint. It has encouraged a different awareness, a different understanding, a differently directed curiosity. I have learnt to shake hands with people as I'm introduced to them and to progress to a kiss on each cheek – or three or four in the Midi. I have learnt how to choose a camembert and what to do with wild leeks. I have cooked and eaten snails and celebrated *le quatorze juillet*. I have picked grapes and gathered wild strawberries. I am on my way to becoming a food writer and I have developed an interest in history that would gratify my grandfather. I might be sad to leave, but regrets? Absolutely none.

Epilogue

Since that *séjour* I have returned to France countless times. I have lived and worked in Paris, studied medieval manuscripts in the bowels of the Bibliotheque Nationale and, in the Archives Départementales in Avignon, transcribed 18th-century documents beneath the fading frescoes of the 14th-century Palais des Papes. I have traversed the length and breadth of the country, sometimes returning to favourite places, sometimes delighting in new surprises, such as the salt marshes of Guérande on the Atlantic coast. But the France I used to know and understand has vanished. Progress, like creeping sand in the desert, has carelessly covered the France of the 1970s.

Badgers have no place in the Jardin d'Acclimatation today. The wild strawberries of Rimberlieu are no more, and the dark forest opposite our house has given way to a row of neat white houses with regulation grey roofs. In Compiègne, La Belle Epoque is now a five-star bed-and-breakfast. Real estate in the centre of town was deemed too valuable to waste on a twice-weekly market, and the site has been redeveloped as a modern and soulless shopping complex, complete with parking for a couple of hundred cars.

In the Midi, however, a new pride in its lost heritage is now evident, and throughout the south of France the sign at the

entrance to every town and village displays its names in both Occitan and French.

Madame's house at Caromb has been renovated and the Anduze pots have disappeared. The big fig tree has spread even further, but the cherries have all gone and Vincent's garage has been converted into a pool pavilion. In the town there is no trace of the butcher or baker, and a new *maison de tourisme* offers maps to guide visitors through the maze of medieval alleys. Foreign residents, once so rare, are now everywhere. The English-speaking population of Provence has exploded and a free English-language newspaper, published twice a month, circulates 10,000 copies.

Claret has become a tourist destination, with a new museum showcasing French glassmaking traditions from the 15th century and displaying contemporary artisan glassware. No longer an obscure, end-of-the road village, it is surrounded by Michelin-recommended restaurants that attract weekend visitors from Montpellier and nearby.

Machines have taken the place of Spanish *vendangeurs* around Nizas and no one dares proclaim the benefits of wine. Instead, cautionary slogans advise moderation, and even café menus warn of the dangers of drinking alcohol. Mas Laval has been repurposed as four independent residences and a new family sleeps and eats and watches television on the site where Jean-Pierre made wine. Only one small, ragged patch of vines remains opposite l'Escoute, now surrounded by new villas with swimming pools. Nizas has almost doubled in population but there is nowhere in the village to buy bread or milk. Ironically, a small lending library operates from a building almost opposite the old Co-op.

Yet one vestige of the old Nizas remains: the shepherd and his flock of scraggy sheep and brutish bucks, their little bells still tingling in harmony. It's not the shepherd I knew, but now his son who still lives *sur les causses* above the village, pasturing his

animals on the edges of the airstrip and continuing the simple pastoral traditions of his father. The only difference is that he speaks French, not Provençal.

Reflecting on these changes, I appreciate even more deeply my experiences of France in the 1970s, 21 months in the Languedoc, Provence, and the north. I was privileged to have lived there at a time when the 19th century almost touched hands with the 21st. In the villages we came to know intimately, the old way of life has now disappeared, vanished with the generation that survived two world wars. The old customs and traditions, the folklore and superstitions I was introduced to by elders such as Madame Molla and Madame Nicolaud, by friends such as Vivette and Jean-Pierre, have faded like a summer sunset. Even more today, I appreciate their guidance that helped me to understand France and the French in a way that would not have been possible by simply reading books.

The lasting legacy of my time in France was the way it changed my life. Had it not been for a chance meeting with a simple shepherd I might never have realised the existence of a Provençal language. Had I not lived in the south of France I might never have appreciated its individual history, its rich traditions, its past proud glory. Without the opportunity to explore libraries in Paris and Compiègne I might never have realised the fascination of old cookbooks, never envisaged a career as a food writer and culinary historian. Without all of these, I might never have been inspired to research the foods and cuisine of southern France in the 14th and 15th centuries, would never have written *The Original Mediterranean Cuisine*. Had I not stepped on to that UTA plane all those years ago . . .

My thanks go to Michael Bollen of Wakefield Press, who published my first book, *The Original Mediterranean Cuisine*, in 1995; in a way, this book is the prelude. I am also grateful to Kerryn Goldsworthy for her astute and intelligent reading of an earlier draft; to Margot Lloyd for her careful editing; and to Liz Nicholson, designBITE, for her evocative cover. Clinton Ellicott has once again provided an elegant and sympathetic design.

BS

Recipe index

French

Bœuf aux carottes 69
Ragoût de mouton aux haricots blancs 71
Pot-au-feu 111
Bouillabaisse d'épinards 117
Rôti de porc à la sauge 119
Haricots verts à la provençale 121
Soupe de poissons à la marseillaise 123
Clafoutis 133
Lapin à la provençale 137
Oeufs farcis à l'ail 147
Tomates farcies 181
Pommes de terre au lard 215
Gratin dauphinois 216
Anchoïade 238
Madame Mourichon's gâteau aux poires (ou prunes ou pêches ou abricots ou raisins) 252
Quatre-quarts 257
Tarte au sucre 258
Sorbet aux fraises 264
Confiture de vieux garçon 266
Poulet farci en gelée 272

English

Beef with carrots 69
Lamb with haricot beans 71
Pot-au-feu 111
Spinach and potato stew 117
Roast pork with sage 119
Green beans, Provençal-style 121
Fish soup, Marseilles-style 123
Clafoutis 133
Rabbit, Provençal-style 137
Garlic-stuffed eggs 147
Stuffed tomatoes 181
Sauté potatoes with smoked speck 215
Potato gratin 216
Anchovy spread 238
Madame Mourichon's pear cake (or plum or peach or apricot or grape) 252
Simple butter cake 257
Sugar tart 258
Strawberry sorbet 264
Bachelor's jam 266
Stuffed chicken in aspic 272

Wakefield Press is an independent publishing and distribution company based in Adelaide, South Australia. We love good stories and publish beautiful books. To see our full range of books, please visit our website at wakefieldpress.com.au where all titles are available for purchase. To keep up with our latest releases, news and events, subscribe to our monthly newsletter.

Find us!

Facebook: facebook.com/wakefield.press
Twitter: twitter.com/wakefieldpress
Instagram: instagram.com/wakefieldpress

www.ingramcontent.com/pod-product-compliance
Lightning Source LLC
Chambersburg PA
CBHW031800220426
43662CB00007B/476